PRACTICING PHILOSOPHY

PRACTICING PHILOSOPHY

Pragmatism and the Philosophical Life

RICHARD SHUSTERMAN

ROUTLEDGE
NEW YORK AND LONDON

Published in 1997 by
Routledge
29 West 35th Street
New York, NY 10001

Published in Great Britain by
Routledge
11 New Fetter Lane
London EC4P 4EE

Library of Congress Cataloging-in-Publication Data

Shusterman, Richard.
Practicing philosophy: pragmatism and the philosophical life/
Richard Shusterman.
p.   cm.
Includes bibliographical references and index.
ISBN 0-415-91394-2 (hb). — ISBN 0-415-91395-0 (pb)
1. Pragmatism. 2. Methodology. I. Title
B832.S53 1996
144'.3—dc20   96-30438

For Erica Ando

Beauty and spirit must be kept apart, if one does not wish to become their servant.

Our qualities, not our peculiarities, are what we should cultivate.

—Johann Wolfgang von Goethe
Maxims and Reflections

CONTENTS

ACKNOWLEDGMENTS

This book argues for extending the conception and practice of philosophy beyond the borders of its professionalized academic establishment. To demand more of philosophy is not to deny the worth of its current academic practice and institutions. But, to prevent such confusion, I here explicitly acknowledge the value of those institutions, and especially my particular debt to them in the writing of this book.

Temple University, my academic home for almost ten years, has been generous in its support. Moreover, like the best of homes, it graciously permitted, even encouraged, me to wander. This allowed me to develop and test my arguments through a variety of foreign visiting appointments, where the task of presenting American pragmatism can be particularly challenging and rewarding. I thank my colleagues and students at the Freie Universität Berlin, the École des Hautes Études en Sciences Sociales in Paris, the University of Helsinki, and Quebec's Université Laval for helpful discussions, and particularly Albrecht Wellmer, Hans Joas, Pierre Bourdieu, Gérard Genette, Arto Haapala, and Roger Chamberland who arranged my invitations. The Collège International de Philosophie deserves special mention, not simply for giving me a more permanent forum in Paris but for providing a uniquely flexible format for presenting new philosophical ideas to a very open and diverse public.

Work on this book was also supported by two extra-university academic institutions that combine national cultural interest with the aims of internationalism. A grant from the Deutscher Akademischer Austausch Dienst first helped bring me to Germany, while a year's Fulbright appointment allowed me to sustain residence in Berlin for eighteen months. Drinking deeply from the often dark wonders of this bewitching city, I could better appreciate, through distance and contrast, the virtues of America embodied in pragmatism. Berlin's rich yet painful history also compelled me to relive and rethink issues of Jewish identity broached in the book's final chapter. How could I avoid them as I regularly rode the S-Bahn line that runs from Wannsee (of the Final Solution) to Oranienburg (site of the Sachsenhausen concentration camp)? Repeatedly asked whether I was truly of German stock (as my family name might suggest), how could I forget the Jewish question?

As conferences help form the fabric of institutional philosophy, I gratefully acknowledge four that particularly inspired this book. In August 1991, as I was finishing the proofs of *Pragmatist Aesthetics*, Richard Bernstein organized a three-day retreat of a dozen pragmatist philosophers, historians, and social scientists to discuss the theme of Dewey and democracy in the Adirondack mountains where Dewey spent some summers teaching philosophy outside the university framework. Our impassioned discussions and sense of continuity with Dewey's progressive project were heightened by the thrill of sharing the aesthetic experience of Dewey's mountain retreat. This book's account of Deweyan democracy owes much to that meeting, particularly to discussions with James Kloppenberg, Richard Rorty, William Sullivan, Cornel West, and Robert Westbrook.

Likewise inspiring was an an intimate week-long meeting of Wittgensteinian aestheticians organized by Kjell Johannessen and Tore Nordenstam in May 1995 on Norway's Sogne Fjord, whose tranquil yet breathtaking beauty Wittgenstein so loved. I can hardly imagine a better place and audience to discuss the issues of Wittgenstein's ascetic yet aesthetic philosophical life.

Chapter Five began with an invitation to speak at a Nelson Goodman conference elegantly organized by Daniel Soutif of Paris's Centre

Pompidou (in March 1992) and enriched by Goodman's stirring participation. The austere chateau of Cerisy-la-Salle, set in the soft, green rolling hills of Normandy and host to a rich tradition of intellectual conferences, was the site of a July 1993 meeting on the issue of modernity/postmodernity for which the first version of this book's fourth chapter was written. The meeting, organized by Jacques Poulain and Françoise Gaillard, was largely structured as a confrontation between Habermas and Rorty, whose comments on my views have been helpful in rewriting. It was also a model of good yet simple living, where the distinction between professional philosopher and ardent amateur was overcome in the spirit of communal life. My faith in the aesthetic nature of philosophical life stems partly from the beauty of such occasions of philosophy.

This book is indebted to many colleagues and students, far too numerous to list. Since Richard Rorty, Hilary Putnam, and Stanley Cavell are all prime targets of this book's citique, I should begin by thanking them not only for instructive discussion and encouragement, but also for the provocation of their theories. Preliminary drafts of the chapters on pragmatism, liberalism, and democracy were also improved through the critical attention of Seyla Benhabib, Raymond Boisvert, Vincent Colapietro, James Conant, Daniel Conway, Chuck Dyke, James Kloppenberg, Tracy Strong, and Charles Taylor. The chapters dealing with art, truth, and practice profited especially from the comments of Houston Baker, Pierre Bourdieu, Noël Carroll, Arthur Danto, Hans-Peter Krüger, Jerrold Levinson, Armen Marsoobian, Jean-Michel Rabaté, Rainer Rochlitz, and Jean-Marie Schaeffer. George Downing, William Earle, and Marx Wartofsky gave me helpful comments on an early version of my chapter on somatic experience, and Jean-Pierre Cometti's French translation of it exposed problematic ambiguities, thus enabling their correction. I am grateful to David Goldberg and Michael Krausz for first asking me to write about Jewish identity and to David Adler, Marjorie Jolles, and Dmitri Shalin who kept me thinking about it. Comments from Brian McHale, Dan O'Hara, and Astrid Franke were helpful on several chapters.

Richard Bernstein, James Miller, and Alexander Nehamas all graciously undertook the taxing burden of reading this book at an early stage, when it was a much more unwieldy and unpolished manuscript.

Their expert knowledge, uncompromising criticism, and enduring encouragement resulted in important improvements. Miller also shared with me his transcripts of Foucault's unpublished final lectures at the Collège de France in 1984, an act of generosity for which I am further grateful.

Early versions of parts of this book have been published in *Political Theory*, *Les Cahiers du musée national d'art moderne*, *Philosophical Forum*, and in the Goldberg and Krausz collection, *Jewish Identity* (Temple University Press). I am grateful for the opportunity to present this material in a much revised form.

More than just a cheerfully patient editor, Maureen MacGrogan offered valuable structural suggestions. Working with her was both a pleasure and an education. Erica Ando has improved my life and thought in countless ways, partly by challenging their Eurocentric limits. For living with my project of philosophical life while leaving me the space to live it myself, she deserves more than words express.

Berlin
May 1996

Introduction

THE PHILOSOPHICAL LIFE

A Renewed Poetics of Philosophy

I

Why undertake the practice of philosophy? Even readers already deeply engaged in this practice are not spared the question: the critical, self-reflective nature of philosophy demands it. Teachers seeking to convince their students of philosophy's value must repeatedly examine it themselves. Students deciding to devote their lives to philosophy should explore what exactly it offers and amounts to, particularly given its uncertainty as an academic career.

"There are nowadays professors of philosophy, but not philosophers. Yet it is admirable to profess because it was once admirable to live." These words from Thoreau's *Walden* pose as much a question as a reproach.[1] What does it mean to be a philosopher? Is it not enough to study, write, and teach this subject in some academic institution, or does being a philosopher require something else, perhaps a special way of living? Defining the philosopher as one who practices philosophy only returns us to the questions of what that practice entails and what is its value. This book is an exploration of these questions, though it can illuminate only a small fraction of their immense scope.

Philosophy resists conclusive definition not only because of its historical diversity and open future, but because its precise nature, limits, and best exemplars are continuously debated. While some claim philosophy as science and others as poetry, it has also been identified with ideology,

1

therapy, and even autobiography (as the systematic articulation of one's own experience and/or wishes of the world). Most of the best philosophy seems to have most of these elements.

Since the productive richness of its complex, contested nature more than compensates for its definitional frustrations, it seems wrong to force philosophy into a single form or function. Two is not much better. So without claiming they exhaust the field, let me distinguish two basic philosophical forms that seem salient in philosophy's tradition and can introduce the argument of this book. One practice, call it "theory," concerns the formulation or criticism of general, systematic views about the world—including human nature, knowledge, and the institutions of human society. Anyone who treats the standard topics of academic philosophy (e.g. theories of meaning, being, truth, knowledge, value, justice, art, and the like) is practicing philosophy in this theoretical sense—no matter whether the vision formulated is scientific, poetic, or ideological, or whether it expresses autobiographical or therapeutic interests.

Thoreau's complaint evokes, in contrast, another way of practicing philosophy: as an art of living. His experiment of living at Walden Pond can best be appreciated in such terms. More than an eccentric flight of romantic primitivism, it is a radical effort to recover the ancient idea of practicing philosophy as a concrete way of life that is as rewarding as it is demanding. His reproachful contrast of false academic philosophy to the true practice of *living* philosophy builds on a long tradition that was extremely powerful before modernity's academic professionalization of philosophy, and it still echoes in moderns like Kierkegaard and Nietzsche.

In this tradition, philosophers like Cicero, Epictetus, Seneca, and Montaigne disparage pure theorists as mere "grammarians" and "mathematicians" who, devoting more "care and attention to their speech ... than to their lives," "teach us how to argue instead of how to live." Philosophy, in this tradition, derives her value and "authority over other arts" because she is "the mistress of the art of life itself." Consequently, "this most valuable of all arts, the art of living well," is tested more in the quality of one's concrete life than in that of one's theoretical writings. "Philosophy," says Seneca, "takes as her aim the state of happiness" not of book learning, whose zealous pursuit can be not merely useless but harmful. Some eminent philosophers, Diogenes Laertius reports, "wrote nothing at all," and, like Socrates, conveyed their teaching primarily through the conduct of their exemplary lives rather than by formulated doctrines. As Montaigne writes: "To compose our character is our duty, not to compose books … Our great and glorious masterpiece is to live appropriately."[2]

Since Thoreau's time, this alternative tradition of philosophy as an art of living has become even further eclipsed, suppressed by the institutions of professional philosophy. The idea of philosophy as a deliberative life-practice that brings lives of beauty and happiness to its practitioners is as foreign to professional philosophy today as astrology is to astrophysics.[3] This is not good for professional philosophy, increasingly marginalized in our pragmatic society by its apparent irrelevance to our lives and by growing doubts about its scientific value. Nor is it good for the millions of intelligent people who must look to far less thoughtful sources than philosophy in trying to develop what the vernacular terms "a philosophy of life." The idea of philosophy as "self-help" in the art of living may bring a scornful smirk from most professional philosophers.[4] But self-help was once philosophy's prime goal, and it remains a worthy one, whose attraction and utility go far beyond the narrow circle who hope to earn their living in the academy. In reviving this idea of philosophy's art of living, this book hopes to broaden the meaning and appeal of practicing philosophy.

Though one may usefully distinguish between philosophy as theory and as artful living—between books and life—one must not erect this into a false dichotomy. First, writing is not only a mode of living, but, already by the Hellenistic age, an important tool for artfully working on oneself—both as a medium of self-knowledge and of self-transformation.[5] Hence the very advocates of philosophy as an art of living made writing (in such diverse forms as letters, diaries, confessions, essays, treatises, handbooks, poems) a central part of that art. Moreover, writing provides a means of recording, communicating, and thus preserving the philosopher's model of life far beyond the immediate circle of his living presence. What would Socrates be for us without the writings of Plato and Xenophon?

Secondly, philosophical theories of the world typically serve as logical grounds or guiding orientations through which philosophical arts of living are developed and defended. Epicureanism is a case in point. Holding that philosophy's prime aim was to achieve a life of happiness (conceived in terms of unmixed tranquil pleasures and best achieved through a simple, retiring life), Epicurus produced a complex theory of nature and human reality that both justified and facilitated his art of living.

Since the greatest obstacles to Epicurean happiness were anxieties caused by beliefs concerning the gods' interference in our affairs and concerning the soul's life after death, Epicurean theory tried to remove these fears by arguing that all there is are only atoms and the void. Nature is thus governed not by divine volitions but by mere mechanical causes of atoms and space. Moreover, by claiming that even the soul is corporeal, Epicurus could argue that there is no sentience, hence nothing to fear, after its dissolution in death. Again, since we often worry how hard it is to get pleasure or endure certain pains, Epicurean natural theory—by indicating the nature and limits of human pains and pleasures—shows how a pleasurable life may be attained through simple measures. Thus even if theory had "no other end in view than peace of mind," Epicurus still held it necessary for the art of living, for without its "study of nature there was no enjoyment of unmixed pleasures."[6]

Stoic ethics, which emphasized living in simple consistency with nature and in tranquil acceptance of its providence, were likewise supported by a philosophical theory (far more extensive than the Epicurean) that viewed the whole natural world as a perfect, living organic unity, whose parts, as necessary to the whole, must be accepted. Similarly, it would be hard to detach Aristotle's ethical ideal of *theoria* from the metaphysics which provided its divine object; and how could Plato urge a life of quest for a vision of the Forms, without presenting a philosophical theory that showed their supreme existence and value?

The point I am making is that there is no essential opposition compelling us to choose between philosophy as theory and as artful life-practice. Indeed, we must *not* choose between them. For even if we doubt that every art of living entails a full-blown philosophical theory and every theory expresses a way of life, we surely should build our art of living on our knowledge and vision of the world, and reciprocally seek the knowledge that serves our art of living. Philosophy is strongest when both its modes of practice are combined to reinforce each other as they did in ancient philosophy.

One great difference between us and the ancients is that philosophical theory no longer seems a major source of knowledge of the world.

The various natural and human sciences that emerged from philosophy have assumed this function, while its role as an art of living has been forgotten and repressed through academic philosophy's anxious insistence on its scientific, theoretical status (even while often claiming its autonomy from "ordinary" science).[7] To make its case, academic philosophy typically stresses the purity of its theoretical stance. Knowledge of truth is the highest end and is sought for its own sake; hence "applied" philosophy is regarded as inferior.

Questioning the thirst for knowledge for its own sake, Hellenistic philosophers like Epicurus or Seneca were more appreciative of philosophy's practical utility. Knowledge was often regarded as having mainly instrumental value for something higher—such as happiness or virtue—that was not reducible to truth and could override the quest for truth when they conflicted. Nonetheless, precisely because (and to the extent) it was instrumental to the good life, knowledge was highly prized and sought. Montaigne displays the same respectful subordination of knowledge to utility for self-care and good living, and he judged the ancient philosophical schools accordingly: "some sects have rather followed truth, others utility, whereby the latter have gained credit."[8]

II

Pragmatism, as I see it, represents a return to this practical perspective and thus deserves its Jamesian description as "a new name for old ways of thinking." It is no "evasion of philosophy," but the revival of a tradition that saw theory as a useful instrument to a higher philosophical practice: the art of living wisely and well. This is evident in the way Dewey champions science while claiming that it, like all knowledge, is but a "handmaiden" to art—conceived widely as the experiential enrichment of life. Pragmatism therefore forms the focus of this book and its guiding orientation in combining philosophical theory with a plea for the reconstrual of philosophy as an art of living. Though its value is best measured by the book's results, I can offer some introductory reasons for my pragmatist focus—apart, of course, from the intrinsic interest in pragmatism itself as an increasingly vital, influential philosophy.

Since the art of living must be a practical art, pragmatism's emphasis on the practical seems particularly suitable. Moreover, it was through my work on *Pragmatist Aesthetics: Living Beauty, Rethinking Art* that philosophy as an art of living first emerged for me as a crucial, contemporary theme.[9] Noting our culture's current concern for lifestyles rather than moralities, my book charted the aestheticization of ethics in recent Anglo-American and continental theory. Philosophers showed growing recognition that ethical decisions of how to live could not be logically derived from man's essence or from uncontestable principles, but instead require, like aesthetic judgments, creative and critical imagination. Michel Foucault and Richard Rorty, however, urged a far stronger claim: the aesthetic life as an ethical ideal. Adopting Nietzsche's injunction to make oneself a work of art, they advocated philosophical life as radically original aesthetic self-creation.

But why should something clearly practical like an art of living (*techne tou biou*) be specifically aesthetic? Doesn't the term "art" here (as in the terms "martial arts" or "medical arts") mean a useful skill, technique, or knowledge rather than the aesthetic creation of fine art (which the Greeks called *poiesis*)?[10] Shouldn't philosophy as an art of living be therefore assimilated to a more "technical" model like the medical model of healing souls (as indeed it often was), rather than to an aesthetic-poetic one? Indeed, how can one recommend that the practical art of living be pursued as an aesthetic life when philosophy generally defines the aesthetic precisely by opposition to the practical, just as it defines art by its oppositional contrast with real life? Is the aesthetic life, then, not a withdrawal from social reality and praxis? And is the private beauty of one's self the best a philosopher can hope or strive for? Moreover, why must radical originality be required for stylizing the self aesthetically? Since very few people can meet this demand, must philosophical living be limited to a very narrow elite?

Pragmatism, as I conceive it after Dewey, offers a distinctive way of defending the aesthetic model of philosophical life against these troubling questions by undermining the traditional, stifling oppositions on which they are based. Recognizing art's deep roots in life's needs and interests—both natural and societal—pragmatism incorporates the practical and cognitive, along with the somatic and social, as contributing elements in aesthetic experience. Urging the greater integration of life and art for their mutual improvement, pragmatism's natural direction is the art of living. Moreover, by locating aesthetic value in the coherent richness of lived experience, not in radical originality or elite refinement, pragmatism suggests a way of making this living art more accessible and democratic than either Rorty or Foucault construes it.

Whether these suggestions amount to anything more than naive optimism and vague slogans can be seen only by pursuing the detailed working out and application of the arguments found in this book. The pragmatist vision sketched here is not, of course, shared by all pragmatists. Far from a uniform school, pragmatism has always displayed different views and interests, while regarding plurality as an advantage more than a weakness. My comparative analysis of different pragmatist thinkers on topics relating to the philosophical life displays this productive variety and, by playing their different views against each other, hopes to forge still more useful strategies.

This melioristic impulse is central to pragmatism and provides another reason for treating the philosophical life through a pragmatist perspective. If we are truly interested in practicing philosophy as an art of living, we should not simply want to know what that practice is or was. We should be especially interested in making it better. This does not imply that pragmatism has or needs a pregiven, univocal answer to what exactly "better" means. "Better for whom?" is always a valid question, and differing characters and life-conditions may favor different directions for philosophical living, as well as different levels of advancement in a given direction. Acknowledging this pluralism, pragmatism should urge that philosophy's art of better living not be construed so as to confine it in principle to a small elite. For pragmatism's democratic faith is part and parcel of its meliorism.

Pragmatic meliorism also explains my narrow focus on a handful of twentieth-century philosophers. Of course, the long tradition of philosophical life must be more thoroughly explored. Earlier ages, particularly ancient times, deserve special study. For then the idea of philosophy as an art of living was developed with greater care and detail, because it was far more central to philosophical practice. Through the path-breaking research of Foucault and Pierre Hadot, and the more recent scholarship of Peter Brown, Martha Nussbaum, and Arnold Davidson, such study is fortunately well under way.

But for all its helpful reorientation, ancient thought is far too dated to provide real options for today's pursuit of philosophical life. As Foucault himself warns, "there is no exemplary value in a period which is not our period."[11] Since a philosophical life must be pursued under certain life-conditions, those philosophical lives practiced closer to our present conditions are more likely to be useful in fashioning our own.

This does not, of course, mean that the latest philosophy is necessarily the best. Preoccupation with new pressures and methods may blind us from older but still vital values that need a fresh formulation. Dewey's concern for nondiscursive experience, I shall argue, deserves reclaiming after its dismissal by philosophy's "linguistic turn," though it also needs to be substantially revised. Another example is his view of community and political engagement as central to aesthetic self-construction. Though Rorty plausibly argues that the disintegration of traditional organic communities makes Dewey's view outdated, I suggest how it may be reinterpreted in terms of newer political and communal forms developing in postmodern times.

Thus, focusing on the almost completed twentieth century still involves enough historical range to show how different views of the art of living reflect changing socio-cultural conditions that generate different aesthetic demands and models. I have not, however, confined my discussion to philosophers standardly identified with American pragmatism. Dewey, Goodman, Putnam, and Rorty clearly belong to that tradition, and Cavell's Emersonian perfectionism and thematization of America link him closely to it. But, construing pragmatism more widely, I have also included case studies of Wittgenstein, Habermas, and Foucault. For their placing of social practices and pragmatic interests at the core of philosophy—even in its most theoretical problems of meaning, truth, and knowledge—not only warrants their connection to pragmatism but has often earned them that label.[12]

Enhancing its cultural impact by enlarging its scope, pragmatism finds good pragmatic reason for seeing itself as more than a purely American, merely academic, philosophy. Hence I devote one chapter to showing its presence in the rap philosophy of African-American popular culture. Still, the book remains well inside the orbit of Western philosophy. This is particularly regrettable, because other cultures (e.g. those of Asia) have extremely rich philosophical traditions that closely integrate (perhaps far better than we do) the practice of theory with a complex, rigorous, and refined art of living.

III

Advocacy of my pragmatist perspective must thus be tempered with recognition of its severe limitations. The philosophical life involves so many dimensions and philosophical issues, and has been practiced or preached by so many philosophers of diverse traditions, that the following seven essays can only scratch particular bits of a wide surface whose deeper exploration would demand several books. Together these essays raise (but cannnot adequately answer) a series of complex questions that I list as a guide to reading and a spur to more systematic treatment.

1. What is the connection between the views of a philosopher and his or her life? To what extent are one's positions a product, justification, or instead a contrasting compensation for one's life? Long before Nietzsche claimed philosophy as disguised autobiography (a vision that justified one's life), Diogenes Laertius had explained philosophical views in terms of the philosopher's life-experience: the pre-Socratic Pittacus's advocacy of humility, for example, as the product of his marrying above his social rank. Was Pittacus justifying the humility his wife made him practice or instead advocating a humility that compensated for his initial pride in taking her on? Philosophy's reflection of life can take the form of inverted images. To what extent, then, do philosophical ideals of unity and tranquillity serve as a compensation for lives of trouble and division? Do they ever function as a disguise or balance for lives that secretly sought variety and excitement? Such questions call for empirical study of the lives of philosophers, and so, in the first chapter, I consider three different exemplary philosophical lives: those of John Dewey, Ludwig Wittgenstein, and Michel Foucault.[13]

2. In what measure can one's philosophy be refuted or validated by one's life? *Argumentum ad hominem* is today considered a glaring logical fallacy and is surely irrelevant to philosophy's more formal, abstract issues. But in premodern times it was common to test a philosophy's practiced value by the philosopher's life, often with particular emphasis on his way of facing death — life's ultimate test. As Montaigne praises Socrates, Cleanthes, and Seneca for how they managed and ended their lives, so he condemns Cicero for the wretched, cowardly way he concluded his. If we should practice what we preach, and if, pragmatically, the proof of the pudding is in the eating, then how can we exclude arguments that relate a philosophy of life to the concrete life lived?

Yet we cannot simply equate the philosophy with the life. For concrete life involves many irrelevancies as well as important contingencies that, as uncontrollable (hence often unrepeatable), cannot be advocated as part of a philosophy that another could adopt. To identify life and thought completely would mean that two individuals could not share a philosophy. Moreover, fortune's overwhelming power seems to make the quality of a life more than a mere matter of having the right philosophy.

But if we can't strictly equate a philosophy of life with the philosopher's concrete life, to what extent can we judge the philosophy by the life? Finally, if we try to answer this question by distinguishing between essential and irrelevant features of a philosopher's life, we face the further question of how to distinguish between them. Though some features (like education) seem always pertinent, even apparently inessential ones (e.g. physical size or birthday or taste for wine) may be *proved* significant by a convincing interpretation of the life that so portrays them. Here, as elsewhere in philosophy, empirical facts and general rules do not suffice for decisive answers.

3. If being a student or professor of philosophical theory does not entail leading a truly philosophical life, what more is needed? Though not a sufficient condition, is being a theorist at least necessary? Or is it possible to live a philosophical life *in* (and not merely while) doing the work of a poet, priest, or painter, a physicist or politician, or even a plumber or pimp? If limited to only philosophical theorists, is it further limited to great, original theorists? And if practicing theory is not a necessary condition, perhaps greatness or originality is? For Montaigne (echoing the ancients), a life without eminence or novelty could count as philosophical if its careful pursuit of self-knowledge and self-improvement leads to a life of order, beauty, and tranquillity. But is actually reaching these (or other) goals a necessary condition, or does the proper pursuit of them in itself suffice? Such issues determine whether we can advocate philosophy for everyone, as Socrates did when urging that the unexamined life was not worth living.

4. They also amount to asking "what exactly is the philosophical life?" Among the vast variety of individual philosophical lives, can we discern a coherent tradition or genre, perhaps with different subgenres or models (e.g. Epicurean, Stoic, aesthetic dandy)? Or must every truly philosophical life determine its own new genre by its originality? What

are this life's defining features or highest values? While truth and self-knowledge are philosophy's standard ideals, other values of ameliorative self-care have been advocated as equally (and sometimes even more) essential: health and tranquillity, beauty and pleasure, heroic virtue and novelty. Philosophy has often been described as the life of the mind, but to what extent can bodily practices (e.g. diet and exercises of somatic fitness and awareness) form part of the philosophical life?

5. Finally, what are the roots of our notion of the philosophical life, and how has it evolved from ancient to contemporary times? Socrates' heroic life is typically regarded as establishing its paradigm, but one can explore earlier exemplars that may have guided him as they have inspired later philosophers. Such exemplars might include not only earlier philosophers (Pythagoras, Heraclitus), but also priests, poets, and mythological heroes, not all perhaps of Western origin. In what ways do contemporary models of philosophical life depart from the ancient? The ancients, for example, seem more focused on tranquillity, while today there is far greater emphasis on radical originality.

What are the major internal and external pressures that directed the evolution of philosophical life and its significant suppression in recent Western philosophy? Two likely explanations of the latter are the depersonalization of knowledge by modern science and Christianity's appropriation of the central functions of self-examination, self-redemption, and direction of life. But such historical transformations demand far more exploration, coupled with a comparative analysis of the philosophical life's different evolution in non-Western traditions.

IV

The complex research program sketched above guides (though clearly exceeds) the efforts of this book, which has three primary aims. To reanimate interest in the philosophical life—not only for theoretical study but for actual practice. To demonstrate the merits of the aesthetic model of such life. To explore and develop the value of contemporary pragmatism both for showing the importance of philosophy as an art of living and for providing strategies to practice it better.

These aims explain the book's structure. The long first chapter provides my initial case for the aesthetic model of philosophical life. After tracing this model back to Socrates, where it exists alongside a rival medical model of therapy, I analyze its contemporary elaboration in the life-philosophies and actual lives of three great philosophers: Dewey, Wittgenstein, and Foucault. Together they represent the three major currents of twentieth-century Western philosophy (pragmatism, analysis, and continental theory) as well as three different but overlapping generations of it.

These philosophers display not only divergent versions of aesthetic life that stem from differing views of art, but also a common core of values (growth, integrity, courage, as well as truth and beauty). These values are differently expressed in the multiple, interrelated dimensions in which philosophical life is pursued: the cognitive and aesthetic, the ethical, social, and political, and also the somatic. Recurrent problems in (and often between) these dimensions are shown to challenge, in life as well as theory, the viability of the aesthetic model of philosophy. The book then tackles such problems in individual chapters by focusing on their treatment by particular philosophers.

That the dimensions of philosophical life should not be sharply separated is a central theme of this book. But for the linear demands of exposition, I divide them as follows. The section "Ethics and Politics" concerns the tension between philosophy's devotion to care for the self and its need to care for others. The section's two chapters treat this dialectic of self and society by examining the topics of liberalism, community, and democracy in the theories of Dewey, Rorty, Putnam, and Cavell. Offering a variety of arguments (including aesthetic ones) for participatory democracy, I try to combine the Deweyean faith in self-fulfillment through public engagement together with a recognition both of today's fragmented public sphere and of the other-directed dimension of ameliorative work on oneself: the Emersonian idea that the quest for a higher self not only aims at an "other" self but serves as an inspiring example to others.

The next part ("Art, Knowledge, Praxis") attacks the traditional philosophical oppositions that divide the aesthetic from both the cognitive and practical, thus making the aesthetic practice of philosophy seem a double contradiction. Building on *Pragmatist Aesthetics*' detailed critique of these dualisms, I elaborate its argument that pragmatism provides greater power to both art and philosophy, not only by emphasizing the practical and cognitive life-interests in art and defending the legitimacy of art's popular forms, but also by reviving the idea of philosophy as an art of living.[14]

Recognizing that life's aestheticization has been diagnosed as a postmodern danger, chapter four treats the modernity/postmodernity debate through a comparative critique of the theories of Habermas and Rorty. Their conflicting valuations of postmodernity project the idea of an essential opposition between reason and the aesthetic (which they contrastingly privilege). This imposes a false choice for philosophy between Rorty's privatist aestheticism and Habermas's public-centered rationalism. But philosophy can be both aesthetic and rational, while embracing an essential dimension of life that Rorty and Habermas ignore—the somatic.

The next chapter therefore considers a current cultural form that claims to combine embodied aesthetics, rational knowledge, and social praxis, while advocating itself explicitly as a life-philosophy. I refer to the hip-hop genre of "knowledge rap," whose strong positive presence has been obscured by the overwhelming media hype over "gangsta rap." As rap's image as thoughtless, ruthless negativity becomes darker than ever, so *Pragmatist Aesthetics'* case for rap continues to provoke polemical misunderstandings. Chapter five tries to bolster the pragmatist–rap alliance by showing the reciprocally reinforcing affinities betwen Nelson Goodman's pragmatism and rap's philosophical-aesthetic practice. As Goodman argues for art's cognitive value and philosophy's creative art of "world-making," so knowledge rappers like KRS-One and Guru see their art as a practical form of philosophy devoted not only to aesthetic and cognitive transformation but also to ethical and political reform. For such rap philosophers, hip-hop becomes a comprehensive art of embodied living that embraces everything from metaphysics, politics, and economics to the ethics and aesthetics of ethnicity, fashion, sex, and diet.

In the book's final section, I develop the crucial themes of somatics and ethnicity, long repressed by philosophy's commitments to idealism and universalism. Much philosophical resistance to the body derives from its apparent nondiscursive aspects. But rather than taking the currently fashionable "textualist" line of asserting the body's total discursivity, I instead defend the notion of nondiscursive somatic experience through a reconstructive critique of Dewey. After rescuing nondiscursive experience from its abuses in foundationalist epistemology, I suggest some ways that somatics can be usefully incorporated into philosophy both as a topic for critical theory and as a dimension for disciplined practice in philosophy's art of better living through self-examination and self-creation.

Self-examination is surely central to the book's final chapter, which treats the vexed issue of Jewish identity. While engaging the views of others, I also focus on my own Jewish experience. This is not merely because I know it best, or because it seems instructively multiform (including life as Israeli, as diaspora Jew, and, if it may count as a special category, as a Jewish American).[15] I focus on my experience of the problem of Jewish identity because the prime philosophical interest of the problem is an existential one: what should one make, if anything, of one's Jewish identity in the construction of one's life? This means, in my case, *my* life and Jewishness.[16] After advocating philosophy as a self-critical art of living by studying the thought and lives of others, it seems appropriate to conclude by applying this philosophical vision, at long last, to a central, still unresolved problem of my own. To shirk this exercise would contradict the whole pragmatic thrust of the book.

If the final chapter seems a special exercise in the old philosophical genre of self-examining meditation, then the composition of this book as a totality stands as a symbol of the philosophical life's struggle to unite its particular interests and contingent occasions into a coherent whole. All the essays here, written over the last five years, were shaped by the general intuition that philosophy should be a tool for the better practice of life, where "better" was conceived in broad aesthetic terms. But, my idea of producing a book on pragmatism and the philosophical life took decisive form more recently, in 1993, when sympathetic critics urged that *Pragmatist Aesthetics* should have gone farther in fleshing out the model of aesthetic life it advocated against Foucault's and Rorty's.

By then, preliminary versions of four of the book's chapters had already been drafted for the special occasions that simultaneously structure, adorn, and harrass the professional life of a philosopher. In preparing this book, I was urged by some colleagues to simply abandon these individual essays. Though cannibalizing their material, I should start writing the book again from scratch to produce a more seamlessly unified whole—what is still sometimes called, even after poststructuralism, a "real" book. But if philosophy is like life, you cannot really start again from scratch, even if you pretend to. Moreover, the points I wanted most to make remained closely tied to particular problems and thinkers I had either treated or wished later to treat in individual case studies of contemporary pragmatism.

Other friends recommended the standard practice of simply leaving one's essays as they were originally published (even if one has thought far past them) and then justifying this maneuver as being faithful to the history of one's thought while providing a handy documentation of it. Though this may seem the easiest alternative, it was too hard for me. Unable to flatter myself that readers would want such a history, I also felt that it would be unfaithful to my current thinking, which is naturally more important to me and should also be to my readers. For many of my earlier published views were significantly revised and updated through the recontextualizing process of considering them together as part of a book.

If philosophy, like life, is a continual exercise in reinterpreting the experience of one's self and surroundings, then the essays had to be revised as part of such reinterpretation. If the art of life involves appreciating particulars in their particularity while reshaping them so that they better contribute to a richer, coherent whole, then this book's composition is an analogue of life's art—even with its difficulties and failures.

1

PROFILES OF THE PHILOSOPHICAL LIFE

Dewey, Wittgenstein, Foucault

I

Philosophy began not with a paradigm text, but with an exemplary life, a dramatic model of living—and of dying. Though Socrates left no writings, he founded philosophy by the inspiring example of his courageous quest for truth and self-knowledge that not even threat of death could deter. This quest was largely focused on the question of "how should one live?" and its underlying premise was that the unexamined life was not worth living. Dedicating his life to relentlessly examining Athenian dogma on this question of *savoir vivre*, Socrates never provided a substantive ethical code of his own. Apart from the gnomic injunctions to know and care for oneself, he left no definitive doctrines, though his disciple Plato would later formulate many through his dramatic persona.[1]

Instead, Socrates' prime legacy was his exemplification of "the philosophical life." His quest for the wisdom of how best to live embodied his paradoxical answer to this philosophical question. His life was his teaching; its practice his philosophy. If this primacy of practice makes Socrates look like a proto-pragmatist, then so does the motive of his search for wisdom. The aim is not truth for truth's sake, but rather ameliorative care of the self (*epimeleia heatou*), and, as a consequence, the betterment of the society in which the self is situated. Philosophy's

17

embodiment in concrete concern for the concrete good of the individual does not preclude its universality. For everyone has both a life to lead and the possibility to reflect on how it should be organized. Yet to the extent that every life is different, philosophy as a life-practice may reflect that difference.

As concretely embodied practice rather than formulated doctrine, how is philosophy to be taught and learned? Practical knowledge, Aristotle tells us, is learned only by doing, by practice. But with no formulated rule-book as official manual, what can guide our philosophical life-practice? The only obvious answer is the emulation of distinguished exemplars, who attract us to philosophy and structure its pursuit. Socrates, who called the philosopher a "master of erotics," provides the seductive paradigm of the philosophical life. His living presence — of incisive wit, tireless inquiry, humorous charm, and unconventional style — captivated many of Athens' brightest youth. But his charismatic figure was even more heroically transfigured through the martyrdom of his death. This heroic image, for the hero-loving Greeks, gave life to philosophy, just like other martyrdoms animated religions. Inspiring Plato's *Dialogues*, its seductive power is so enduring that we still introduce philosophy to our students through his captivating account of Socrates' trial and death.

But there are problems with hero worship as a model of philosophy. For even taking only *one* philosophical hero to emulate, there remains the question: What is to be imitated? Clearly, we are not supposed to worship the person of the philosopher or imitate his particular appearance, for such an idea would turn philosophy into idolatry and affectation. It is obviously not the particular person nor specific deeds of Socrates, but the philosopical life-practice we are to emulate. Yet it is far from obvious how to separate this from the particularities of the person and the contingencies of his life. Interpretation is especially needed because Socrates refused to codify his practice, but insisted on *living* rather than writing philosophy.

Plato therefore tried to abstract and expand the essential core of Socrates' philosophical practice by articulating certain views through the Socratic persona of his *Dialogues*. For teaching that is clearly formulated and inscribed in doctrines can be more easily preserved (*littera scripta manet*) and more widely communicated. Plato, unlike Socrates, founded a school based on a set of abstract theories.

But if philosophy is a life-practice rather than a mere field of theoretical knowledge, then separating philosophical thought from the lived context of the philosopher could constitute a gross distortion of its actual meaning and value. So there is danger in writing philosophy (as Plato himself warns in the *Phaedrus*), because the reproducibility and apparent autonomy of textual expression could make the philosophical life that evoked it seem irrelevant.[2] But how, then, is philosophy to be communicated beyond the exemplary philosopher's living presence?

One answer is by portraying his life as well as his thought and by relating the two as much as possible. If philosophy is to be lived, the teaching of its exemplary dead is perhaps best taught by philosophical biography, a genre suggested but never fully achieved by Plato's account of Socrates.

We seem to be witnessing a renaissance of philosophical biography, but I shall focus on only three representative philosophers of the twentieth century: John Dewey (1859–1952), Ludwig Wittgenstein (1889–1951), and Michel Foucault (1926–1984).[3] The wide appeal of their biographies indicates two promising phenomena. First, that philosophy, despite its apparent decline in prestige and authority, continues to fascinate our intellectual culture, so that philosophers can still function as heroes whose lives can be read for edification. If they fail to function as the lives of saints, nor are they reducible to the lives of the rich and famous that make the staple of contemporary biography. If Foucault became something of a media celebrity, this could not be farther from the character of Wittgenstein. And if interest in these two lives builds upon sensationalism regarding their charismatic eccentricity and social, sexual deviance, this will not explain the interest in the sober, wholesome life of John Dewey.

Secondly, the great success of their biographies suggests a growing dissatisfaction with professional philosophy's institutionalized separation of philosophical thought from concrete personal life. Since this dissatisfaction is easier to express outside the ranks of institutional philosophy, it should not surprise us that the biographers are mostly not professional philosophers. Nor is it surprising that their biographical subjects themselves stressed the intimate link between philosophical thinking and personal experience, and, partly for that reason, maintained a rather ambivalent, sometimes scornful, attitude toward professional philosophy.

Dewey confessed outright that his philosophy was mainly the product of personal experiences. It came "from persons and situations more than from books—not that I have not, I hope, learned a great deal from philosophical writings, but that what I learned from them has been technical in comparison with what I have been forced to think upon and about because of some experience in which I found myself entangled" (LW 5:515). Though he enjoyed a very successful professional career (climbing the university ladder from Minnesota to Michigan, then Chicago to Columbia, and serving as President of the American Philosophical Association in 1905), Dewey soon lost interest in the professional game. He made no effort to direct the philosophy department at Columbia (as he had done in Chicago) and became increasingly alienated by the profession's narrow preoccupation with traditional academic questions, particularly those concerning the "intellectual lockjaw called epistemology" (MW 4:138n).

Dewey sharply chided his professional colleagues for shirking the duty of bringing philosophy to bear on "the living struggles and issues of its own age and times," confining its practice to old academic problems so as to "maintain an immune monastic impeccability, without relevancy and bearing in the ... contemporary present" (MW 4:142). Condemning philosophy's retreat into smug, scholastic professionalism, Dewey insisted that it would recover its true worth (as a life-centered enterprise) only "when it ceases to be a device for dealing with the problems of philosophers and becomes a method, cultivated by philosophers, for dealing with the problems of men"(MW 10:46).[4]

Foucault's relation to the academy is similarly ambiguous. A shrewd strategist who skillfully played the academic game to reach the most prestigious position of Professor at the Collège de France, Foucault faithfully discharged his professional duties. But he made no effort at all to reinforce his academic power by establishing an additional base in one of the several Parisian research centers, as many of his colleagues had done. An avid *chercheur* and connoisseur of power, Foucault seemed surprisingly indifferent to its academic variety, and throughout his career "he continued to evince no interest whatsoever in recruiting disciples" (Mi 185).

Wittgenstein was the most outspoken in his scornful loathing of the profession and its clever but shallow "philosophical journalists" (CV 66) who reported on philosophy rather than living it; he thus shunned professional meetings. Though he held the prestigous chair of philosophy at

Cambridge, Wittgenstein's reason for taking it was simply to acquire British citizenship, since his status as an Austrian "Jew" had become precarious after the Nazi *Anschluss* of Austria.[5] Rather than seeking to recruit students, he exhorted (often bullied) them to leave academic philosophy for a worthier occupation, especially medicine, whose concrete benefit to life made academic philosophy look, by comparison, indecently idle. Wittgenstein himself often considered training as a doctor to escape the empty "deadness" of academic philosophy. "I cannot found a school," he wrote, "because I do not really want to be imitated. Not at any rate by those who publish articles in philosophical journals" (CV 61).

The emulation and influence he desired was in how people thought about and conducted their lives—in the practice of philosophy as a way of life. Rather than a continuation of his logical investigations, he wanted to effect "a change in the way people live which would make all these questions superfluous" (CV 61). Rather than propositional content, Wittgenstein wanted to communicate a model of how to live philosophically.

> My lectures are going well, they will never go better. But what effect do they leave behind? Am I helping anyone? Certainly no *more* than if I were a great actor playing out tragic roles for them. What they learn is not worth learning; and the personal impression I make does not serve them with anything.

"What help is it," he asks, "to solve philosophical problems, if [one] cannot settle the chief, most important thing"—how to live a good and happy life? (Mo 506–507). "Live well!" (CV 52) is the supreme philosophical commandment.[6]

In short, Wittgenstein's disrespect for mere academic philosophizing stems from a view he shared with Dewey and Foucault, that philosophy had a much more crucial, existential task: to help us lead better lives by bettering ourselves through self-knowledge, self-criticism, and self-mastery. Philosophy, for these three great thinkers, was more than thought; it was a life-practice where theory derived its real meaning and value only in terms of the life in which it functioned, in the concrete pursuit of better living.

Dewey's pragmatism highlights the ultimately practical, life-enhancing function of philosophy. As "the comprehensive art of the wise conduct of life itself," philosophy is a criticism of "life in the interest of a more intense and just appreciation of the meanings present in experience.... Its primary concern is to clarify, liberate, and extend the goods which inhere in the naturally generated functions of experience" (LW 3: 25; EN 304–305). Rather than a specific science, "philosophy is a form of desire, of effort at action — a love, namely, of wisdom," where wisdom is not factual knowledge "but a conviction about moral values, a sense for the better kind of life to be lived" (MW 11:43–45). As a "passionate" but critical interpretation of life, philosophy involves "a moral resolution to prize one mode of life more highly than another," and it dons the garb of learning and logic "in the wish to persuade other men [and "perhaps the writer himself"] that this was the wise way of living." Rival philosophies "are different ways of construing life," whose differences can be both valid and valuable since they are often based on very different conditions of living which inspire different "passionate desires and hopes"; hence philosophy must involve change because the world is always changing (MW 11: 43, 44, 46).

Two crucial ideas are suggested here: the close connection of philosophical thought to one's conditions of living, and philosophy's effort to improve those conditions of both life and thought by changing the condition of oneself through critical reflection.

Wittgenstein and Foucault make these points with even greater force. Throughout his notebooks, letters, and conversations, Wittgenstein confirms his conviction that philosophy is ultimately more concerned with "the problem of life" (CV 4) than with the logico–linguistic puzzles whose treatment made him the idol of Oxbridge. Nor can philosophy's life-answers be simply theory or propositional truth; they must instead be concretely lived through the practice of self-transformation: "The fact that life is problematic shows that the shape of your life does not fit into life's form. So you must change the way you live" (CV 27). As philosophy's value emerges from its life-context and pursuit of better living, so "the delight I take in my thoughts is delight in my own strange life" (CV 22).

Philosophical writing is likewise assessed through its role in the totality of living as "a complete human being," which "is why the greatness of what a man writes depends on everything else he writes and *does*" (CV 65, my italics).[7] It is also why no great philosophical work can be definitive for all times and people: different conditions of living will pose different problems and demand different philosophical efforts (CV 67).

Affirming this unity of philosophical thought with the concrete practice of philosophical living, Foucault exhorts us to take the *bios philosophicus* as the privileged genre of philosophy. Avowing that his own philosophical views could best be understood only in terms of certain episodes and practices in his life, he generalizes that "the key to the personal poetic attitude of a philosopher is not to be sought in his ideas, as if it could be deduced from them, but rather in his philosophy-as-life, in his philosophical life, his ethos" (FR 374).[8]

More important, however, than scrutinizing the lives of others, each philosopher must direct critical attention and creative imagination to her own concrete deeds and life-experiences as well as to her own ideas. "At every moment, step by step, one must confront what one is thinking and saying with what one is doing, with what one is" (FR 374). And if philosophy was always in the business of self-knowledge, Foucault insists that this must be taken as more than propositional knowledge of static truth. Philosophy becomes an embodied life-practice in which the self is transfigured through experiment, discipline, and ordeal. "The critical ontology of ourselves has to be considered not, certainly, as a theory ... [but] as an attitude, an ethos, a philosophical life in which the critique of what we are is at the same time the historical analysis of the limits that are imposed on us and the ordeal [*épreuve*] of their possible transcendence [*franchissement*]" (FR 50).

Foucault, Dewey, and Wittgenstein obviously pursued rather different philosophical lives, no doubt because of different life-conditions. But perhaps there are some crucial common features that are worth examining. For the philosophical life has at least, in Socrates, a shared, founding exemplar and the shared though diverse tradition that he generated in Greco-Roman antiquity.[9] My aim, however, is not to establish a definitive genealogy or shared, defining essence of the philosophical life but rather to explore instructive models for our own attempts at philosophical living.

II

Philosophical Living as Aesthetic

If the philosophical life is not a simple quest for knowledge but a quest for better living and a better self, how should these aims be understood?

What are the models for enhanced life and self-improvement? Apart from the vague notions of wisdom and virtue (and partly to explain them), Socrates (as Plato represents him) proposes two different and influential models that still thrive in later antiquity: a quasi-medical one of health and an aesthetic model of art and beauty.[10]

In several dialogues (e.g. *Crito*, *Gorgias*, and the *Republic*), he suggests that the philosopher's role is analogous to the physician's. As the physician cares for the body's health, the philosopher aims at improving the soul's. But philosophy appears superior to medicine, since the physician's quest is doomed, in the end, to failure. While the body's health must be ultimately undermined by death, the immortal soul's is not so limited. Thus the philosopher's quest may be permanently triumphant, even if the cost is commitment to the soul's immortality and its troubling division from the body.

The aesthetic model of self-betterment is less dependent on these problematic doctrines and even more potently portrayed. In the *Symposium* (198C–213D), Socrates praises love's desire for beauty as the source of philosophy, and he lovingly describes the philosophical life as a continuous quest for greater beauty that ennobles the philosopher. This quest is not simply to view or possess higher beauties but to create or "give birth" to the beautiful: "beautiful and magnificent speeches and thoughts"; "beautiful pursuits and practices"; "beautiful learnings." These beautiful progeny are inspired (like the begetting of children) by our life-drive for immortality, and they help us achieve it by remaining after our death as beautiful memorials of our life. Heroes have readily sacrificed their lives to acquire that "immortal memory of virtue."

But the philosopher hopes for still more. He seeks not merely particular memorials of beauty and virtue, but an abiding vision of the perfect Form of beauty itself. For this vision provides not only the greatest joy of beauty but also the perfect knowledge to give "birth to real virtue," rather than simply beautiful images or memories of it. This life of beauty, Socrates concludes (in the words of Diotima) is "the only life worth living" and makes the philosopher "the friend of God and immortal, if any man ever is."[11]

Given this aesthetic model of philosophy, it becomes important for Socrates and Plato to differentiate their subject from art and to assert its superiority for the practice of living. The poets and their interpreters are therefore condemned for not really knowing the arts of living of which they speak. Even Aristotle's defense of art as *poiesis* (external making) serves to distinguish it sharply from *praxis* and ethics. The result has been a long tradition of sharply separating art from philosophy and the serious conduct of life.[12]

But today's moral scepticism — not only about the major ethical traditions but about the hope for a compelling new theory derived from human essence — has revitalized the aesthetic model, the idea that life should be practiced as an art. Baudelaire and Nietzsche were its nineteenth-century prophets, urging the individual to artfully stylize and recreate oneself so as "to become what one is."[13] Wittgenstein, Dewey, and Foucault carry this idea firmly into the present, inspiring a host of aesthetic thinkers.

As his biographers make clear, Wittgenstein's philosophical aims far exceeded the technical theorizing that won him fame. Even his early, most logic-centered work was, he confessed, deeply inspired by ethical concerns and boldly claimed that "ethics and aesthetics are one" (T 6.421).[14] His continued commitment to an aesthetic vision of philosophy and life is evident from remarks posthumously collected in *Culture and Value*: "I think I summed up my attitude to philosophy when I said: philosophy ought really to be written only as a *poetic composition*." For like "the work of the artist," the philosopher's thought may succeed in "capturing the world sub specie aeterni," providing a vision wherein he might see "his life as a work of art" (CV 4–5, 24). "Working in philosophy — like work in architecture in many respects — is really more a working on oneself. On one's interpretation" (CV 16). But such work is not merely the work of thought, for philosophy's solutions to life's riddles are not propositional knowledge but transformational practice. "The answer to the problem you see in life is a way of living that will make what is problematic disappear" (CV 27). As "Live happy!" is the philosophical goal, so "the beautiful is what makes happy"; and art, which "looks at the world with a happy eye" has beauty as its "end" (N 75, 86).

Dewey is also an advocate of aesthetic living. His revisionary theory of art as experience is aimed at overcoming art's compartmentalization and "recovering the continuity of esthetic experience with the normal processes of living" so that art can be better integrated into life. This is not only because aesthetic experience provides us with "necessary ingredients of happiness" (AE 16), but because he construes art widely as the organizing refinement of any medium, including the medium of life itself. The art of living, for Dewey, is "an art of organization of human activities as such" (like "the art of politics and morals as conceived by Socrates and Plato") that ultimately aims (like fine art) at making our experience more aesthetic, our lives more enjoyably rich and unified (AE 31).

Like Dewey, Foucault sees the ideal of aesthetic living as deeply rooted in ancient Greek culture, which practiced "a kind of ethics which was an aesthetics of existence," the expression of "the will to live a beautiful life, and to leave to others memories of a beautiful existence" (FR 341, 343). Like Dewey, he complains that this model of life as art has been neglected through art's modern specialization:

> What strikes me is the fact that in our society, art has become something which is related only to objects and not to individuals, or to life. That art is something which is specialized or which is done by experts who are artists. But couldn't everyone's life become a work of art? Why should the lamp or house be an art object, but not our life? (FR 350)

Foucault answers this last question by urging "the idea of the *bios* as a material for an aesthetic piece of art." "From the idea that the self is not given to us," he argues, "I think that there is only one practical consequence: we have to create ourselves as a work of art" (FR 348, 351).

But what does it mean to live aesthetically and create oneself as a work of art? Even if all agree that the philosophical life should follow an aesthetic model, this is still far from determining what type of life to lead. As the notions of art and aesthetic are deeply ambiguous and contested, we find very different genres of aesthetic living.[15] For instance, while the classical Greek aesthetic demanded beauty, harmony, measured moderation, clear limits, and easily intelligible unity, the dominant modernist aesthetic is far less concerned with realizing these values and often seems bent on challenging them. Shaped by the ideologies of romanticism, individualism, and the avant-garde, our high art aesthetic instead makes radical novelty and individuality the prime requirement of an artwork, though this demand is not made by the aesthetics of popular art.

Such differences translate into differences as to what is demanded of the art of living. Is it enough to shape one's life into a satisfyingly harmonious, well-integrated, and dynamic whole? Or does making one's life a work of art require something more—a radical originality that transcends previous models and limits, as the avant-garde artwork aims to do? Advocates of artful living typically fail to distinguish these different notions of the aesthetic life, a confusion whose effects can be as harmful for life as for theory.

Foucault exemplifies this problem. He devotes a major scholarly effort to reconstructing the ethical ideal of aesthetic living embodied in ancient Greek practices of self-stylization.[16] Here the precise ways of managing one's sexuality, marital relations, diet, and so forth, were not dictated by universal commandments whose violation meant sin, but rather were aesthetically chosen "to give [one's] existence an honorable and noble form" (CS 185). Such choices involved a measure of free aesthetic self-expression. But because of Greek society's solid sense of what was noble and admirable, they were also clearly guided and constrained by conventional models. Artistry was exercised in aesthetically deploying established models to give attractive form to the particularities of one's life. Not everyone could succeed in living an aesthetic life, for most had neither the taste nor means to do so. Yet, even if difficult, it did not demand that one invent a whole new style of living. On the contrary: radical nonconformity to accepted models would constitute tasteless barbarism.

Foucault, however, ends up advocating and living an aesthetic life that is far more extreme in its demands, taking as its model the avant-garde artist or Baudelairian dandy who refuses all established models in the aim of creating something radically new. Such an artist is not content with self-stylization; he "tries to invent himself" (FR 42); to "create a new way of life," "something radically Other." "What must be produced," Foucault urges, "is something that doesn't yet exist and about which we cannot know how and what it will be.... It's ... the creation of something entirely different, a total innovation": something, we must suppose, on the order of *Ulysses* or the *The Waste Land*.[17] Though showing how much the Greek art of living relied on a limit-respecting aesthetic, Foucault recommends an aesthetic of transgressive experimentation to test and transcend our limits. This idea of creative transgression for radical self-invention is not simply traced to Baudelaire's modernist aesthetic but ingeniously linked to Kant's Enlightenment project of critique of limits for the sake of knowledge. Perhaps more than anything else, Foucault's own close connection with the Parisian musical and literary avant-garde (e.g. as friend of Boulez, lover of Barraqué, and collaborator with the *Tel quel* group) naturally drew him to identify the aesthetic with radical innovation and transgression.

Foucault's "interrogation of the limit and transgression" was not merely theoretical.[18] It was pursued through the means of extreme limit-experiences—with drugs and sadomasochistic sex, but also in radical politics. Such experiences can shatter our familiar sense of self and so pave the way for its reinvention. But they also, in their violence, court madness and even death, the ultimate limit. Foucault's early death from AIDS is thus portrayed by biographer James Miller as the (unintended) culmination of a life devoted to making oneself a distinctively novel work of art through transgressional explorations.

Dewey offers a very different view of life as art. No less an advocate of freedom than Foucault, he wanted art (and aesthetic living) to be free from the demand to be radically new and uniquely distinctive. This compulsion, with its cult of isolated genius, he regarded as the unhappy product of art's increasing compartmentalization and professionalization under capitalism. Deprived of its traditional social roles, art is reduced to the production of gratuitous commodities ("specimens of fine art and nothing else") put up for sale in "the impersonality of the world market" and forced to seduce buyers through novelty and uniqueness (AE 15). Artists are thus impelled to develop a peculiarly acute individualism that makes their works increasingly difficult for the general public to fathom and enjoy—an intolerable situation for the democratic Dewey.

Rather than individualistic innovation, his art theory highlights unity, communicability, and dynamic, developing richness. The same balance shapes his ideal of aesthetic living. Though his liberalism advocates self-realization, Dewey insisted that the individual best realizes himself not by consciously cultivating his own peculiar distinction but by immersing himself in associated life. For concentrating narrowly on the project of self-creation will rob one of the wide sympathies and materials needed to transform the self in richer ways. Similarly, self-transformation was aimed not at radical novelty for its own sake but rather at continuous, coherent growth.

Wittgenstein lies between these two forms of aesthetic life. More than Foucault, he recognized the charm of the ordinary, but, far more than Dewey, he valorized and practiced the extraordinary. His whole philosophy mediates between the transcendental sublime and the common, a practice captured by his metaphor of condensing a cloud of metaphysics into a drop of grammar. Wittgenstein could praise the joys of simple living and useful work as the key to a balanced happy life, when urging his students to abandon the rarified narrowness of a philosophical career; yet he himself exhibited no such balance. Though his "concern was to stress life's irreducible variety," condemning "a one-sided diet" of similar examples as "a main cause of philosophical disease," we learn that he often chose an "unvarying diet" of food and philosophy. Declaring that "he did not care what he ate so long as it was always the same," Wittgenstein apparently feared that food would distract his excruciatingly intense, "almost pathological" concentration on the abstract philosophical problems he was treating (Mo 536, 537, 552; PI para. 593; Ma 69). Though he favored "restful beauty" and claimed "the happy life [as] more *harmonious*," his own life insists on restlessness and tension (Ma 11; N 78). Why show such hard-edged passion and stressful striving, even while claiming tranquil peace of mind ("*Friede in den Gedanken*," calm "coolness" without "hardness and conflict") as his philosophical ideal (CV 2, 9, 43)?

The cause may be the same modernist ideal of genius that motivated Foucault.[19] Wittgenstein discovered this ideal not in Baudelaire or Nietzsche, but in Otto Weininger, who held that genius "is the highest morality, and, therefore, it is everyone's duty" (Mo 24). He could also find it in his high-cultured Viennese family, which, through its great wealth, taste, and talent, regularly entertained and fostered artistic genius. Brahms, Mahler, and Klimt were among them, and two of Wittgenstein's older brothers showed amazing musical gifts. Whatever the source, Wittgenstein's preoccupation with genius is manifest not only in repeated attempts to analyze this concept (chiefly in terms of talent, character, and courage), but in self-confessed fears that his talent was only for "reproductive" clarification rather than the radical innovation that genius required (CV 18–21, 35, 38).[20]

For the genius-model of aesthetics, the qualities of good taste, clarity, harmony, and even happiness are not enough. Instead, radical novelty and uniqueness are required of true art, and, in consequence, of aesthetic living. His prime interests being "only *conceptual* and *aesthetic* questions" (CV

79), and knowing that he had no originality in the arts ("in my artistic activities I have nothing but *good manners*," [CV 25]), Wittgenstein drew the philosophical conclusion. He devoted his quest for original genius to philosophical work, even when he realized how painfully abstract, narrow, and lonely this work could be, how miserably it could be misunderstood and distorted. Fears that his talent might not suffice to vindicate his quest drove him to frequent thoughts of suicide and self-castigation. "I ought to have done something positive with my life, to become a star in the sky. Instead of which I remained stuck on earth, and now I am gradually fading out."[21]

Assuming that true aesthetic living could only mean the stardom of original genius, Wittgenstein pursued it to the manic extremes that give his life a romantic mystique like Foucault's. Both ignored other aesthetic options (more dominant in premodern culture and popular art), probably because they were hardly live options for such products of Europe's *haute bourgeoisie* whose sensibilities were steeped in the high culture of modernism. With Dewey, raised as the son of a Vermont grocer before the reign of modernism, the case was clearly different.[22]

Can we revive these alternative aesthetics for philosophical living in today's postmodern culture? This question requires probing further dimensions of philosophical life as revealed by our three exemplary philosophers.

III

Philosophical Living as Somatic

If philosophy is not mere theory, but an entire life-practice, it must be essentially embodied in physical life. If philosophical life is aesthetic, this implies a concern for the body both as a medium of aesthetic self-fashioning and as a means of aesthetic pleasure. Somatic aesthetics, in its sense of external bodily representation, can play a crucial role in a philosopher's charismatic exemplarity, lending not only his life but his theoretical views considerable conviction. G.E. Moore's "sublime beauty" and vehement body language gave him enormous power of persuasion with students and colleagues.[23] So apparently did Wittgenstein's: "His face was lean and brown, his profile was aquiline and strikingly beautiful.... His look was concentrated, he made striking gestures with his hands.... His face was remarkably mobile and expressive when he talked. His eyes were deep and often fierce in their expression. His whole personality was commanding, even imperial" (Ma 23–24).

But somatic aesthetics involves more than the philosopher's external form and comportment. It includes a more controversial dimension of bodily experience, a quality of somatic feeling that lies beneath linguistic formulation and often resists it. To philosophy's image as an essentially linguistic discipline devoted to pure *logos*, the nondiscursive somatic dimension of life poses a challenge.

One excuse for avoiding this challenge and eschewing the nonlinguistic is that too much philosophical nonsense has resulted from trying to look beyond language so as to theorize reality "in the raw" and see how language and cognition relate to it. Wittgenstein showed the futility of such attempts. The result has been an identification of experience with linguistic experience, so that philosophy performs its role of defining the limits of our thought and world by defining the limits of language. There is, of course, no way of standing outside language to describe the world and our experience. Yet nonlinguistic dimensions of experience seem nonetheless crucially important to our lives.[24] How can philosophy acknowledge and treat them?

Dewey, who reached philosophical maturity before the linguistic turn, had no trouble recognizing nonlinguistic experience and celebrating its importance both for cognition and for aesthetic satisfaction. His theory of inquiry and action ultimately rests on nondiscursive experience that is "had" but "not known," a noncognitive lived-dimension that provides the needed background and direction for thought and action (EN 198). Dewey likewise insists that aesthetic experience is rooted in prelinguistic somatic rhythms, in the most "basic vital functions" that we share with "bird and beast," and that art should aim at enhancing embodied experience as well as our minds (AE 19–20).

Practicing the somaticism he preached, Dewey became a devoted student and advocate of Alexander Technique—a system of subtle, gentle exercises of the upper body that realign posture and facilitate motion and breathing, while increasing awareness and conscious control of bodily action and affect. Over twenty years of Dewey's later life were spent exploring his body through this technique, and he wrote enthusiastic introductions to three of Alexander's major books.[25] Making this body-developing discipline part of his philosophy of self-enrichment and growth, Dewey lived a gratifyingly healthy life into his nineties and attributed his longevity to such philosophical living. In 1950 he declared, "it is in the capacity of a philosopher that I am a Nonagenerian" (LW 17:84). Four years earlier, he explained more specifically that without continued exercise in "Alexander's work ... I'd hardly be here today—as a personal matter."[26]

For Wittgenstein and Foucault, major philosophers of the linguistic turn who coined the seminal notions of "language-games" and "discursive formations," recognition of nondiscursive experience is more complex. But the soma nonetheless forms an integral part of their ideal of philosophical living. "The human body is the best picture of the human soul" (PI, II:178); moreover its passions help constitute the human soul that philosophy has the task of reforming. Hence, "it is my soul with its passions, as it were with its flesh and blood, that needs to be saved, not my abstract mind" (CV 33). For the young Wittgenstein, as revealed in Ray Monk's biography, "sensuality and philosophical thought were inextricably linked—the physical and mental manifestations of passionate arousal." At one point he confessed that when it came to sharing his new philosophical thinking, he "could talk only with somebody who holds his hand" (Mo 117, 243).

Monk's biography reveals a still more startling and significant fact about nonlinguistic experience: the great philosopher of language "did not even start speaking until he was four years old" (Mo 12). Was the "language-less" Wittgenstein so long deprived of meaningful experience or understanding? If this is incredible, then it seems hard to limit meaningful experience and understanding to the dimension of language. This long period of prelinguistic experience could explain Wittgenstein's passionate concern for the limits of language, suggesting a source for the central intuition that links the logic and the mysticism of the *Tractatus*—the idea of unutterable truths that make themselves manifest, that cannot be strictly expressed by propositions but only shown, yet are nonetheless crucial to our experience (e.g. logical form and the values of ethics and aesthetics).

Translated into Dewey's terms, Wittgenstein is celebrating what can be meaningfully *had* but not properly *known*, yet which provides the necessary experiential backgound for all knowing: "Perhaps what is inexpressible (what I find mysterious and am not able to express) is the background against which whatever I could express has its meaning"(CV 16). Somatic experience was one such site of the mysteriously proximate but propositionally unutterable: "the purely corporeal can be uncanny" (CV 50).

Even when the logic and metaphysics of the *Tractatus* were abandoned for a more flexible, capacious array of language-games, Wittgenstein continued to recognize the importance of nonlinguistic experience, particularly in the aesthetic and religious dimensions of life (LC 2–13; CV 70, 79, 85). In exploring the limits of language, Wittgenstein seemed acutely sensitive to the value of what lay beyond them, something that had an almost utopian resonance. The philosopher's tendency to "run against the boundaries of language," "against the walls of our cage" may be "absolutely hopeless" and produce linguistic nonsense. But it represents a noble yearning for something genuinely precious (at once sublime and simple) outside that discursive cage, something that Wittgenstein "personally cannot help respecting deeply" (LE 11).

In Foucault, even more than in Wittgenstein, preoccupation with language bears the glowing penumbra of a utopian nonlinguistic desire. Language remains a cage or labyrinth that "exists everywhere," structuring our experience from its "sovereign position" and binding us in the mind-forged manacles of socio-political domination and repression, which are reflected and sustained in the very discipline of its categories, rules, and evaluative terms. Though we may analyze its diverse forms, language's sovereign secret always "escapes us ..., its face inclined toward a night of which we know nothing," "a place of which no one can speak." (FL 25–26; LCP 86). This suggests that breaking out, even momentarily, from the linguistic labyrinth could afford us an intense emancipatory pleasure and new vision.

Radical somatic experience thus becomes an important complement to philosophy's standard study of discourse. The wish to transgress the limits of language, coupled with the guilty anxiety that its fulfillment would arouse, is beautifully captured in a recurrent nightmare Foucault had suffered since childhood—the inability to read a text or even project on it a linguistic meaning: "I have under my eyes a text that I can't read ... I pretend to read it, but I know that I'm inventing; then the text suddenly blurs completely, I am no longer able to read anything or even invent; my throat constricts, and I wake up" (FL 25).

While urging us not "to exclude any effort to uncover and free ... 'prediscursive' experiences" (AK 47), Foucault emphasizes how problematic such efforts must be. If bodily experience seems to offer a way out of language, Foucault is careful to insist that this experience is itself typically structured by the linguistic-social background (the dominating language-games, practices, and categories) through which we conceive and deploy our bodies. No site of pure, nondiscursive freedom, the soma is where society inscribes its disciplinary practices to form its subjects, its socially functional selves. But if we cannot fully escape the labyrinth of language, we can still use the body's nonlinguistic experiences to escape or explode some particular discursive yoke that oppresses or constrains our pursuit of the philosophical life of inquiry and self-enrichment.

The body serves Foucault's project in at least four ways. One philosophical task (for which he praised Kant's critical spirit of Enlightenment) is to test the limits of discursive thought and its ordinary modes of experience. For Foucault, such limits cannot be adequately tested by standard rational arguments which should, perforce, respect them. They can, however, be challenged by genealogical unmasking to show their contingent genesis in history. But they are perhaps best tested by powerful, transgressive experiences that transcend them—by physical *épreuves* (the French word conveying at once the ideas of test and experiential ordeal).[27] Thus, "the essence of being radical is physical" (FL 191), using the body in emancipatory critique of the discursive order by pushing it toward extreme "limit-experiences" which seem to defy or shatter the experiential structures of that order. Foucault viewed this somatic quest for limit-experiences as part of what he called "the erotics of truth," a "relentless search for a certain truth of pleasure ... pursued through its reverberations in the body and the soul."[28]

In challenging the discursive limits that define our experience, we are also testing the limits which define ourselves as subjects. Corporeal experimentation thus serves the classic philosophical quest of "knowing oneself," while also serving Foucault's special aim "to call into question the [signifying] subject." Such somatic exploration, if radically and relentlessly pursued, could achieve "an experience that might be [the subject's] real destruction or dissociation, its explosion or upheaval into something radically 'other'" (RM 46). Foucault so pursued it, according to Miller, through powerful drugs and sadomasochistic sex.

Without condemning these means, one can appreciate other, less violent forms of somatic exploration that also challenge and dissolve entrenched subjectivities by disturbing their entrenched somatic habits. By a demanding yet tender *askesis* of slow, subtle exercises of upper body and torso, combined with changing breathing, one can (I learned) suddenly feel new parts of one's spine, discover new possibilities of motion and action that overcome oppressive inhibitions by breaking through their reinforcing musculature and movement. This new somatic freedom can, in turn, radically alter one's sense of self. Foucault seems to overlook this option of a gentle yet transformative somatics (developed in the work of Alexander, Feldenkrais, and other body therapists), though he may have simply rejected it as too mild for his radical aims.

For Foucault, the body's third role is to help transform the self through new, undisciplined, decentering pleasures. Foucault both practiced and praised S/M for "inventing new possibilities of pleasure with strange parts of [the] body," seeing it as "a creative enterprise" "to make of one's body a place for the production of extraordinarily polymorphic pleasures, while simultaneously detaching it from a valorization of the genitalia," so that one could "invent oneself" in an altogether new manner. For S/M challenged not only the traditional top-down hierarchy of the body ruled by the head, but also Sade's hierarchy that privileged the genitalia and thus remained "an eroticism appropriate to a disciplinary society."[29]

What Foucault presumably sought in such somatic experiments was "to invent with the body, with its elements, its surfaces, its volumes, its depths, a nondisciplinary eroticism: that of the body plunged into a volatile and diffused state through chance encounters and incalculable pleasures." Describing this creative somatic explosion in more detail, Foucault portrays it as "a multiplication and burgeoning of bodies," "an exaltation of a kind of autonomy of [the body's] smallest parts." The result "is a creation of anarchy within the body, where its hierarchies, its localizations and designations, its organicity, if you will, is in the process of disintegrating.... It is the body made totally plastic by pleasure: something that opens itself, that surrenders, that throbs, that beats, that gapes."[30]

This anarchic somatic pleasure is something very different from Foucault's fourth recommended use of the body—as a medium of aesthetic self-stylization through demanding discipline and critical control. One model of such disciplined self-fashioning was "the moderate subject" of ancient Greece whose "aesthetics of existence" required mastery of self in relation to one's body, to one's wife, to boys, and to truth. It required a tasteful, imaginative compliance with "certain formal principles in the use of pleasures, in the way one distributed them, in the limits one observed, in the hierarchy one respected"(UP 89). Foucault's more radical model of embodied aesthetic self-fashioning—the Baudelairian dandy—is just as disciplined. Though refusing the conventionality and moderation of the Greek self-fashioner, *dandysme* involves (in Baudelaire's own words) "rigorous laws that all its subjects must strictly obey," expressed in the injunction to fashion oneself in an original, modern, poetic way.[31] Transgressive aestheticism thus involves, for Foucault, a somatic "asceticism," "a discipline more despotic than the most terrible religions" designed to make "of his body, his behavior, his feelings and passions, his very existence, a work of art" (FR 41–42).

Somatic anarchy and somatic discipline can be complementary as well as oppositional. Experimental dissolution of a repressive body-set can be a necessary first step for the disciplined reconstruction of a better one. Such a two-stage treatment is implicit in body therapies like bioenergetics (which begins with the shock of falling exercises and convulsions to break the hold of the entrenched body-set).[32]

Perhaps Foucault sought the same kind of strategy for the somatic dimension of philosophical life. But he also suggests a more daring way of linking discipline and dissolution: to make a discipline of the pursuit of undisciplined somatic dissolution, making oneself a radical artwork by submitting one's body to the programmatic demand for ever more risky and uncontrolled experimentation in anarchy. This conflation of somatic discipline with anarchic experimentation seems as dangerous (and as tempting) as Foucault's conflation of art with the violent novelty of the avant-garde.

Foucault's early death from AIDS (an accident, after all!) surely does not invalidate the somatic dimension of his aesthetics of existence. However, without moralizing, one can recognize that his specific style of somatico-aesthetic philosophy not only has risks but some interesting alternatives, the kind suggested by the life of the body that Dewey pursued.

IV

Self-Transformation, Growth, and Integrity

If philosophy is not an abstract theory but an embodied life, it essentially involves time and change. If it is also art, it demands not merely change but attractively coherent development or growth. Self-transformation is thus central to the philosophical life. Since every individual organism must adapt to survive, Dewey argues that change is built into our most basic natural needs and physiological rhythms. But it emerges, in any case, as a deep psychological need and moral imperative for all three of our philosophers. Moreover, since they deny that self-realization is defined by a fixed human essence, self-transformation becomes a distinctly individual challenge.

By his own confession, Wittgenstein went to war in 1914 not for the sake of country but through an intense desire "to turn into a different person."[33] Even in his later years, he still remarked that he could feel really active only when he changed his philosophical position and went on to develop something new (Mo 467), a fact that helps explain why he was constantly reworking his texts rather than being satisfied enough to have them published as they stood. Wittgenstein even argues that the active stimulus of change improves one's philosophy, preventing thought from growing smugly stagnant and stiffly one-sided: "I find it important in philosophizing to keep changing my posture, not to stand for too long on *one* leg, so as not to get stiff" (CV 27). Whether standing or sitting, he did in fact have trouble keeping still.[34]

Not only important for a sense of active living, change represents a way of escaping a self that does not please us. For Wittgenstein, who had recurrent bouts of moral self-loathing about his "baseness and rottenness," to be unhappy is ultimately to find fault with oneself.[35] If "life is problematic," "you must change the way you live" (CV 27). Foucault exhibits the same need for change as escape from self. "Do not ask me who I am, and do not tell me to remain the same. More than one person, like me no doubt, writes in order to have no face," escaping one's face, one's self, by changing it (AK 17). Self-transformation becomes the guiding goal of the philosophical life: "the main interest in life and work is to become someone else that you were not in the beginning" (TS 9).

But mere change for its own sake is not enough to define a life-project. For change can be blind, chaotic, insignificant. To some extent, it is anyway inevitable. Change must therefore be stylized into a coherent, meaningful project, which Foucault describes as making one's life a work of art: "the idea of the *bios* as a material for an aesthetic piece of art" (FR 348). This aesthetic refashioning has a clearly meliorative aim: "to improve oneself, to surpass oneself, to master the appetites that risk engulfing you" (FF 5). Yet one's creative transformation should not remain impenetrably solipsistic; it should, at least by suggestive example, "clear the way for a transformation, a metamorphosis which isn't simply individual but which has a character accessible to others" (RM 38–39).

The intelligibility and appeal of self-transformation require some degree of unity through change. Traditionally, this need was often expressed through the ideal of integrity, whose important aesthetic sense of *wholeness* has been unfortunately occluded by its more recent moralistic sense of honesty. Aquinas in fact makes *integritas* the first of his three conditions for beauty, along with *harmonia* and *claritas*. A beautiful object must stand out as a complete and unified whole — with no part missing or out of place. A beautiful life requires that its changes hang together to make an attractive whole.[36]

Like Foucault, Wittgenstein advocated coherent self-transformation and self-mastery, not only as a worthy end but as a crucial means for improving the lives of others. "Improve yourself," Wittgenstein would often say, and you will "improve the world"(Mo 17–18). He urged this not simply because of his intimate linking of self and world ("the world is *my* world" [T 5.62]), but because exemplary self-mastery is necessary for convincing others to change their lives as well: "That man will be revolutionary who can revolutionize himself"; for "no one can speak the truth, if he has still not mastered himself" (CV 35, 45).[37] The desire to transform not only himself but to effect "a change in the way people live" may seem inconsistent with Wittgenstein's apparently quiescent view that philosophy neither formulates new truths nor should interfere with our use of language, but simply "leaves everything as it is" (PI para. 124).

The resolution of this seeming contradiction is that formulated truth does not, for Wittgenstein, exhaust the practice of philosophy. By shrewdly collecting "reminders," assembling appropriate examples of existent facts and meanings in a "perspicuous representation," one can be brought to *see* and *inhabit* the world differently. This, indeed, is the real philosophical transformation. Not merely an expert at assembling examples, the philosopher should himself *be exemplary* of right living, inspiring others toward a similar life of self-betterment. "How can I be a good philosopher," asks Wittgenstein, "when I can't manage to be a good man?"[38]

For Dewey, who advocated "self-realization as the moral ideal" (EW 4:42), the aim of coherent, enriching change was captured by the ideal of creative growth. Rejecting not simply the idea of "a fixed, ready-made, finished self" but even the notion of any fixed or final ends for self-realization, Dewey concluded that "*the* end is growth itself," since this would include the development of new ends previously unimagined. One must "fight against induration and fixity" in the self so as to "realize the possibilities of [its] recreation" (E 306). "The growing, enlarging liberated self ... goes forth to meet new demands and occasions, and readapts and remakes itself in the process. It welcomes untried situations," for those precisely are what best provides it with possibilities of change and growth (E 307).

Transformative, enriching growth thus seems the highest moral injunction. Moral goodness, argues Dewey, is not an absolute state or quality but a comparative measure of striving to be better. One who has a high level of moral self-development but seeks to go no farther is thus less moral than a less developed self faithfully working toward self-improvement: "direction of movement, not the plane of attainment and rest, determines moral quality" (E 307). Self-satisfied smugness and stagnancy are thus mortal sins of philosophical living. "Resting on your laurels," Wittgenstein echoes, "is as dangerous as resting when you are walking in the snow. You doze off and die in your sleep." Complacency in the improving self is like "a beautiful garment that is transformed ... into worms and serpents if its wearer looks smugly at himself in the mirror" (CV 22, 35). Chided for driving himself too hard in seeking perfection, Wittgenstein proudly replied, "*Of course* I want to be perfect."[39] Foucault's project of continuous self-transcendence presents the same perfectionist ethic of self-overcoming—an ethics of overachievement suitable for the philosophical overachievers who are its advocates.

We should not forget, however, that other advocates of philosophical life propose less sublimely heroic ambitions. Montaigne, for example, prefers the beauty and pleasure of tranquillity and ordered harmony achieved through circumscribing one's ambitions. "The value of the soul consists not in flying high, but in an orderly pace. Its greatness is exercised not in greatness but in mediocrity." Resisting the temptations of fame through distinctive extremes, the beauty of good-living can show "its elevation by liking moderate things better than eminent ones." "The most beautiful lives," he concludes, "are those that conform to the common human pattern, with order, but without miracle and without eccentricity."[40] Even these aims, however, cannot be achieved without ameliorative work on ourselves. So how, then, is such self-transformation accomplished?

The first step is self-knowledge: probing one's present limits so as to grasp the needed dimensions and directions of change. As Wittgenstein advocates, "If anyone is unwilling to descend into himself, because this is too painful, he will remain superficial."[41] Courage is thus a necessity for growth, "the grain of mustard that grows into a great tree" (CV 38). It is required both for probing the self's imperfections or limits (through agonizingly honest self-confession) and for confronting the unknown dangers involved in its transformation. Endorsing Kant's Enlightenment motto of *Aude sapere* (dare to know), Foucault emphasizes the same need for courage in facing "the limits that are imposed on us and the ordeal of their possible transcendence" (FR 50).

The particular techniques of "working on oneself" for self-transcendence are multiform. Enlarging one's self by losing oneself in community action was one of Dewey's valuable suggestions. Foucault recommends not only the limit-experiences of body practices and militant politics, but also the tamer medium of writing: one writes "to become someone other than who one is." "There is an attempt at modifying one's way of being through the act of writing," an effort "to get free of oneself," "to let go of oneself" (*se déprendre de soi-meme*) (DL 182; UP 8). For Foucault, the essay's residual sense of "attempt" or "trial" best captures this textual aspect of philosophical living. "The essay—which should be understood as the assay or test [*épreuve*] by which, in the game of truth, one undergoes changes, and not as the simplistic appropriation of others for the purpose of communication—is the living substance of philosophy, at least, if the latter is still what it was in times past, i.e. an 'ascesis,' *askesis*, an exercise of oneself in the activity of thought" (UP 9). But other textual genres of philosophy (like "the confession") can embody this idea of effortful self-transformation that is never final, always open to question and revision. It is also evoked in the unending dialogue of critical self-questioning that characterizes Wittgenstein's later texts.[42]

Though evidently appealing, the ideal of self-realization through self-transformation poses a problem. What will sustain the unity of the self through such a program of change? If the self is but a series of transformations, the project of self-realization would seem to collapse with the dissolution of an enduring self. This is not merely a logical puzzle of referential identity for which one could, of course, provide certain formal solutions.[43] The real problem is existential and aesthetic: how can one live coherently or happily through radical and complex change without the security of what Dewey called "a fixed, ready-made, finished self"?

While Hellenistic philosophers could advocate integrity by appealing to one's "true self" or "ruling principle," and by prizing the tranquillity of uniformity over the hazards of change, this strategy of unity seems no longer available.[44] How, then, can we reconcile the demand for change with the aesthetic need for integrity and harmony? How to combine the goal of radical self-transformation with the (self-directed) Wittgensteinian plea "Only don't lose yourself! Collect yourself!"?[45]

The answer Dewey recommended was that the self's changes should be coherently organized around "sincere, enduring interests," held together by some unifying strand or pattern of development. One's "personal identity is found in the thread of continous development which binds together these changes" (E 302, 306). Our stable sense of self thus hangs by a thread. For Dewey this thread was adequately sustained by entrenched habits and the self-image we receive from our enduring community relations and intimate family ties, unities whose availability and value Dewey never seriously doubted.

The case is very different with Wittgenstein and Foucault, who seem far more sensitive to the violent ruptures and discontinuities of the changing self: perhaps because they lived in more discontinuous, self-fragmenting times; perhaps because they simply led, because of their homosexuality and other factors,[46] more divided and unstable lives, deprived of the (increasingly questionable) stability of conventional marriage and children to which Dewey seemed addicted. Whatever the reasons, Wittgenstein and Foucault (like many of us postmoderns) could not take the unity and even the sanity of the changing self for granted.

Recognizing that philosophy's very quest for self-knowledge

through self-analysis threatens the fragile unity of self, Wittgenstein poignantly notes: "The folds of my heart always want to stick together, and to open it I must always tear them apart" (CV 57). In the easily decipherable code of his notebooks, he confessed: "I am often afraid of madness," and his subsequent entry clearly links this fear with abrupt, discontinuous self-transformation. "Madness," he writes in an uncanny anticipation of Foucault, "need not be regarded as an illness. Why shouldn't it be seen as a sudden—more or *less* sudden—change of character?" (CV 53–54).

Foucault's confessions of disunity and proximity to madness were more public. From his podium at the Collège de France in 1976, he questioned the very coherence of his life and writings, doubting whether beneath the apparent disorder of very varied research and disruptive limit-experiences, "he follow[ed] a more profound, coherent, and reasoned trajectory" (PK 79). In an interview he later avowed that he had "had a personal, complex, direct relationship with madness" (RM 38). Years before, in considering the dissociative limit-experiences of Georges Bataille and perhaps his own initial experiments in radical, subject-shattering self-transformation, Foucault recognized the dangerous but distinct "possibility of the mad philosopher" (LCP 44).

The unity needed to hold oneself together as an enduring, attractive *oeuvre* had somehow to be supplied. Not guaranteed by a fixed human essence, it was instead constantly challenged by the variety of Foucault's activities and quest for radical transformation.[47] He eventually sought this integrity in the idea of aesthetic self-stylization. But what could supply the aesthetic glue to bind, integrate, and animate Foucault's variety of self-transformative experience into an appealing whole, one living work of art? His answer is like Wittgenstein's: a single-minded passion for philosophy, pursued with a singular, untiring desire to live a memorably unique and extraordinary philosophical life.

V

Death, Truth, and Heroism

The generative premise of any memorable life is death. Not only does the very notion of life depend on its contrast and conclusion, but the idea of living memorably gets its urgency from the fact that one will pass away and so need to be remembered. If philosophy is a life-practice taught through its exemplarity, the philosopher must create an exemplary monument of that life (typically through writing) in order to reach an audience beyond her death.

Not surprisingly, death is central to the tradition of philosophical living. Already in Plato's *Phaedo*, philosophy is defined as the pursuit or "practice of dying"; and this theme pervades philosophical antiquity (particularly in Stoicism). As Montaigne observes, the ultimate test of the truth and power of a philosophy of life was how it prepared the philosopher to face her death, where there is no more place for "sham" and "pretending."[48] Even after philosophy's modern professionalization as scientific discourse eclipsed the traditional model of philosophical living, we still find the notion of philosophy as an anticipatory meditation on death—perhaps most famously in Heidegger's account of authentic existence in *Being and Time*.

Though neglected by Dewey, death looms large in the philosophy of Wittgenstein and Foucault. Preoccupied with death on the personal level, both seriously contemplated suicide. It had been the solution for three of Wittgenstein's older brothers and two of his early heroes (Weininger and Bolzman); and it so fascinated Foucault that he not only attempted it several times, but studied it and publicly advocated its legitimation.[49]

Moreover, both gave reasons why death is central to the philosophical life. First, as Wittgenstein learned at the battle-front, death provides a strong spur to philosophical reflection (Mo 137): the urgency, in facing life's loss, of examining its meaning. Secondly, by the structural logic of semantics, death gives the concept of life its very meaning by providing its contrast and defining its range or limit, while also providing its directional trajectory and narrative terminus. If, as Wittgenstein wrote from the trenches, "only death gives life its meaning"(Mc 240; Mo 139), then exploring the meaning of life should take account of this defining contrast and structural frame. Foucault thus argues, "It is only starting from death that a science of life is possible ... [just as] it is from the perspective of folly that a psychology of intelligence can be constituted."[50] For, as Wittgenstein notes in a phrase remarkably suggestive of Foucault's two major obsessions, "in life we are surrounded by death, so too in the health of our intellect we are surrounded by madness" (CV 44).

Since understanding life involves probing its limits, and since philosophical probing means more than theoretical contemplation but also the concrete experience of practical ordeals, the approach to the experience of death through self-risking limit-experiences becomes a central discipline for Foucault's philosophy. Such experiences (which, for him, include those of writing) not only risk "the sacrifice of life itself" (LCP 117), but offer feelings of self-extinction that anticipate the final truth of death and provide a training ground for courage in facing it.

Wittgenstein's remark that "only death gives life its meaning" goes beyond the mere point of structural contrast. Death also gives meaning by providing a challenge—a sublime obstacle to somehow overcome by living the right sort of life. The will to surpass death's limits inspires efforts to immortalize one's life by making it extraordinarily memorable and admirable. By serving as an exemplar for future emulation, such a life transcends one's death. With the Greeks, as Foucault notes, "the will to lead a beautiful life" expressed the wish "to leave to others memories of a beautiful existence" (FR 341) and thereby attain a measure of immortality—an unquestionable object of desire, regarded by Plato and Aristotle as the prime motive for all human and animal reproduction.

One classic form of the memorable, beautiful life is that of heroism, courageously mastering the fears of life that culminate in the supreme fear of death. Death-defying courage was especially admired in the heroic culture of ancient Greece, which explains the enormous appeal of Socrates' philosophical heroism. Incorporating this heroic ideal into their account of philosophical living, Wittgenstein and Foucault insist on the importance of courage, even for intellectual progress.[51]

A highly decorated war hero who still complained of his "infinite cowardice" and "unheroic nature,"[52] Wittgenstein affirms

> Not funk but funk conquered is what is worthy of admiration and makes life worth having been lived. Courage, not cleverness; not even inspiration,—this is the grain of mustard that grows into a great tree. To the extent that there is courage there is a link with life and death. (CV 38–39).

> A hero looks death in the face, real death, not just the image of death. Behaving honourably in a crisis doesn't mean being able to act the part of a hero well, as in the theatre, it means rather being able to look death *itself* in the eye." (CV 50)

Conversely, "Fear in the face of death is the best sign of a false, i.e. a bad, life" (N 75).

Praising his father's gentle death as so "beautiful" that it "was worth a whole life," the young Wittgenstein wished for himself the aesthetic joy to "die in a moment of brilliance."[53] But he later insists that true confrontation of death cannot be thus romanticized or sentimentally softened. Death must be faced in its abrupt and brutal starkness:

> When someone has died, we see his life in a conciliatory light. His life appears to us with outlines softened [the German is "*abgerundet*," literally "rounded off"] by a haze. There was no softening for *him* though, his life was jagged and incomplete. For him there was no reconciliation; his life is naked and wretched. (CV 46)

The life-vindicating heroism offered here is that of tragedy. Death is only mastered by the memorable example of courageously facing its inevitable brutality in cutting life "jagged and incomplete" and frustrating one's efforts to round it all into a harmonious whole.

Foucault seeks a less tragic mastery of mortality. In his Nietzschean "gay science" of artful living, death is not just a brutally abortive, horribly ungovernable limit to be courageously faced. It instead can constitute a unifying, culminating moment to be sought, selected, and even savored as the fitting climax of one's carefully wrought aesthetic life, especially if that life involves a conscious preparation for death. The pursuit of deathlike limit-experiences is one form of preparation. Foucault therefore urged that we "teach people that there is not a piece of conduct more beautiful or, consequently, more worthy of careful thought than suicide. One should work on one's suicide throughout one's life."[54]

In the act of suicide, one masters death by deciding its moment and its means. But living life as an extended preparation for the goal of death provides a deeper mastery. For death then becomes not a threat of arbitrary annihilation, but the structuring end that gives enriching sense to one's life. Thus, in Miller's controversial view, Foucault's clearly unintended death from AIDS is nonetheless the culmination of a life-practice directed at death through its testing of the limits of experience. In this way, Foucault can be seen like Socrates as "dying for the sake of truth"; but for him this idea has a deeper, darker meaning. For a central part of the truth he sought was the truth of death as the limit of life and the subject.[55]

An even better way of mastering death, Foucault suggests, is by positively enjoying it, by experiencing it through pleasure, perhaps in the ecstasy of a limit-experience. In discussing the difficulty of attaining deep pleasure, he confessed: "I would like and I hope I'll die of an overdose of pleasure of any kind"; "the complete total pleasure ... for me, it's related to death." "The kind of pleasure I would consider as *the* real pleasure," Foucault elaborated "would be so deep, so intense, so overwhelming that I couldn't survive it. I would die." He claimed a foretaste of death's pleasure when, after smoking opium, he was hit by a car and "for maybe two seconds ... had the impression ... [of] dying, and it was really a very, very intense pleasure" (PPC 12). Montaigne likewise claimed a foretaste of this "pleasure" of "infinite sweetness," when, after a riding accident, he felt he was dying.[56]

Those who die in paroxysms of pleasure are very fortunate, but surely few. Besides, the pleasure Foucault and Montaigne describe is only that of an *imaginary* death. Yet Foucault apparently faced the approach of his real death, if not with pleasure, at least with laughter and serenity. Perhaps this was because death offered an agreeable, permanent relief from the tyranny of an incredibly demanding, self-critical subject. By definition, when one is dead, one has done all one has to do, gone as far as one can go. As Miller shrewdly suggests, at death, "the limit beyond all limits," Foucault was "free of the need for truth at last"(Mi 303, 374).

Wittgenstein seemed similarly obsessed with mercilessly pushing himself beyond the limit, for the sake of truth. Unable to conceive of living without the continuing struggle of philosophical labor, he seemed relieved to learn that death would finally release him from this wearying toil and from his painful, hopeless battle with cancer. In January 1951, Wittgenstein came to live at his friend Dr. Bevan's home so that he could better work his way unto death. He wrote philosophy up to the moment he fell violently, mortally ill, completing the final remark of *On Certainty* the very day before he lost consciousness forever, and two days before his death on April 29, 1951 at the age of 62.

Upon learning from Bevan that his life would be over in but a few days, Wittgenstein is reported to have exclaimed, with evident relief,

"Good" (Ma 81). Perhaps because of an unfightable enfeeblement, Wittgenstein seems in the end to take a "softened" view of death as rest and reconciliation. The standard biographical accounts describe his last words (to Mrs. Bevan) as "Tell them I've had a wonderful life" ("them" referring to friends who were coming to see him). His close friend Malcolm finds the remark very "mysterious," for "his life was fiercely unhappy" (Ma 81). But this remark, it now seems, was followed by one last plea: that he be quickly buried before his Viennese family could get hold of him.[57] Like Foucault, Wittgenstein seemed rather happy to be finally free from the duty to reach the hardest truths that would prove his genius and justify his life—not merely to himself but to his demanding family, patrons of genius who were both exacting in their standards and severe in their criticism.[58]

The death–defying quest for truth is what most distinguishes the philosophical life defined by Socrates from other models of the good life. Yet Socrates claimed to be seeking truth not for its own sake, nor as a means to assert his unique distinction so as to satisfy the genius-dandy's need for radical, personal originality, for inventing "something radically Other" (RM 121). Truth instead was sought for the sake of better living, for care of the self. Socrates therefore warned against pursuing knowledge not useful to that end, a warning echoed by many later philosophers (e.g. Seneca and Montaigne).[59] Even the paradigmatic ideal of self-knowledge was subordinated to a wider ideal of self-care, which, as Foucault himself admits, was given an "autonomy and even a preeminence" in ancient philosophy outside of Platonism (TS 26).

From this pragmatic perspective, one may challenge the demand for radical distinction and death–defying originality in the quest for truth. Wittgenstein avows that "happiness" rather than truth is the aim of "the life of knowledge" (N 81), and goes on to question the whole value of scientific truth for the more essential care of our selves.[60] Perhaps "the idea of great progress is a delusion, along with the idea that the truth will ultimately be known; that there is nothing good or desirable about scientific knowledge, and that mankind, in seeking it, is falling into a trap" (CV 56). Though Dewey's pragmatic faith in science is unshakably firmer, he likewise insists that truth's value resides in its instrumentality for life. Philosophy's traditional quest for ultimate truths and certainty is thus toned down to a search for better beliefs to foster better living, tempered by a critical respect for the common traditions and values that frame the philosopher's life-world.

Dewey's emphasis on life should raise the question of death. It must have been vivid in his experience (with the devastating death of two young sons), but his philosophical prose strikingly avoids it. If neglecting death is a weakness in a philosophy of life, Dewey's silence is disturbing.[61] Death does, however, figure in his poetry. Never intended for publication (having been mostly discarded but secretly rescued from his wastebasket and old desk by a Columbia librarian), Dewey's poems voice a range of darker emotions and themes that are suppressed in his philosophical writings by a controlling optimism. But taking philosophy as a life-practice, can we simply exclude this poetic reflection from his philosophy simply because it is pursued in verse and in private? Wittgenstein's philosophizing about death (in the *Notebooks* and *Culture and Value*) was similarly private, sometimes even written in code.

Dewey's poetic reflections, however, differ greatly from Wittgenstein's remarks. Death does not loom as the archenemy to be heroically stared down and mastered, but is instead accepted as a natural part of life's cycle. Only once negatively described as "the maddened moment ... of icy passion," death is often embraced in the poems as a haven of repose and reintegration with nature, where one is finally free from individual struggle and personal desire. For such reasons, Dewey can poetically address death as "my love,"[62] even while championing life and the struggle for ameliorative growth.

Dewey's meager attention to death is most charitably construed as pragmatic optimism: a concentration on life (that one can change) rather than death (the limit beyond which one can do nothing). It also aptly reflects death's relative retreat in contemporary life. Concentration on death was surely more justified in ancient and early modern times, when premature and painful death was a ubiquitous source of suffering and was far more in the public eye. Nonetheless, since we all experience death — if not in the moment of dying, then at least implicitly throughout life as its structuring horizon and conclusion, neglect of this theme is a weakness.

Granting this, one should distinguish between *recognition* of death and *intense preoccupation* with its mastery. We can then question whether the latter remains crucial for philosophical living, or whether it is only essential for providing it with the sort of spectacular, death-defying heroic pathos that allowed a plebian like Socrates to compare himself to the princely Achilles (*Apology* 28b–d).[63] With Wittgenstein and Foucault, this classic model of heroism is reinforced by the high modernist aesthetic of distinctive genius to generate their demand for memorability through spectacular singularity and courageous confrontation of death.

Can the philosophical life transcend the limits both of tragic heroism and of high modernist aesthetics yet still sustain its own central virtues? We may demand that this life be memorable, critical, and imaginative in experimentation, and that it bravely face our mortal condition—which includes the sad banality of aging as well as the sublimity of death. But these demands can be construed in less grandiose terms. Why should the memorableness of a philosophical life require centuries of global fame and not merely the vivid, generative memories of appreciative students and colleagues? In *Immortality*, Milan Kundera seems to suggest this option by distinguishing between "great immortality" and "minor immortality."[64]

There is also the option of construing the memorableness of living not simply as leaving memories for others, but primarily in terms of providing oneself with richly satisfying experiences whose memories justify one's life to oneself. One might speak here of a difference between two legitimate aesthetics: one of representation for others versus one of experience for oneself. Adopting the second, one would choose the beauty of a moderate life (that, viewed from the outside, seems unattractively dull) over an extremely dramatic life that may be sublime to observe but mostly an ugly torture to endure. Of course, to the extent that one's own experience of self is colored by a sense of one's image in the eyes of others, the difference between living for ourselves and living for others becomes diminished. But, here precisely is a role for philosophy's creative, experimental self-criticism—to help one reconstruct who one is and how one best lives.

Similarly, though death-battles evoke the most spectacular heroism, we should not discount the opportunities for courage in the ordinary business of living and its relentless struggles. (Aging may require as much courage as dying.) Nor should the idea of creating oneself be confined to making oneself radically unlike anyone else. Finally, the somatic testing of experiential limits also admits of less violent varieties than those Foucault advocated. Through gentle experiments in breathing and subtle movement (whether in yoga, Alexander work, or newer techniques of exploratory somatic awareness), ordinary people can come to feel parts of their bodies as never before, inducing an experience that for all its gentleness can be dramatically exciting and transformational.

In short, the strategy suggested here is to democratize the virtues of the philosophical life so as to make it a more appealing and feasible ethical project for more members of society. The difficulty is that philosophical living was not originally conceived in democratic terms, but instead was shaped by the deeply aristocratic character of Greek culture and its valorization of the spectacular and heroic. Part of the charm of philosophical life was its otherness, its defiant distinction from the conventional or ordinary, which embodied philosophy's crucial role of critique.

Construing this life in terms of modern aesthetics does not solve the problem. For our dominant aesthetic ideology is likewise elitist in demanding radical originality, with the artist-genius emerging as a new hero of superior imagination and self-sacrificing dedication.[65] If the philosophical life is to be exemplary and memorable by its aesthetic appeal, how can this appeal survive without radical, dazzling distinction? Can we democratize philosophical living without "normalizing" it, as Foucault would say, into unaesthetic banality? Must it, therefore, be confined to a small elite?

If there is a solution to this problem, it involves recognizing and developing a popular aesthetic that finds beauty and creative self-expression in more common, less spectacular forms. Though the sixteenth-century Montaigne could claim the greatest beauty for lives conforming to "the common human pattern ... without miracle and without eccentricity," this aesthetic has been undermined by modernity's quest for perpetual progress through singular genius and radical originality. For most contemporary philosophy, the notion of a popular aesthetic remains discredited yet unexplored. But its legitimation and amelioration (as advocated in *Pragmatist Aesthetics*) seem essential to the culture of democracy.

VI

Self and Society

Democracy is an issue here, because philosophy is lived in a social context. In contrast to the hermetic sage, the philosopher not only belongs to the *polis* but is one of its teachers. How then does he fit the personal quest for self-knowledge and self-perfection into the larger fabric of social life, so that care for the self intersects with care for society? For there is an obvious danger that preoccupation with self would involve a retreat from public life, as Epicurus indeed advocated.

Philosophy, Foucault argues, arose as a special form of courageous, critical truth-telling (*parrhesia*) precisely because this could no longer be safely pursued in Athenian political life, which was governed neither by truth nor by the few who sought to know it. Claiming in the *Apology* that he would have long ago been killed had he spoken out in official politics, Socrates instead ventured his truth-saying in more personal dialogical encounters, where he could seek self-knowledge while urging his interlocutors to undertake the same critical project of knowing and caring for themselves. He hoped that his words here could be more effective and that the consequent philosophical self-perfection of individuals would eventually yield a better *polis*. Philosophy thus appears as a higher, purer, alternative politics.[66] Its "care for the self," Foucault concludes, "is also a way of caring for others," since self-perfection "renders one competent to occupy a place in the city" (FF 7).

But since society exerts such a formative influence on the self and on its very idea of self-realization, how can we change society simply by concentrating on self-perfection without trying to transform those social factors that structure our very efforts at knowing and perfecting ourselves? Hence the wish for a philosopher-king who has the princely powers and knowledge to socially implement philosophy's care for the self and so create a society more suitable for philosophical living. But, even with such fantasies, the problem remains: how should philosophical life integrate self-improvement with reconstructive social work?

When conceived in terms of high art's aesthetic, yet pursued in modern societies of egalitarian ideology, philosophical living faces still more acute problems of social integration. If the criterion for success of a philosophical life is creating oneself into a dazzling work of unique genius, then how is this life-work to serve as an exemplar for general emulation? Pursuit of extreme originality risks rendering it too painfully lonely and esoteric to be widely understood. Moreover, even if understood, how could its demand for radical distinction be endorsed as an ethical model for society at large? If we take both egalitarianism and philosophy's exemplarity seriously, some other model of success must be provided for philosophical living. For even if we rightly reject the idea of conformist society and defend a pluralism of individually chosen lifestyles, we can hardly demand or even desire that everyone be radically, spectacularly different.

Wittgenstein, Dewey, and Foucault all wrestle with this problem of integrating self-perfection with the quest for democratic society. Their lives here are as instructive as their theories, and Wittgenstein's seems the most troubled. Born to a family devoted to public service as well as aesthetic distinction, torn between an acute sense of intellectual superiority and an equally strong spirit of egalitarianism, Wittgenstein struggled to reconcile his high-strung aesthetic sensibility with his deep, Tolstoyan longing for the ordinary, simple, and humble.[67]

Philosophical distinction was pursued through work so very abstruse, innovative, and individualistic that he always claimed to be misunderstood, even by the great philosophers who were his close associates, like Russell and Moore. Disturbed by the loneliness and misunderstanding involved in his quest for original genius, Wittgenstein frequently reacted by planning to abandon philosophy altogether and instead become a simple, useful member of common society. After completing his first masterpiece, the *Tractatus*, he tried a career as an elementary school teacher in rural Austria. But this project horribly miscarried because of his overly high teaching expectations, his severe manner of enforcing them, and his contempt for the narrow-mindedness of the parents and local officials. Later, during World War II, he left his chair at Cambridge to work as a mere dispensary porter at a London hospital.

Wittgenstein's most striking attempt to leave the lonely heights of philosophy and join the common ranks was his strenuous but unsuccessful effort in 1935 to find work as a manual laborer in Soviet Russia, refusing the philosophy posts that were offered him there. Though he continued to defend the Soviet ideal of a classless society and claimed to be "a communist at heart," he also confessed that the nitty-gritty of living in such a society was too distasteful for his upper-class taste, too full of petty dishonesty for "people of our upbringing" (Mo 343,353). It was one thing to idealize the people, it was another to live with them on their own terms.[68] Similarly, though he enjoyed Hollywood films and detective stories, they were taken more as escape than as objects of serious aesthetic study.[69]

Blocked by the uncompromising limits of his refined taste, Wittgenstein never tried to integrate his philosophical and democratic interests by writing more popular philosophy. He saw with Russell's popular works (which he strongly disliked) that such philosophy could reach a wide public. Even if unable to achieve large-scale social transformation, it could at least provide a way of getting one's ethical message to more people and spur them toward reform. Neither Dewey nor Foucault renounced this route of popular writing and journalism, but Wittgenstein eschewed it. To circulate an accessible formulation of one's life-philosophy outside the concrete context of its lived practice risked banality, sermonizing, and exhibitionism—apparent flaws of taste, if not morality.[70]

Compounded by his sense of living in an alien culture, Wittgenstein's high aesthetic imprisoned him in the romantic myth of the genius who must separate himself from (smaller-minded) society so as to produce the masterwork that will somehow redeem it. His philosophy and populist sentiments were never successfully synthesized, and his life, though a triumph of individual genius, was, for the most part, unhappily lonely.

Dewey felt no such qualms of aesthetic distinction and cultural difference in pursuing philosophical self-realization within the democratic society he championed. An unashamed popularizer whose technical writings display the same concern for easy accessibility, he devoted most of his ethical and political theory to showing that liberal democracy not only affords the best framework for individual self-realization but that this self-realization is best achieved through active commitment to the liberal democratic community. Because the self, even in its individual expression, is a product of social life, the kind of self formed through rich social engagement and concern for others "will be a fuller and broader self than one which is cultivated in isolation from or in opposition" to them. Preocccupation with one's own self-perfection will be counterproductive; not only because it blinds us to resources already present in others that can promote our growth, but also because it prevents us from helping others to perfect themselves and so enrich the fund of resources that can benefit our own lives as well as theirs. Oppression harms not only the oppressed: "the whole social body is deprived of the potential resources that should be at its service" (E 302; LW 11: 219).

Appropriately, Dewey's own life reveals no private preoccupation with distinctive, original self-creation.[71] Personal self-realization is pursued through a life of continuous public service for the causes of democracy. Having created, in Chicago, his famous Laboratory School which deeply influenced American education, Dewey later helped establish the New School for Social Research, the ACLU, and the NAACP. A key figure in the Outlawry of War movement and other international causes, he also served as president of two organizations aimed at establishing a third political party in America to promote democratic socialism. Moreover, he chaired the Commission of Inquiry on the Trotsky trial and the Commitee for Cultural Freedom.

His philosophical care of the self seems to be expressed so completely in care for the community, that important incidents of his private life — which include the heart-rending death of his two younger sons and a passionate, though unconsummated extramarital affair with a young Polish immigrant writer — are essentially dissolved, in Westbrook's and Ryan's biographies, into the larger social narrative of democracy. While downplaying the private is part of their biographical stance, it certainly reflects Dewey's own emphasis on the public dimension of philosophical self-perfection. Even biographers like Steven Rockefeller who probe most deeply into Dewey's private life end up confirming that Dewey's personality was firmly structured by a systematic repression of personal desires in the name of higher social ideals. Dewey's repression, also expressed in his extreme shyness and lack of spontaneity, is often attributed to the formative influence of his devoutly religious, zealously high-minded mother who exerted "too much moralistic emotional pressure" on the young Dewey, constantly demanding whether he was "right with Jesus."[72]

This, of course, does not mean that self-fulfillment through the social always requires such strong repression. It does show, however, that Dewey's rejection of self-centeredness rests on more than the logical grounds that this narrows the self. It stems also from his own psychological experience that relentless self-scrutiny is unpleasant. In his sixties he confessed that "being too introspective by nature" he had to control the tendency to "autobiographical introspection ... as it is not good for me."[73]

Here we have the paradox of a great philosopher shying away from the standard philosophical ideal of self-knowledge. But Dewey's pragmatist retort would insist that this goal, like any other, has no absolute validity apart from the consequences it engenders and that philosophy's demand for self-knowledge faces the limits of its goal of self-care. Self-scrutiny is only valuable to the extent that the organism can productively deal with it. As Montaigne and Nietzsche argued before Dewey, the values of life and enriched experience override the demand for knowledge, even though knowledge is often a necessary tool for their realization.[74] If the philosophical life has typically identified knowledge (particularly self-knowledge) with self-care and happiness, we now see that these ideals admit real tensions that can be expressed in the choice of different life-philosophies that differently privilege them.

Similar tensions are evident in Dewey's social theory. Though celebrating liberal democracy for its triple ideal of "liberty, equality, and fraternity," he recognized that the tensions between them pose "the great ethical problem: How to harmonize the development of each individual with the maintenance of a social state in which the activities of one will contribute to the good of all the others?" No general theory or "fixed method" could provide the answer, because the actual conditions of personal and social life differ with changing context. In short, since the art of living in democracy is not an exact deductive science, "the approach must be experimental" (E 349–50). Philosophy's harmonizing solutions and choices must be constantly tested and revised in the concrete practice of life.[75]

Foucault presents the most interesting case of integrating philosophical life with democratic social praxis. Far from Wittgenstein's frustrations, he also diverges from Dewey's unturbulent (if repressed) model of success. An experimentalist more radical than Dewey, he offers riskier strategies for translating the quest for self-perfection into the struggle for democratic reform. Moreover, in contrast to Dewey's example and maxim, Foucault seems self-consciously focused on himself and far less inhibited about self-expression.

Foucault lived the life of a public philosopher every bit as much as Dewey. Relishing his role as a philosophical media celebrity, he was keen to supplant Sartre as France's leading philosophical persona, appearing at numerous demonstrations and press conferences along with the aging existentialist rival. Like Dewey and Sartre, Foucault was willing to popularize his thought, not only granting frequent interviews in the popular press, but writing articles on topical political issues for newspapers like *Le Monde*, *Le Nouvel Observateur*, and *Corriere della Sera*.

While rejecting humanist ideology, Foucault was a militant activist for democratic and humanitarian causes, and, in the late sixties and seventies, became primarily interested in radical, popular political movements: the student revolt, prison protest, the Iranian revolution, and the struggle for gay rights. He was closely associated with the revolutionary French Maoists of the *Gauche Proletarienne* and organized the Prison Information Group. In a number of protests with students and GP militants, he risked bodily injury in violent confrontation with the police. Foucault clearly savored these communal limit-experiences of revolutionary abandon, just as he preferred the gay scene in California because its "experiences were experiences of community."[76]

Whatever the precise reasons, by 1980 Foucault, like many other French intellectuals, had abandoned militant extremism. Instead, he came to commend liberalism for valorizing privacy, pluralism, and the *negative* liberty of freedom from external rule—the ideal of minimalizing society's government so as to allow maximal self-government. This new appreciation of liberalism was linked to his increasing preoccupation with the ethics of care for the self, a topic which would henceforth dominate his work and lead him to devote far more research to the philosophical life than either Wittgenstein or Dewey ever did. His final course of lectures at the Collège de France was mainly devoted to this topic, tracing it from Socrates through the Cynics and Stoics and then into Christian times.

Miller's account suggests that Foucault pursued political radicalism largely for its transformatory limit-experiences of transgression, but then abandonned it when he saw a more promising strategy for self-transformation in the ethics of self-stylization. Appropriating a much earlier phrase of Foucault, he glosses this development as a "turn from an interrogation of the limit and transgression to an interrogation of the return of the self" (Mi 318). Should Foucault's political praxis then be dismissed as too narrowly self-centered and self-serving to be truly democratic? Should we regard it not as real politics but as "radical chic" aimed at elitist self-distinction?

This would be a mistake: first, because Foucault remained politically active (albeit not as radically militant) to the very end of his life.[77] Secondly, because he saw the "private" self as intrinsically a site and political battleground of the political. This self is both the effect and the enduring, reinforcing presence of the socio-political forces that constitute and shape us as individual subjects. Just as socio-political institutions mold us into disciplined, docile selves, so these "normalized" selves serve in turn to reconstitute and sustain those very institutions. For institutions cannot exist without their animation by acting subjects. To attack the normalized self through limit-experiences aimed at its radical transformation is thus to attack the essential underpinnings of repressive disciplinary institutions. To pursue such transformatory limit-experiences by radical transgression against those very institutions seems a most promising strategy, attacking them at once from both the outside and the inside.

Promising, but ultimately not satisfying for Foucault. His own formative subjectification as a highly refined, successful bourgeois intellectual was perhaps too deeply entrenched to be permanently transformed into a life of radical transgressional politics, with its all too frequent brutality, confusion, and failure—aversions which mainstream politics also offers in abundance. In any case, Foucault's ideal of self-creation as a radically original artwork is best seen in this political context. Not as a selfish withdrawal from politics, but the pursuit of transformational politics by other means—those over which the individual has more (though far from complete) control. Political resistance to oppressive normalizing powers is pursued by transforming the normalized self into something radically different and more attractively powerful. The avant-garde artist is the revolutionary's *confrère*; both are claimed by Foucault as modern avatars of the ancient philosophical life of heroic self-transformation for the sake of truths and values that extend beyond the self.

The innovative artwork is an exemplary model for self-governance because it defies prescribed external rules yet succeeds as an effective, attractive law unto itself. But the aesthetics of radical novelty carries its own disciplinary norm: the injunction to be altogether original and unique. Only a few exceptional individuals can fulfill it. If Foucault saw the Greek aesthetics of existence as possible only "for a small elite" that had the requisite material means, his modernist aesthetic of original genius seems even more exclusive. It thus undermines his egalitarian ideal that art not be merely "something done by experts who are artists," his hope that "everyone's life be a work of art" (FR 341, 350). But if we renounce the aesthetics of radical distinction as our model for self-transformation, how do we avoid falling back into normalized complacency, accepting the aesthetic shape we already have or the one that society has already prescribed as the norm?

Foucault's dilemma—and one for any democratic aesthete—is that self-transformation must be different enough to resist the homogenizing pressures of normalizing powers and yet be accessible enough to be understood and adopted by ordinary subjects normalized by those powers. Some way must be found to transcend standardized norms without exceeding the reach of common people. In his very last lectures, Foucault sought such a way through study of the ancient Cynics.

Like the exemplary modern artist and revolutionary, the Cynics advocated a radical change of one's lifestyle and a repudiation of society's standard values. This idea of challenging social conventions is nicely captured in Diogenes' famous injunction (from the oracle of Delphi) to "change the face of the currency." Yet the direction of this change was not toward elitist sophistication, rather toward the most simple, humble, popular experience. Reducing life to its most basic functions and reducing its own philosophy to very elementary practices and doctrines, Cynicism could be practiced by anyone who really wanted to make the effort. It required neither wealth, education, nor intellectual brilliance—only the will power to endure the raw realities of simple living and the demanding physical training used to perfect the capacity for endurance.

Cynicism could therefore be advocated for everyone, no matter how poor and humble. In contrast to other ancient philosophies, it insisted on universality and was militant in its missionary zeal. The term "Cynic" (from the Greek word for "dog") suggests not only the doglike simplicity and shamelessness of its way of life, but a watchdog's attention to care of the self and a dogged aggressiveness in attacking rival lifestyles and values. The goal of universal conversion gave Cynicism's doctrine of self-care a promising political dimension. For if everyone adopted the Cynical life that scorned society's conventional hierarchies and aristocratic values, then political transformations would seem sure to follow. Demanding such radical reform not simply from a single soul or *polis* but from the whole world, pursuing it not only by discourse but by action, does not this philosophy, Foucault asks with Epictetus, "constitute the true political activity" (Lecture of March 21, 1984)?

Cynicism's philosophical life fascinated Foucault because its telling and testing of the truth was physically embodied and courageously pursued through continuing experimentation at the human limits of raw living and physical endurance. Cynicism was similarly heroic in its flagrant defiance of convention. Diogenes not only violated Greek norms by eating and sleeping on the public street; he even masturbated there, bravely enduring not only the physical elements but the scornful abuse of conventional society.

If philosophy's goal was to show that truth was other than what was commonly accepted, then this truth need not be located in a transcendental other world (like Plato's). It could rather be found in a radically other form of *earthly* living, by courageously abandoning our most familiar but artificial social conventions so as to live life's raw truth. This heroic, dramatic nonconformism made the Cynic's life distinctively spectacular and memorable as well as true. Yet, because such distinction not only comes through bare simplicity but also aims at leveling social divisions by converting everyone to it, no philosophical quest for self-perfection could appear more democratic.

Cynicism, however, had its flaws. One problem was aesthetic. To inspire emulation, the philosophical life should be beautiful—a life that could engage and gratify the aesthetic taste of those who contemplated its example. Though Cynicism was admirably heroic, memorable, and even (in Foucault's words) "spectacular by its savagery," the crude simplicity of its radical return to basics (as evidenced by the extremes of Diogenes self-exposure) made Cynicism too ugly for the beauty-conscious Greeks—and for Foucault. By pushing the beautiful idea of simplicity to its radical extreme, it introduced vulgarity and ugliness into the philosophical life.[78] Likewise, in taking the noble idea of independence to its limit by forsaking the securities of conventional employment and accepting whatever chance provided, Cynicism led to a life of dependent mendicancy that the proudly aristocratic Greeks found insupportably dishonorable. For similar reasons, today's street-people could hardly be proposed to us as models of the good life.[79]

But could there be a life of simplicity that would avoid the ugly excesses which rendered Cynicism aesthetically repugnant? In his survey of Cynicism, Foucault briefly notes the second-century Demonax, who achieved great popularity and influence by adopting "a gentle practice" of Cynicism that, despite some demanding privations and physical *aske-sis*, avoided the scandalous extremes of Diogenes with their "violence, aggression, and affront" to the sensibilities of the poor as well as rich. Foucault similarly notes how the Stoic Epictetus defends Cynicism by maintaining that its ugly scandalous traits are not esssential to its practice, that "the Cynic doesn't have to be dirty, disgusting" but should, to the contrary, avoid offensive indecency so as to attract more converts (Lectures of March 7 and 21, 1984).

This more modest, inoffensive Cynicism does not, however, win Foucault's endorsement, because its modesty seems to rob the Cynic's life of its dramatic spectacularity, its heroism, and its radical otherness.[80] But heroism, even memorable heroism, can be practiced with modesty and does not require the clamorous exhibitionism of Diogenes. Modesty, however, *does* seem out of line with the spectacular, with what Foucault calls "*l'éclat*" and identifies as a necessary feature of successful philosophical living. Yet why must a successful philosophical life be spectacular? Beauty and exemplarity do not really require it (as even Dewey's example shows). Nor does the exercise of philosophy's other central virtues: integrity, rational critique, courage, and the quest for self-improvement and for the knowledge it demands.

Why, again, must the philosophical life flaunt a radical otherness?[81] Implicit in both these demands is an aesthetics of avant-garde genius that is not content with beauty but requires dazzling distinction, the creation of "something radically Other," "a total innovation" (RM 121–22). Despite its ugliness, Foucault is strongly drawn to Cynicism because it displays an aesthetic of spectacular, original distinction (in which radical ugliness paradoxically seems a part). Unlike Montaigne and Dewey, he is unable to recognize the possibility of a popular aesthetic of simplicity that can be beautiful without being dazzling and radically original.

We are never given any argument why such an aesthetic is impossible or why it must be inadequate for shaping an attractive philosophical life. Surely it suggests a way to reconcile the ideal of aesthetic living with the ideology of egalitarian (though not homogenized) democracy. The question of a popular aesthetic becomes thus crucial not only to the art of democracy but, ultimately, to its ethics and politics as well.

VII

Remaining Questions

Before pursuing such issues in the coming chapters on democratic and aesthetic theory, let me note another hard question. Even if a popular aesthetic proves possible, doesn't the very idea of democratizing the philosophical life simply rob that notion of meaning? Only by distinguishing philosophy from other practices or ways of life can the philosophical life have any sense. But if democratization means that not only "real" philosophers but ordinary folks can practice philosophy, then doesn't the meaning of "philosophical life" just evaporate into a uselessly empty notion of good living? Don't we need to provide a clear definition of the philosophical life, some distinctive list of essential features or necessary achievements, in order to ensure it really means something?

Of course not; just as we don't need a definition of art to talk meaningfully about artworks. In both cases, clear definitions are unavailable because the concepts are not only vague and open, but also essentially contested and essentially historical (hence changing). Like "art," the concept of philosophical life can have its meaning clarified by presenting and explaining some paradigm cases and offering some genealogical narrative to link its different cases to a shared yet divergent tradition.

Nonetheless, let me further clarify my idea of the philosophical life by suggesting something crucially shared by our three contemporary paradigms: the ideal of critically reflective self-care as self-improvement through the disciplined pursuit of relevant knowledge. If this ideal is likewise held by premodern philosophical-life exemplars—from Socrates and Epictetus to Augustine and Montaigne, they do not further share the Dewey-Wittgenstein-Foucault model of self-improvement as endless growth through perpetual self-transformation.

Democratizing the philosophical life means that anyone could make this ideal her guiding principle of life. Most people, however, do not choose to—not even if they seek a good or an aesthetic life. For there are other styles of good and aesthetic living that, unlike philosophy, are not as demandingly amelioristic and concerned with knowledge; for instance, complacent lives of simply enjoying the good things and aesthetic pleasures that come one's way. If most people don't want to make the meliorative effort required of philosophical living, then such living can function as "a critical other" to smugly conventional lives without being undemocratically limited to a professional elite or clique of eccentric geniuses.

Just as aesthetic lives need not be philosophical, so conversely, not all philosophical lives must direct their meliorative quest by the aesthetic ideal. The ancient medical model of self-improvement as better psychic health and virtue through disciplined self-knowledge can also serve; so can a more scientific model of self-perfection through dedicated pursuit of objective truths (as intimated in Max Weber's notion of "science as a calling").[82] Though these three models can overlap (e.g. mental therapy and science being either conditions or means for artful self-creation), the aesthetic model for philosophical life seems today the most compelling.

Such points show that "philosophical life" means something more definite than merely "thoughtful or good or aesthetic living," but there remains an objection often pressed by my fellow professors of philosophy. To construe philosophical living as critically reflective and ameliorative self-care practiced through the disciplined pursuit of knowledge seems to leave this practice disturbingly unconnected to the specific field called "philosophy" in the standard, disciplinary sense. Shouldn't the philosophical life be somehow connected to the reading and writing of distinctively philosophical texts concerned with traditional philosophical problems? Shouldn't its pursuit of "relevant" knowledge be concerned with Aristotle and Adorno rather than Archie and Asterix comics or baseball trivia?

Philosophical living needs strong links to the disciplinary tradition of philosophical writing for three good reasons. First, these texts are typically directed toward the sorts of knowledge most relevant for the self-ameliorative practice of philosophical living. Moreover, they have often been written by individuals engaged in the philosophical life and as an integral part of it. The practice of philosophical life is not only enhanced by a consciousness of belonging to a venerable theoretical and literary tradition named "philosophy," but is also in fact empowered and sustained through that tradition's exemplary stature. We must not forget, however, that this stature partly derives in turn from philosophy's striking exemplars of life-practice.

Nor should we forget that the disciplinary bounds of philosophical writing are historically open, vague, and essentially contested. For those who construe philosophical writing primarily in terms of a focus on questions of "wisdom" and "the meaning of life," this genre includes not only essayists like Cicero, Montaigne, Emerson, or Nietzsche but even philosophical poets like Dante, Goethe, or Wordsworth, and novelists like Dostoyevsky or Proust. Philosophers who dismiss such authors as mere literature face the countercharge that writers like Carnap and Frege are mere mathematicians or logical grammarians. Philosophy's history is full of such charges and countercharges because it is a richly diverse and essentially contested tradition. If only by connection to this tradition, the concept of philosophical life is likewise essentially complex and contested. This makes it pointless to pose questions like whether a philosophical life can satisfy its reading requirements through Plato, Spinoza, and Shakespeare without also including Locke, Russell, and Quine. Philosophical life is further complex and contested in having dimensions apart from writing, which, as we saw, can be exemplifed in rival ways and different degrees by different philosophers.

Complex, contested "range concepts" like that of art or democracy are more usefully treated with a logic of gradations than of categorical "yes-no" demarcations.[83] Futile debates about whether a particular government is really democratic can be transformed into more specific, answerable questions like "is it more or less democratic than some other regime and with respect to which dimensions of democracy?" The gradable approach thus directs us to more fruitfully concrete questions of how to render the problematic government more democratic.

In thinking about philosophy and the philosophical life, such a gradable approach makes more sense. I can imagine someone who worked on philosophical theories of truth, meaning, or personal identity but did nothing about relating this work or any other disciplined thinking to the project of self-improvement. Such would be a philosopher without a philosophical life. By the gradable approach, getting a philosophical life would not suddenly turn him into a *real* philosopher but simply into *more* of a philosopher; while leading that life with greater scope and devotion would make him still more of a philosopher. In this sense, one might consider Wittgenstein more of a philosopher than Frege or Quine, even if not a better or "truer" one. In the same sense, Tolstoy might be considered more of a philosopher than our imagined truth-theorist even though he might be a much worse philosopher in the technical sense. The gradability of a multidimensional range concept also accommodates the fact that though the practice of philosophical life is open to everyone, those with more knowledge of philosophy's tradition can, *ceteris paribus*, practice it more fully and richly.

Prizing useful pliability, pragmatism favors the gradable approach in preferring projects of melioration to rigid demarcation. Precisely defining the philosophical life (and its aesthetic model) is less useful and interesting than exploring strategies for practicing philosophy as ameliorative, aesthetic self-realization. The issue of democratizing philosophy's aesthetic life is best treated not as an abstract question of logical possibility but as a project to pursue by critically probing and developing actual pragmatist proposals for democratic politics and popular aesthetics—topics of the following essays.

Part I

ETHICS AND POLITICS

2

PRAGMATISM AND LIBERALISM
BETWEEN DEWEY AND RORTY

I

Throughout the Reaganite eighties and into the post-Soviet nineties, Richard Rorty has been using pragmatism to praise and defend the virtues of contemporary American democracy and to advocate a political philosophy which he has dubbed "postmodern bourgeois liberalism."[1] At every turn, he invokes John Dewey as its inspirational source and appeals to Deweyan arguments for its justification. Claiming his liberalism is fully "continuous with Dewey's," he locates his differences with Dewey in "the account of the relation of natural science to the rest of culture, and in stating the problem of representationalism versus antirepresentationalism in terms of words and sentences rather than in terms of ideas and experiences" (ORT 16). More bluntly put, Rorty rejects what he sees as Dewey's privileging of natural science over literary culture, just as he refuses to countenance philosophy that traffics, as Dewey's does, in nonlinguistic entities like experiences or ideas. Apart from such differences, Rorty claims to be advocating the same sort of "democratic, progressive, pluralist community ... of which Dewey dreamt" (ORT 13).

By celebrating American bourgeois democracy while condemning the pretentious yet futile "subversiveness" of leftist intellectuals, Rorty's liberalism has offended Marxist and post-Marxist radicals all over the world. But it has also shocked many American Deweyan liberals. Long-term friends and pragmatist fellow-travelers like Richard Bernstein are dismayed at how Dewey's radical and clearly anticapitalist liberalism is being distorted and assimilated into "an *apologia* for the status quo—the very type of liberalism that Dewey judged to be 'irrelevant and doomed.'"[2] Opposing Rorty's complacent view that bourgeois liberalism requires only small-scale improvements through minor "reformist tinkering" (ORT 16), Bernstein invokes Dewey's *Liberalism and Social Action* (1935), which ardently insists that "liberalism must now become radical, meaning by 'radical' perception of the necessity of thoroughgoing changes in the set-up of institutions and corresponding activity to bring the changes to pass. For the gulf between what the actual situation makes possible and the actual state itself is so great that it cannot be bridged by piecemeal policies undertaken *ad hoc*."[3]

Rorty responds by dismissing such contemporary attempts to maintain Deweyan radicalism as empty "exercises in nostalgia," given the fact that today there are no real alternatives to capitalist economies (SH 22). And he scorns the way radical intellectuals portray themselves as socially concerned champions of the oppressed, when their global theories of radical reform have no touch with concrete political realities and practical proposals, but serve only to flatter their own self-image as avant-garde revolutionaries whose special, esoteric knowledge could save the world.

This chapter will compare Rorty's and Dewey's liberalism, while paying particular attention to their meaning for this book's central issue: the philosophical life of self-realization in contemporary liberal society. The purpose of my comparison is not to grade Rorty's fidelity or to police the purity of Dewey's views. Such historical purism is false to the forward-looking spirit of pragmatism. In trying to understand how Dewey's radical liberalism has evolved into Rorty's conservativism, I hope to promote a better balanced liberalism by playing their views off one another.

To probe the deeper philosophical roots of their differences, I shall consider such issues as the nature of liberty, contingency, and philosophical justification, the value of aesthetic unity, the social construction of the self, and the relation of means to ends. Moreover, since pragmatism is historicist and recognizes that philosophical differences are often the product of social change, I shall explore how the differences between

Rorty and Dewey may be understood in terms of their different worlds. Finally, I shall suggest how we liberal pragmatists may go beyond the Dewey-Rorty stand-off by splitting their differences, keeping the Deweyan hope for philosophically inspired social reform and more participatory democracy, along with the Rortian sense of the limits and abuses of philosophy in treating our current social predicament. This, of course, includes our "private" social predicament as philosophers seeking the best way to live.

II

Foundations and Justification

Dewey and Rorty share the aim of freeing liberalism from its traditional philosophical foundations in Enlightenment metaphysics. The standard liberal strategy, established by Locke and Kant, was to ground human freedom ontologically through some doctrine of natural rights, ultimately derivable from our God- or nature-given gift of reason, which requires freedom in order to realize itself in rational choice and action. Individual liberty is thus guaranteed as what people should have and what societies must protect, because it is built into the very nature of things as part of the rational essence of human nature. Dewey refused to ground liberalism in such a metaphysical doctrine of inalienable rights and necessary human essences. As pragmatist, he rejected metaphysics' fixed world of essences, insisting instead on the plasticity, change, and contingency of our universe.

Rorty thus praises Dewey for making liberalism "look good" to contemporary antiessentialist philosophers by giving it "philosophical articulation" without "philosophical backup," by "debunking the very idea of 'human nature' and of 'philosophical foundations'" that political theories like liberalism were supposed to require (ORT 178, 211). For Rorty, there are no ontologically fixed essences or inalienable truths to appeal to as philosophical foundations, so there is no place for philosophical justification of politics or any other practice. Any attempt to provide one will only serve to discredit the relevant practice by calling attention to the fact that it is weak enough to require false philosophical support.

Rorty, however, is wrong in thinking that Dewey's attack on the metaphysics of traditional liberalism was primarily aimed at making liberalism safe for philosophers. It was aimed at making liberalism safe for the masses by curbing its rapacious individualism. If individual liberty rested on inalienable ontological givens of human nature, then that would imply it is always already present in us. There would thus be nothing to do but to leave it, and individuals, alone; the worst thing to do would be to impose external constraints on it. Liberty here is identified as negative liberty, as freedom from interference; and liberalism is equated with a laissez-faire politics that refuses to constrain the freedom of the few to take advantage of the many, denying the many a positive freedom of empowerment to lead a better life.

Dewey rejected the idea of natural rights because it saw liberty as an abstract metaphysical *given*, not as a concrete good that depended on contingent societies and required their improvement. For Dewey, "freedom ... is something to be achieved" rather than "something that individuals have as a ready-made possession"; its achievement is "conditioned by the institutional medium in which an individual lives." Hence "organized society must use its powers to establish the conditions under which the mass of individuals can possess actual as distinct from merely legal liberty" (LSA 21).

Rorty ignores this motive in Dewey's rejection of liberalism's philosophical foundations because he is far more appreciative of negative liberty, defending it against its communitarian critics who share Dewey's emphasis on positive freedom and communal life. Rorty also ignores that Dewey's rejection of the old metaphysical foundations of liberalism is not a rejection of philosophical justification *tout court*. Dewey in fact worked hard to provide his vision of liberal democracy with a convincing "philosophical back-up." He elaborated this in terms of basic human desires for consummatory experience, growth, self-realization, and community. He further showed the need for collaborative effort to achieve greater frequency and security for these desired ends in a changing contingent world whose future can in some measure be influenced and improved by human action and experimental intelligence.[4] Though repudiating any transcendental deduction of democracy from necessary essences, Dewey was concerned whether "nature itself, as that is uncovered and understood by our best contemporaneous knowledge, [could] sustain and support our democratic hopes," giving them a convincing "intellectual warrant" (MW 11:48).[5]

Rorty's neglect of this nonfoundational option of philosophical justification is not surprising, because he wants to deny such justification any logical space. Revealing what Bernstein rightly diagnoses as a residual "positivist strain," Rorty sharply dichotomizes the universe of justificatory discourse into "real" philosophical justification (hard-edged, technically argued deductions from shared first principles) and mere rhetorical urging through polemics and storytelling.[6] While historicism and contingency make the former vulnerable or question-begging, the latter does not really qualify as philosophical argument that can logically establish what it urges. Given this crippling dichotomy, it is easy to see why Rorty reads Dewey as offering a story rather than "philosophical backup." But it is is harder to understand why Rorty maintains this positivist dichotomy while rejecting positivism.

One answer may be the more technical professionalism of Rorty's philosophical world in contrast to Dewey's, a contrast that lurks behind many of the differences in their pragmatist liberalisms. Rorty's philosophical institution, professionalized under the aegis of positivism and increasingly isolated from the mainstream of American cultural life, prides itself on the technical rigor and logical precision of its deductive arguments, on its quest for certain knowledge which is part of its logic of legitimation through assimilation to science. By such scientistic professionalist standards, justificatory arguments in the murky (and dangerously practical) domain of political theory, arguments that were moreover articulated in nontechnical language and clearly motivated by political ideals, could hardly count as professional philosophical proof. And if not professional philosophy, they were simply not philosophy at all, but only ideological polemics and culture criticism.

III

Freedom and Self-Realization

Both Deweyan and Rortian liberalism privilege not just the individual but what one might call her individuality: her particular freedom and self-realization. While Dewey differs from Rorty in demanding active communal life for self-realization, he stresses that the democratic ideal of equality is not a leveling uniformity of societal function or status, but can only "be measured in terms of the intrinsic life and growth of each individual" (E 346). For Dewey no less than Rorty, "democracy means that personality is the first and final reality," and its satisfaction through self-fulfillment should be the aim of both the individual *and* society. Though society establishes the environing conditions for its realization, "personality cannot be procured for any one, however degraded and feeble, by any one else, however wise and strong"; and "only ... the man who is realizing his individuality is free in the positive sense of the word" (EW 1:244; EW 3:344).

Dewey further insists that a liberal democracy must lead its members to achieve this positive freedom of active empowerment. Rorty demurs, fearing that any public preoccupation with how individuals realize themselves will painfully intrude on their personal negative liberty. For him, the prime value of liberalism is its privileging of negative liberty over any positive conception of self-realization or empowerment, its "ability to leave people alone, to let them try out their private visions of perfection in peace" (ORT 194). This different valorization of positive and negative liberty underlies the most salient differences between Dewey's and Rorty's versions of liberalism.

It explains why Dewey will risk radical reform of the politico-economic system so that the mass of individuals will have adequate conditions, i.e. the positive freedom, to realize themselves; while Rorty, afraid to damage the negative liberties that already exist, instead urges the politics "of Tolerance rather than that of Emancipation" (ORT 213). It also explains why Rorty defines liberalism's ideal *negatively* as the "desire to avoid cruelty and pain," and sees its society as "a band of eccentrics collaborating for purposes of mutual protection" (CIS 59, 65), while Dewey defines it positively in terms of the creation of a real community devoted to the positive joys of self-fulfillment in associated living and committed to collective action so that each member can realize herself while (and through) contributing to the common good.

Finally, their different emphasis on positive and negative liberty explains why Dewey's liberalism seeks to bridge the private and public, while Rorty's resolutely refuses to. Dewey's utopia aims "to harmonize the development of each individual with the maintenance of a social state in which the activities of one will contribute to the good of all the others" so that very different individual self-fulfillments can contribute to "a fund of shared values" (E 350); Rorty more modestly and negatively wants to leave individuals to their own devices, whatever (and however meager) they be. He sees "the aim of a just and free society as letting its citizens be as privatistic, 'irrationalist,' and aestheticist as they please so long as they do it on their own time—causing no harm to others." The ideal is "to equalize opportunities for self-creation and then leave people alone to use, or neglect, their opportunities" (CIS xiv, 85). Dewey would respond that for such opportunities to really be equal (i.e. equality of positive empowerment rather than of freedom from interference) society cannot simply leave people alone to neglect them but must create the conditions and habits that encourage their use.

Such differences seem more than a mere function of personal preference. They reflect the historically different societies that Rorty and Dewey inhabit and the role these societies accord the philosopher. In Dewey's time, people still believed that radical reconstruction of society was possible and that philosophers could play a major role in mapping it out. This faith is now almost totally eroded. Philosophers in America no longer play the prominent public role that Dewey did. The structure of society (including that of their own profession) does not empower them to do so; they are free to theorize, but foolish if they think they can positively implement their theories through influential political action.[7] In such conditions, it is natural to privilege negative and private liberty because it seems the only liberty we still have to exercise. Viewed in this way, Rorty seems not so false to Dewey as he is true to his own social reality.

Though they differ on the type of individual freedom they privilege, Dewey and Rorty agree that self-realization is the highest value for liberal democracy, and that such self-fulfillment is distinctively individual and aesthetic. Realizing oneself is not a matter of fulfilling any fixed general essence of human or citizen, conforming to a predetermined moral or social formula legislated by nature or society. It is rather a particularized creative project of individual growth, a Nietzschean project of becoming what one is, by utilizing one's particular conditions, talents, inclinations, and opportunities to mold oneself into a fuller, more attractive person who will enjoy more rewarding experiences with greater frequency and stability. Rorty's advocacy of "the aesthetic life" of constant "self-enlargement," "self-enrichment," and "self-creation" aimed at realizing one's "distinctive individuality" may seem the more outspoken (EHO 154, 158; CIS 41). But Dewey was just as ardently explicit on these aesthetic themes. He recognized "self-realization as the ethical ideal" and insisted that it "demands the full development of individuals in their distinctive individuality," which can only be achieved through continuous "growth, learning, and modification of character" (E 302, 305, 348).

The primacy of aesthetic self-realization is sometimes occluded by Dewey's valorization of science and political concerns. But these, for him, are simply means (though valued means) for the satisfying consummatory phases of experience that he identified with aesthetic experience and prized as the joy that makes life worth living. Dewey thus affirmed that "art, the mode of activity that is charged with meanings capable of immediately enjoyed possession, is the complete culmination of nature, and that 'science' is properly a handmaiden that conducts natural events to this happy issue" (EN 269); just as he claimed that "art is more moral than moralities" since its imagination discovers and realizes new goods and ideals rather than trying to enforce outworn conventional ones (AE 350).[8]

Though both Dewey and Rorty advocate the ideal of aesthetic self-realization, they differ as to how this ideal is embodied; and this results in their strikingly different political views, especially on liberalism's need for participatory democracy and the division between the public and private spheres. For Dewey, self-realization requires active participation in the public sphere and in the business of government. The individual can fully realize her freedom, distinctive selfhood, and talents only in "fixing the social conditions of their exercise," only in "direct and active participation in the regulation of the terms upon which associated life shall be sustained and the pursuit of the good carried on" (MW 5:424). Self-government is thus essential to self-realization. Since the individual is always affected by her environing conditions, she must take an active interest in the managing of her community and in the common good of her fellow citizens who interact with and impact on her. Hence "any liberalism that takes its profession of the importance of individuality with sincerity must be deeply concerned about the structure of human association," and the canny liberal concerned with her own self-realization should recognize that its success depends also on that of others (LSA 31; E 302).

Dewey thus aims at harmonizing liberty and equality with fraternity. Rorty instead seeks "to dissociate liberty and equality from fraternity," and self-realization from self-government (ORT 210). Drawing a "firm distinction between the private and the public" (CIS 83), he insists that self-realization is an essentially private affair, a question of "what should I do with my aloneness?" (ORT 13). The public, political functioning of liberal democracy is merely an external protective framework—though the best we know—for individual self-creation but not an intrinsic, formative element of it.

We can better assess these different visions of liberalism and self-realization by exploring their roots in more basic issues concerning the nature of the self, its social construction, and the type of aesthetic that should guide its reconstruction.

IV

Contingency and Unity

Dewey and Rorty both view the self as an individual, contingent, and changing creation, not the necessary expression of an ontologically predetermined and universally shared human essence. For Dewey "there is no such thing as a fixed, ready-made, finished self" (E 306), because every self not only produces actions but is also the product of its acts and choices. Such choices depend not only on the changing contingencies of its environment (natural and social) which limit the range of choices, but also on the contingencies of the consequences of action which influence future choices. For Rorty, however, "the contingency of selfhood" becomes still more extreme. If there is no ahistorical essence of human nature or "permanent ahistorical context of human life" which dictates what the self must be, then it is entirely "a matter of chance, a mere contingency," a "random," "accidental coincidence" (CIS 26, 37; EHO 155, 157).

Rorty's argument conflates contingency as "not logically or ontologically necessary" with contingency as "entirely random and idiosyncratic"; it reflects the false presumption that we have either absolute necessity or total randomness.[9] Dewey refused to make this leap from denying ontological necessities based on metaphysical essences to affirming that selfhood is a random matter of chance. He instead recognized historicized essences (e.g. in the form of powerfully effective biological and social norms) and contingent necessities—regularities or needs that are virtually necessary given the contingent evolution and current structures of human biology and history. Thus, in contrast to Rorty, he could not only speak of "the intrinsic nature of man" (E 308), based on current knowledge of biological and social sciences, but could argue from this historicized nature to justify the sort of life and government that would be most conducive to human flourishing.

Moreover, while both philosophers affirm a "moving, dynamic self" (E 308) aiming at continual growth, Dewey insists far more than Rorty on the unity and coherence of self-development. In advocating growth as the highest moral ideal, Dewey recommends change to "fight against induration and fixity, and thereby realize the possibilities of recreation of our selves." But he also urges that the self's changes be structured through "sincere, enduring interests" and held together through some unifying strand. For our very sense of self, "our personal identity is found in the thread of continuous development which binds together these changes" (E 302, 306). Rorty's program of "radical change" for "self-enlargement" refuses to let self-coherence and unity constrain "the desire to embrace more and more possibilities" by constantly redefining the self in new, often conflicting vocabularies. We shouldn't worry about the self's losing its unity, because it never really had any. We are simply "random assemblages of contingent and idiosyncratic needs," and what we take as the single self is in fact a composite of conflicting "quasi selves," "a plurality of persons ... [with] incompatible systems of belief and desire" (EHO 147, 162).

Rorty's fragmentation of the self builds on a Davidsonian reading of Freud and dovetails with postmodernism's deconstruction of the subject, so can we claim that his liberalism is sounder than Dewey's because it rests on a more sophisticated, psychologically updated view of the self?[10] Rorty himself must reject this argument, for he repudiates the very idea of basing ethics on some underlying theory of human nature. He even maintains that such theories of self instead derive their power by conforming with our preferred ethical views, with the ideals and institutions we find most attractive (ORT 192–93; TT 577–78).

Where, then, is the attraction of self-enlarging self-realization without a self unified enough to hold it all together? It admirably conforms to contemporary society's (well-advertised) ideal of maximal, multitrack consumption, the ingestion of an overabundance of commodities, images, information bits—far more than can be digested and brought together in a coherent whole.[11] Rorty's view of the self as a random composite of incompatible quasi selves constantly seeking new possiblities and multiple changing vocabularies seems the ideal self for postmodern consumer society: a fragmented, confused self, hungrily enjoying as many new commodities as it can, but lacking the firm integrity to challenge either its habits of consumption or the system that manipulates and profits from them.[12]

To sum up, Rorty's radicalization of contingency engenders a far more narrowly individualistic idea of self-realization than Dewey's. Both deny that self-realization can be conformity to a universal, ahistoric human essence (since there is none). But Rorty alone concludes that self-realization must therefore lie in maximizing one's distinctive idiosyncracy by highlighting the contingent differences which distinguish us from other members of our community and by confining our efforts of self-creation to the private sphere, to the question of "what to do with our aloneness" (CIS 24–25; TT 13). Working on oneself *by* oneself *for* one's self-distinction is Rorty's answer to this question. Dewey instead would urge us to find a friend, a community. For in order to create ourselves, even our private selves, we need to work with others on our environing society; because its fairly stable contingencies are far more formative of self than the random vagaries of chance that Rorty emphasizes. Indeed they significantly limit the range of the latter.

V

Society and Philosophy

Although Dewey gives teleological privilege to the individual, society precedes and shapes its constitution. "Individuals will always be the center and consummation of experience, but what the individual actually *is* in his life experience depends upon the nature and movement of associated life" (LW 14:91). This social construction of the self is central to Dewey's argument that personal self-realization demands an active public life: If "the mental and moral structure of individuals, the pattern of their desires and purposes" (I 80) depend largely on the habits, thoughts, and values that society encourages, then improving our society seems essential to improving the quality of the selves we realize. Moreover, if humans are intrinsically social animals, both needing and enjoying social life, then an individual can only fully realize herself by going outside herself and taking an active part in associated life. Dewey thus concludes: "Only by participating in the common intelligence and sharing in the common purpose as it works for the common good can individual human beings realize their true individualities and become truly free" (LSA 20).

This argument to fuse "self-creation and justice, private perfection and human solidarity, in a single vision," is precisely the sort of philosophical thinking that Rorty repudiates as hopelessly misguided (CIS xiv). But in doing so, he neither denies that the self is shaped by society nor that individuals, in order to achieve the end of self-realization, should work to assure the sort of democratic society that provides the best framework or means for this end. What Rorty denies is that the project of self-realization requires engaging in public life as *part of the end*. Yet this is exactly the sort of integration of public and private that Dewey demands: "to get rid of the habit of thinking of democracy as something institutional and external and to acquire the habit of treating it as a way of personal life" (LW 14:228).

Why does Rorty reject Dewey's democratic ideal which ultimately identifies personal self-realization with public action for the public good, which binds the ethics of self with the politics of the other? Why does he insist that individuals in liberal society need no social glue to bind them together other than the desire for a social organization which will "leave them alone to try out their private visions of perfection in peace"? Why is he especially suspicious of *philosophical* claims to unite the quest for private perfection and public democracy?

First, Rorty wants to protect our cherished negative liberties from *philosophical* tyranny. No philosopher, no matter how sure of his ideal of self-perfection, should be able to prescribe how different individuals must live their own *private* lives, beyond what is necessary for letting others live theirs. Moreover, no such ideal should be advocated as necessary for the *public* welfare. Theories which link self-perfection with the public good promote precisely that claim. Even to insist that self-perfection requires active participation in public democratic process is, for Rorty, to violate democracy by imposing on our negative liberty a specific ideal of private self-fulfillment.

For Dewey, negative liberty is not liberty enough to guarantee true democracy. Democratic public concerns must be incorporated into the ideal of self-realization. He would further claim, against Rorty, that self-realization cannot be adequately full if narrowly self-seeking and focused on the private:

> The *kind* of self which is formed through action which is faithful to relations with others will be a fuller and broader self than one which is cultivated in isolation from or in opposition to the purposes and needs of others. In contrast, the kind of self which results from generous breadth of interest may be said alone to constitute a development and fulfillment of self, while the other way of life stunts and starves selfhood by cutting it off from the connections necessary to its growth. But to make self-realization a conscious aim might and probably would prevent full attention to those very relationships which bring about the wider development of self. (*E* 302)[13]

Here the debate seems to reach a stand-off where choice of theory depends on a more or less aesthetic judgment: is self-realization without involvement in public life really rich enough to truly satisfy or realize the self? But Rorty then brings a second argument against making participation in public life an essential part of personal self-perfection: its futility. How can we formulate our quest for self-realization in terms of the public's quest for greater democracy and other common goods, when the public seems something so abstract, remote, and unfathomable that it can hardly give rich, concrete content to our personal lives? The substance of public life, Rorty argues, is just too thin, bland, and generalized to afford the individual adequate material for distinctive growth. Dewey may believe that public politics feeds a wider, broader self, but for Rorty it supplies only unexciting commonalities, standardized procedures, and bureaucratic institutions, which, though necessary for governance, are not the thick, interesting particularities through which the self can develop and articulate its distinctive voice.

We may again look behind the conflicting views and arguments to the different social conditions which structure them. Dewey wrote in an age when community life was more substantial and coherent for the individual, and when philosophers like himself played a more active and visible role in public life.[14] In such a context, the idea that full self-realization required participation in social life made more sense. By contrast,

Rorty's contemporary America makes no public demands on its philosophers. Rather than being urged to develop ourselves through service to society, we are cloistered in the universities and impelled to adopt (through societal and peer pressure, including the structuring pressures of tenure and differential salaries) a narrowly professional model of self-realization, whose trajectory involves little more than writing articles for professional journals and books for university presses. In such a context, it is natural to think that professional distinction and private pleasures are, in pragmatic terms, all there is to self-realization. So if Dewey is a philosopher of the *polis*, then Rorty is a "campus" philosopher, which may be the only kind of philosopher that contemporary American society is willing to have.[15]

The responsibility for the public desuetude of American philosophy does not lie only with the global (and perhaps democratizing) societal forces that have been undermining the authority of intellectuals. American philosophy's domination, since the 1940s, by the ideology of logico-linguistic analysis—a domination against which Dewey cautioned and struggled—has also played a major role in isolating philosophy from social praxis. This formalist approach intensified compartmentalizing professionalization by reconstructing philosophy in terms of technical discourse and metaproblems far removed from the actual language and problems of society. It further privileged the areas of "pure" philosophy (those closer or better reducible to strict logico-linguistic analysis), while marginalizing others as "applied." This pushed political and social thinking toward the margins (though not as far out as medical or business ethics).

Finally, all real philosophical problems (even those that seemed deeply and stubbornly about life) were conceived as essentially problems of language that could be resolved or dissolved by logico-linguistic treatment.[16] Given this fundamental premise, philosophy can do very little for concrete social and political problems, which typically embody empirical and normative rather than merely linguistic complexities. This is precisely the conclusion that Rorty urges and where his liberalism differs sharply from Dewey's.[17]

Dewey thought philosophy should be central to socio-political reform, not by deducing ontological foundations for such reform but by imagining the best ends and means for it. Chiding contemporary philosophers for "lack of imagination in generating leading ideas,"

Dewey claimed that philosophy could prove its value only "with the formation of directive hypotheses instead of with a sweeping pretension to knowledge of universal Being" (PC 11; QC 248). In proposing concrete means and ends, philosophy should be "thinking which is operative — which frames and defines ideas in terms of what may be done, and which uses the conclusions of science as instrumentalities" (QC 227).

By contrast, Rorty accepts philosophy's lack of socio-political utility. His pragmatism shares the Deweyan refusal to empower by appeal to ontological essences and natural rights, but it abandons the idea that philosophy can compensate by proposing effective means for social empowerment. Rorty "cannot find much use for philosophy in formulating means to the ends which we social democrats share." Instead he sees "its main use" in thinking through our personal utopian visions, in supplying vocabularies which we can appropriate, transform, and transcend in our quest for self-realization. So "philosophy has become more important for the pursuit of private perfection rather than for any social task" (TT 569; CIS 94).[18]

VI

Public/Private and Means/Ends

Rorty's privatization of philosophy is most often explained as uncaring moral complacency, as trying to justify our selfish preoccupation with private gain and narcissistic self-fulfillment. But such charges seem unhelpfully simplistic, especially given his frequent critique of our society's selfishness and greed.[19] A more useful critique would be to argue that Rorty denies philosophy's contribution to politics because he harbors an exaggerated expectation of what this contribution should be. He must know that philosophers are sometimes consulted on public issues and that they educate generations of public servants. But this is evidently not enough for Rorty's project of distinctive self-realization, which seems to demand, on the political front, either new visions of social ends or at least new methods of implementing those ends our society already shares. He quite reasonably does not expect such innovative contributions to issue from professional philosophers. But it is far less reasonable to assume that meaningful politics must take this grand form of invention. Rorty's view that the options of public life are just too bland to supply significant content for self-realization suffers from the same sort of exaggerated expectation, which identifies meaningful self-realization with radical innovation and distinction.

The best way to defend Rorty's privatization of philosophy is to argue that by directing philosophy from public problems to private perfection, we are more effectively redirecting it from means to ends. For Rorty, as for Dewey, the ends or consummations which make life worth living are realized only in individual experience. Liberal democracy and its public institutions are thus not ends in themselves but means to provide individuals the freedom and wherewithal to enjoy their chosen ends and realize themselves as ends in their own preferred ways. If philosophy can serve these ends directly by providing vocabularies and exemplars of self-creation, why should it have to serve them indirectly by worrying about the public means?

Dewey's reply, we recall, is that the public means of democratic life is an intrinsic part of the end of self-realization. Part of this reply rests on aesthetic grounds of fullness and unity. Private pleasures are not rich enough to satisfy. "Shared experience is the greatest of human goods" (EN 157); and civic life contributes indispensable satisfactions and dimensions of self-perfection. Moreover, since the self is shaped by its environing society, the Deweyan goal of self-unity or "fullness of integrated personality" demands the integration, not the Rortian split, of public and private life.

But beyond these aesthetic considerations, Dewey's refusal to separate the end of private perfection from the means of public participation involves his distinctively holist view of the means/end distinction. True means are not simply necessary, external conditions for the end, but rather integral parts of it—as the colors and lines that are the means of a painting also form part of its end. Dewey saw the traditional sharp distinction between ends and means as correlative with the division between theory and practice, both of them born from Athenian class-hierarchy that identified means and practice with the lower laboring classes, while ends and theory were given to the leisured elite who had the conditions to enjoy them. Opposing the privileging separation of theory from practice, pragmatism should also oppose the separation of ends from means, and consequently of private from public.[20]

Rorty's focus on philosophy for private ends seems precisely such a privileging strategy of division, though it is disarmingly disguised by debunking philosophy's old metaphysical claims. If we really care about ends, Dewey urged, we must equally care for the means to produce them; hence "ends separated from means," private perfection divorced from public action, are the "sentimental indulgences" of the leisured elite. "It is a doctrine which can appeal only to those who are already advantageously situated" (QC 223; E 202).

Rorty can answer this charge of "sentimental indulgence" with that of "sentimental nostalgia." It is not that public means are less important than private ends. It is rather that, realistically speaking, philosophy today can do very little to improve those means, while it can do much to realize private ends. So, pragmatically speaking, it makes better sense to use philosophy where it can be profitably used.[21] As public philosophers in the postmodern, post-Soviet world, "we have little sense of how to make ourselves useful," because we can neither ground bourgeois liberal democracy on philosophical foundations nor concretely imagine any superior alternatives (SH 13). As marginalized intellectuals in a bafflingly complex society, we philosophers simply lack the practical means to transform public life and improve solidarity, so to theorize vaguely about such transformations would be a far greater sin of separating theory from practice, means from ends.

Perhaps Dewey's age was somewhat different. But to think that our multicultural, postmodern, liberal society will heed our philosophical urgings for a public sphere of close-knit community, a good "old timey *Gemeinschaft*" (ORT 209) bound together by shared ends and values, is to indulge in nostalgic fantasies of legendary days when philosophers could pretend to orchestrate the harmony of the *polis*. For Rorty, this "communal and public disenchantment [with its concomitant disenchantment of public philosophy] is the price we pay for individual and private spiritual liberation" (ORT 194).[22] Not only is it a price worth paying; it has already been paid, and there is no return.

VII

Cultural Politics

Dewey offers liberal philosophers a vision of democratic life where they can realize themselves as free, distinctive individuals by serving their society's quest for freedom, where private perfection is fused with and enriched by community action, and where philosophical training contributes to public reform, not just to private growth. It is very hard to give up this liberal utopia, with its rich integration of the self and the social, of freedom and community, grounded on the Deweyan axiom that democracy "is the idea of community life itself" (PP 328). Abandoning this vision is particularly hard for leftist intellectuals of my generation. For participation in such communal action for socio-political reform (whether campus sit-ins, national protest marches, or socially conscious, sleep-in music festivals) was precisely what gave us our very identities as free individuals capable of distinctive self-creation. Such communal political action was how we transformed ourselves from obedient children to free adults, from solitary readers and TV viewers absorbing parentally assigned texts to group activists keen on creating our own distinctive culture and modes of living, one of which was the commune.

Though Dewey's liberal ideal is hard for us to abandon, the contemporary reality Rorty portrays is equally hard to deny. American postmodern society simply does not constitute the sort of closely integrated public or caring-sharing community on which Dewey's democratic ideal of private-public self-realization is based.[23] But even if Rorty is right to abandon hope in a philosophically inspired Deweyan "Great Community," he is wrong to conclude that private pleasures are all we theorists can hope to derive from philosophy. The error in Rorty's logic is to think that loss of *the* public as one true community leaves us nothing but the private. Between the Great Community and the private individual there is also the notion of smaller communities or publics. These are small enough to be real communities of meaningful interpersonal relations and yet large and powerful enough to connect the individual to the wider social world and afford him a true arena to enact and enhance his freedom.

The university community constitutes one such public and has become the focus of concrete political reform with respect to issues like affirmative action and multiculturalism in the curriculum.[24] Moreover, such curricular reform is often philosophically inspired by genealogical critiques of the canon, deconstructive arguments for the centrality of the marginal and of difference, and pragmatist critiques of fixed, absolute values. It is easy to see how the radical student activism of the sixties, after two decades of political frustration and increasing despair for substantive reform in more central political areas, has turned its energy to the politics of culture and education.

Rorty is quick to condemn us "tenured radicals" for conflating cultural politics with *real* politics, for substituting the problems of privileged campus dwellers for the problems of the poor and homeless. He chides us for pretending that cultural transformations in the university "will eventually, somehow, link up with solutions to the problems" of "real leftist politics," which he glosses as "initiatives for reducing misery and overcoming injustice" by "redressing the balance of power between the rich and poor"(IP 488–89; SH 7). He blasts our focus on cultural politics for implying, and thus promoting, a total despair of reformatory action through our extracurricular political system and a rejection of liberal democracy for being incorrigibly corrupt.

But this implication strikes me as silly as arguing that concentrating on the local college team implies that the NFL is an unredeemable lost cause that must be dissolved. Moreover, just as it is weird to deny that college (or high school) play is good enough to be real football, so it is odd to argue that because problems of cultural oppression and racism on the campus are so much less acute than in the ghetto, they cease to be problems important enough to wear the honorific term "real." Finally, it seems dangerously simplistic (though typically American) for Rorty to portray political misery and injustice in narrowly economic terms of rich and poor. Wealthy German Jews could not buy an Aryan manumission.

We cultural activists know as well as Rorty the difference between the problems of lesbian feminists at Barnard and those of homeless crack addicts in Harlem, just as we know that our campus reforms offer no substantial help in solving the more painful, pressing, economic problems Rorty identifies with real politics. But conceding this, we can still assert what Rorty denies: "that cultural, and especially academic, politics are continuous with real politics" and should be vigorously pursued (SH 20). For university policies concerning admissions, scholarships for the poor, affirmative action in hiring, and the holding of investments in countries and corporations which foster oppression are not so easily separable from the real politics Rorty commends.

Why, then, should he fight to deny this, especially when continuity is so central to pragmatism's rejection of essentialist dichotomies?

Apparently, it is fear of cultural politics' global pretensions and its elitist, sectarian, negative methods. Rorty thinks that such politics "calls for the total transformation of our society" and that it works to achieve this by ideological unmaskings and cultural trangressions effected through literary theory's specialist tools for deconstructing texts, its mastery of what Paul de Man calls the "linguistics of literariness" (IP 487). The strategy, as Rorty scornfully sees it, is "that upsetting our students' parents will sooner or later help upset unjust institutions" (SH 20).

But Rorty's anxious critique of cultural politics rests on conflating two very different varieties of this species—call them poststructuralist Marxism and postmodernist pragmatism—both of which think that cultural politics is the best thing we humanities professors can currently do for democracy. The Marxists argue that the entire socio-political system of liberalism is so irreparably corruptive that all established means of democratic reform, even the use of ordinary language, are always already contaminated by bourgeois ideology. Hence there is nothing for leftist professors to do but practice academic subversion by writing and teaching against liberal ideology through transgressive analysis of cultural texts, using a technical language that neither bourgeois oppressors nor the brainwashed oppressed can understand. Subversion should be practiced, not only for its moral refusal of complicity, but in the hope that it will aid historical forces working for liberalism's total disintegration.

Pragmatists, on the other hand, reject such totalizing theories of ideological systems and language, and with it the dream of total revolution. They offer no fancy theoretical foundation for thinking that campus and cultural politics should be used to advance democracy; simply the practical point that that is the area where we humanities professors have the most knowledge and power. (As postmoderns, such pragmatists are as appreciative of the local and piecemeal as they are dubious of totalized critique through utopias of a radical Other.)

Cultural politics, for such pragmatists, is not an excuse for abandoning liberal democracy, but simply provides the best domain where we can practice and improve it from within. It offers a more familiar and manageable arena for substantive participation in democratic action and reform, a narrower field of greater control and surveyability where we can experiment with concrete proposals and better gauge their effects. In this arena, our political activity is immediately tangible and often effective, thus offering positive reinforcement to habits of engaged, caring, political action. And these habits, if sufficiently developed and reinforced, can give us the firm political disposition and confident know-how needed to throw ourselves successfully into the wider, more terrifying terrain that Rorty designates as real politics. It would be better if we were already prepared to tackle the world, to help the homeless rather than the culturally slighted. But using this to condemn our attempts to improve our local academic community (and our public selves) is to make "the better" the enemy of "the good" and to ignore the continuity of democratic habit.

These themes of habit and local community are, of course, central to Dewey's liberalism, which held that "democracy must begin at home, and its home is the neighborly community." For only such "face-to face communities" provide "the vitality and depth of close and direct intercourse" through which we learn to respect each other as distinctive individuals and to care for our mutual as well as private welfare (PP 368).[25] For us humanist academics, compelled by market pressures to be gypsy scholars, the university is often our only local community, and culture is where we live. This is a good place to exercise our liberal democratic virtues and the best way to bridge the difference between Rorty and Dewey: using cultural politics to enhance our private perfection by making us better, more active public selves, enjoying the consummations of caring, communal action inspired by our philosophical hopes and convictions.

3

Putnam and Cavell on the Ethics of Democracy

I

Two of America's most prominent philosophers, Hilary Putnam and Stanley Cavell, have recently focused their attention on the question of democracy, studying the arguments for its justification and reconciling its defense with the claims of individual self-perfection. Each of these philosophers explores democracy not in terms of its concrete rules and political institutions, but as an ethical ideal that is central to what they regard as the primal philosophical question, "How to live?" Thus Cavell advocates "the life of philosophy" for its "power to change people" by teaching them to live better; while Putnam declares that "the role of philosophical reflection at its best" is "to change both our lives and the way we see our lives," since "we all have the potential of thinking for ourselves with respect to the question of How to Live."[1]

This, of course, was the burning question of nineteenth-century Harvard-bred thinkers like Emerson and Thoreau, who avidly pursued it not only in theory but through adventurous experiments in living, like Walden. Faithful to this tradition of construing *life* as the central philosophical project, Cavell and Putnam chide professional philosophers for ignoring it to concentrate on metaphysical issues that have virtually no impact on how one lives.

By affirming philosophy's practical orientation to the problems of life, Putnam and Cavell are likewise true to the spirit of pragmatism. Both are especially inspired by Dewey's ethics of democracy and self-realization. But by criticizing its alleged limitations, each attempts a better theory of the democratic philosophical life. To continue this project of reconstructive pragmatist meliorism, I hope to show where their own theories, and Dewey's, require revision and amplification. I begin with Putnam, who, unlike Cavell, firmly identifies himself with pragmatism.

II

Putnam's defense of democracy is explicitly built on two Deweyan lines of argument that he characterizes as *social* and *epistemological*. The social line of argument helps combat the kind of scepticism about democracy that derives from a demand for "absolute" justification, one that would justify democracy in terms of "the world as it is independent of our experience" (RP 81).[2] Dewey's pragmatism—with its insistence that knowledge is always situated and has impact on the plastic, changing universe—rejects the very idea of such an absolute point of view.

There is thus no possibility and no need to justify democracy in terms of something beyond the experience and values that situated members of a community already share. Justification of democracy is always already social, addressed to a community and based on its values. It aims at "giving reason to people already disposed to hear it, to help in continually creating a community held together by that same disposition." It is, as Putnam says, "addressed to *us* as opposed to being addressed to each 'me'" (RP 182). Moreover, the values to which it appeals are essentially social in a further sense: being values of intelligent discourse and action, rather than mere values of physical or psychic fitness (metaphorically described by Bernard Williams as the "ethological standard of the bright eye and the gleaming coat" [RP 182]).

Complementing this "social justification" is what Putnam calls Dewey's "*epistemological justification of democracy*," a line of argument that similarly issues from pragmatism's insistence that knowledge—like the very notion of reality—depends on a community of inquirers.[3] Putnam formulates the claim like this: "Democracy is not just one form of

social life among other workable forms of social life; it is the precondition for the full application of intelligence to the solution of social
problems" (RP 180). How is this strong claim supported?

The argument's first premise, Putnam maintains, is that "*epistemology
is hypothesis.*" Experience has shown that knowledge of the world, including the world of value, is best achieved not through *apriorism* or acceptance of authority but through "intelligently conducted inquiry,"
which includes the formation of hypotheses and their testing in experimentation (RP 186). Secondly, the social condition that promotes the
fullest capacities for forming and testing hypotheses is surely a free collaborative community of inquirers exchanging their different points of
view and results.

Hence, "the need for such fundamental democratic institutions as
freedom of thought and speech, follows, for Dewey, from requirements
of scientific procedure in general: the unimpeded flow of information
and the freedom to offer and to criticize hypotheses" (RP 188). For
Dewey, such freedom means *positive* freedom or real empowerment to
apply one's thought to the government of self and society. Democracy
means active participation by all, rather than simply leaving questions of
governance to experts who are entrusted with the job of ensuring the
freedoms and benefits that we wish to enjoy from society.

Dewey can defend his participationist model of democracy over the
consumerist one of expert-governance by again employing his epistemological justification. Despite their specialist knowledge, experts do not
know everything relevant to the direction of society. Good government
therefore needs the participation of all members of society; because all
these different members, through their diverse situations, possess differently situated knowledge that needs to be heard so as to ensure not only a
wider range of hypotheses about how to direct society, but also a wider
range of criticism of those hypotheses that are actually tested. As Putnam
states Dewey's argument, since the materials used to assess and improve
democracy "cannot be circumscribed in advance," "there is no one field
of experience [or one class of people] from which all the considerations
relevant to the evaluation of democracy come" (RP 189).

Dewey was particularly suspicious of the "cognitive distortion" produced by the privilege of experts: "A class of experts is inevitably so removed from common interests as to become a class with private interests

and private knowledge, which in social matters is not knowledge at all," for it fails to see the experience and interests of other sections of society. "All special privilege narrows the outlook of those who possess it."[4] The argument that experts rule best gets its power by assuming that they *know* best, that they possess more than all others *all* the necessary knowledge for governing society. But this in turn assumes that we know what that necessary knowledge is, that we know, for example, what our essential human nature, needs, and capabilities are. "In contrast," Putnam asserts with Dewey, "we don't know what our interests and needs are or what we are capable of until we actually engage in politics. A corollary of this view is that there can be no final answer to the question of how we should live, and therefore we should always leave it open to further discussion and experimentation. That is precisely why we need democracy" (RP 189; cf. WL 217).

III

Though endorsing Dewey's "social philosophy" of democracy as "overwhelmingly right," Putnam finds his "moral philosophy" inadequate for treating "problems of individual choice" that are central to the core ethical issue of how to live (RP 190). The problems Putnam has in mind are those "individual existential choices" of the kind evoked by Sartre's famous character Pierre (in *Existentialism and Humanism*), who confronts the agonizing choice between joining the Resistance (and thus leaving his aged mother alone on the farm) or remaining with his mother (thus forsaking the Resistance).

Such "problems of individual choice" cannot be handled just like "social problems" of collaborative empirical problem-solving, where we aim "to 'maximize' the good" by choosing the best solution in terms of "estimated utilities." For it is not a question here of obtaining general social consequences that are good but rather of what is good or "right" for the individual (RP 190).[5] Such decisions cannot be determined by scientific method but instead require an "existential" act of freedom or leap of faith beyond any available evidence. As Putnam forcefully puts it:

> Someone who acts only when the "estimated utilities" are favorable does not live a meaningful human life. Even if I choose to do something

of whose ethical and social value there is absolutely no doubt, say, to devote my life to comforting the dying, or helping the mentally ill, or curing the sick, or relieving poverty, I still have to decide not whether it is good that someone should do that thing, but whether it is good that I, Hilary Putnam, do that thing. The answer to that question cannot be a matter of well-established scientific fact, in however generous a sense of "scientific." (RP 194)

Putnam therefore turns to William James who famously argued that with crucial, pressing personal questions (e.g. religious faith), one has the right to exercise the will to believe "in advance of the evidence" (RP 192). Seeing this Jamesian voluntarist idea also in Sartre's and Kierkegaard's views of existentialist self-creation, of "becoming who [one] ... is," Putnam endorses it as the best model for addressing the personal ethics of how to live (RP 191).[6] Dewey's failure to recognize such individual ethics is explained as resulting from a "dualistic conception of human goods" that divides between a social-ethical dimension expressed in terms of rational collaboration and, on the other hand, an aesthetic dimension where the individual finally finds expression but only through her private "consummatory experience."

> For Dewey there are fundamentally two, and only two, dominant dimensions to human life: the social dimension, which for Dewey meant the struggle for a better society, and for the release of human potential; and the aesthetic dimension. To the criticism that he fundamentally saw all of life as social action, Dewey could and did always reply that, on the contrary, in the last analysis he saw all "consummatory experience" as aesthetic. The trouble with this answer is that a bifurcation of goods into social goods which are attained through the use of instrumental rationality and consummatory experiences which are ultimately aesthetic is too close to the positivist or empiricist division of life into the prediction and control of experiences and the enjoyment of experiences to be adequate. (RP 196)

That Dewey's "conception of human goods" involves a rigid dualism between the social and the aesthetic—the one concerned with improving society through scientific rationality while the other concerned simply with private consummatory experience—is a very troubling charge. It is particularly troubling because Dewey's declared pragmatist agenda was to overcome such divisions between science and culture, society and the self, instrumentality and art. But any social/aesthetic dualism can be refuted by looking more carefully at Dewey's aesthetics and highlighting an important argument for democracy that Putnam ignores, one I shall call the *aesthetic justification for democracy*. Before taking this up, we should appreciate the full force of Putnam's claim that neglecting the individual ethics of how to live is not merely a minor omission for a theory of democracy, but a central gap that would undermine the whole democratic project of modernity.

IV

Putnam usefully distinguishes three basic conceptions of equality in premodern Western culture (all inspired by "the Jerusalem based religions") from the modern conception established by Kant. The former he formulates as follows:

(I) There is something about human beings, some aspect which is of incomparable moral significance, with respect to which all human beings are equal, no matter how unequal they may be in talents, achievements, social contribution, etc.

(II) Even those who are least talented, or whose achievements are the least, or whose contribution to society is the least, are deserving of respect.

(III) Everyone's happiness or suffering is of equal prima facie moral importance. (MFR 45)

In all three of these traditional conceptions, Putnam notes, "the value of equality does not have much to do with individual *freedom*" and "can be reconciled with various sorts of totalitarianism" (MFR 46, 51). One can easily imagine a totalitarian theocracy interpreting these equalities in terms of "divine human nature" and then repressively limiting freedom so that this divine nature and its promise of eternal happiness and salvation are not perverted by ungodly temptations. One can imagine secular totalitarianisms making similar moves to ensure "equality."

In contrast, Putnam argues, Kant gives a radically new "content to the notion of equality ... that builds liberty into equality." Human autonomy, for Kant, means more than free will and our capacity for reason. It is also "the idea that we have the further freedom that we have no knowledge of a fixed end of what human happiness is"; since abstract reason cannot determine the content of "an inclusive human end which we should all seek (unless it be morality itself, and this is not an end that can determine the *content* of morality") (MFR 46, 49). Our choice of how to live is therefore not predetermined or constrained by any known essence of human nature, function, or happiness.

Consequently, as Foucault also noted, Kant urged the Enlightenment maxim *Aude sapere*: dare to know by daring to think for yourself.[7] And this need to think for ourselves is likewise where we find a particularly modern democratic conception of equality that also implies freedom. Since we all have to think for ourselves without prior knowledge of what human essence and happiness are, this ability to think becomes "itself the most valuable fact about our lives. *That* is the characteristic with respect to which we are all equals. We are all in the same predicament, and we all have the potential of thinking for ourselves with respect to the question of How to Live"(MFR 50). This "is not just a virtue, but ... the most significant moral capacity that we have," one whose denial in an individual would mean that the denied "has failed to live a fully human life"(MFR 61–62).

If equality is defined in such terms of free-thinking about how to live, then constraints on that freedom would threaten democracy's claim to equality, not just to liberty. And if ethics were simply a question of social planning whose collaborative inquiry provides the knowledge that determines all decisions about how to live, then there would no longer be freedom for the individual to choose how to become who he or she is. Such an ethics would be inconsistent with modern democracy.

These are the deep worries that spur Putnam to attack Dewey for refusing individual ethics through an exhaustive bifurcation of the social and aesthetic. But we can dispel such fears and allegations by recognizing what I call Dewey's aesthetic justification for democracy, a justification based on the strongly personal, yet social, aesthetic satisfactions that democracy provides when pursued as "a *personal* way of individual life" (LW 14: 226).

We should first remember that Dewey's aesthetics denies any dichotomy between social instrumentality and aesthetic consummatory experience. I develop these points in *Pragmatist Aesthetics*, but let me note them briefly here. In contrast to the dominant Kantian tradition that defines the aesthetic in opposition to practical interest, Dewey celebrates the embodied interest and wide-ranging "instrumental function" of aesthetic experience whose stimulating energy both enriches present activity and overflows into other tasks (AE 140, 144). Moreover, in contrast to a privatistic aesthetic, he insists that art's experience is essentially social and communicative: "since it is constituted ... by the common qualities of the public world," art is a communicative "remaking of the experience of the community in the direction of greater order and unity" (AE 87, 275).

Finally, Dewey insists on the ethical dimension of aesthetics, that "art is more moral than moralities" (AE 350). For aesthetic imagination is always suggesting ideals higher than those of conventional morality, new visions or alternative models of life beyond those concretely encountered but to which the individual can aspire in addressing the question of how to live. As if to answer Putnam's worry about the need to go "in advance of the evidence," Dewey declares that art fosters our "sense of purposes that outrun evidence and of meanings that transcend indurated habit"; such purposes and meanings enrich the experiencing self both aesthetically and ethically (AE 350).

If aesthetics is not in opposition to the social, instrumental, and ethically personal, then Dewey can develop an aesthetic justification for democracy based on the idea of enriched experience and self-realization. It involves three related lines of argument. The first is this: Any individual of a community is a social individual, who thus has needs, habits, and desires associated with and affected by communal life. Therefore, the individual's free and active participation in democratic life—in social government as well as in the protection and exercise of her personal freedom—will make her experience and self much richer and more interesting than if she had no opportunity to participate in the government of self and society. Since democracy provides better opportunity for the free and equal participation of more individuals in government, it can provide them a richer life and is thus superior. As Dewey puts it: "Only by participating in the common intelligence and sharing in the common purpose as it works for the common good can individual human beings realize their true individualities"; the "self which is formed through action which is faithful to relations with others will be a fuller and broader self than one which is cultivated in isolation" (LSA 20, E 302).

The second aesthetic justification is closely related. If nothing is "as fulfilling and as rewarding as is concerted consensus of action," then, because participatory democracy promotes such action, it should be valued and pursued for the experiential satisfactions such action brings. Democracy, like communication, "is consummatory as well as instrumental," and "shared experience is the greatest of human goods" (EN 145, 157).

The third argument appeals again to the aesthetic idea of personal experiential enrichment, but develops it through democracy's respect for difference and the right of every individual to have and develop her distinctive perspective on life. Democracy's advocacy of the free and equal (though not always identical) participation of all different types of people in the direction of community life greatly enriches the experience of each. It not only provides the spice of variety, but gives the individual a heightened sense of her own distinct perspective and identity. "To cooperate by giving differences a chance to show themselves because of the belief that the expression of difference is not only a right of the other persons but is a means of enriching one's own life-experience, is inherent in the democratic personal way of life" (LW 14:228).

In defining democracy by the aim that "further experience will grow in ordered richness," and in recognizing that this pursuit will be guided by "need and desire" that go "beyond knowledge, beyond science," Dewey embraces not only an aesthetic justification but an aesthetic ideal of democracy that affirms the role of personal ethics and life-choices in advance of the evidence. "Democracy, as a personal, an individual, way of life" demands "a working faith in the possibilities of human nature," the same sort of will to believe that Putnam appeals to in James (LW 14:226, 229). It also requires faith in one's (and others') aesthetic sense of which existential choices will make a richer but still unified self. These choices of the self, Dewey insists, cannot be legislated by the group for the individual on the basis of scientific findings about social utilities; they are rather a function of one's particular needs and desires. Explicitly linking democratic theory to aesthetics, Dewey claims that just as significant aesthetic wholes must be "constituted by parts that are themselves significant," so "no significant community can exist save as it is composed of individuals who are significant" (AE 207–208).

Blind to this aesthetic justification of democracy, Putnam falsely condemns Dewey for a bifurcation of the social and the aesthetic that leaves no room for a personal ethics of self-creation. Like Rorty, he wrongly identifies Dewey's democratic project with the procedural, institutional democratic theory of John Rawls. But while Rorty finds such a public-democratic/private-aesthetic dualism convenient for aestheticizing the ethics of self,[8] Putnam resists this aestheticism and instead looks to James and existentialism to find a place for individual ethics that defies the alleged Deweyan dichotomy of the social and aesthetic. However, just as the aesthetic/social, aesthetic/ethical, and aesthetic/instrumental dualisms are false, so is the dualism of social/individual. The individual, as Dewey insisted, is always already social. Even one's most private thoughts and personal dilemmas reflect the voices of society one has internalized, which does not, for all that, preclude one's freedom.[9]

Putnam may have overlooked the individual dimension of Deweyan democratic ethics, because Dewey *does* tend to highlight the social—insisting not only on the social construction of the self but also on the essentially social nature of self-realization. Though advocating individual "self-realization as the moral ideal," he argued that the individual self is best fulfilled not by consciously attending to its individuality, but by instead attending to the social relations and shared concerns that shape the self in forming its environment. "Self-realization may be the end" but preoccupation with self is not the way to achieve it. For "to make self-realization a conscious aim ... would prevent full attention to those very relationships which bring about the wider development of self" (E 302).

Hence Dewey's recommendation for individual fulfillment in democracy is not to consciously cultivate one's distinctive self but to enrich it by concentrating on shared interests and "objects that contribute to the enrichment of the lives of all" (E 302–303). This does not deny individual expression in lifestyles: differences in our talents, situations, and inclinations will make for distinctive contributions to the society and values we share. Nor does it mean that every life must be devoted to politics: the realm of shared interests is much wider. But it does militate against extreme concentration on the self's personal distinction and more private gratifications.

Dewey practiced the ethic he preached, translating his personal quest for self-fulfillment into the social struggle for a more democratic society and systematically sublimating (perhaps even repressing) his more private concerns and desires. If his life proved that distinctive self-realization is consistent with selfless social action, it fails to entail that this is the best or only way for self-perfection today. Nor does it really prove that democratic self-realization must always eschew the cult of selfhood. If contemporary society is more fragmented, selfish, and privatistic than in Dewey's day, then self-realization may more likely succeed by taking a more privatist turn. This is Rorty's conclusion, reinforced by the fear that urging a unity of social and personal good will lead either to repressive self-denial or oppressive imposition of one's personal authority on others.

Sharing Rorty's concern for individualism and failing to see it satisfied in Dewey's democratic theory, Putnam, however, wants to connect the projects of self-creation and democracy. He does so by seeing self-creation as expressing the basic equality that modern democracy must guarantee: freedom of thought about how to live.

However, given the basic tensions between freedom and equality that Putnam (like Dewey) recognizes, this strategy seems far too thin to unite the quests for democracy and self-fulfillment. The value of thinking *for* oneself does not entail the value of thinking primarily *about* one's distinctive self. Dewey's worry remains: preoccupation with distinctive selfhood not only impoverishes the self but also deprives others of care and weakens the social bonds of democracy. To relieve this worry there seems no better place to turn than to Stanley Cavell's ingenious ethics of democracy, whose arguments share Dewey's strategies but surpass them.

V

Cavell's 1988 Carus Lectures on "Emersonian perfectionism" seek to reconcile the ideals of self-realization and democracy that together constitute the core of the American dream. Emerson's advocacy of independent, nonconformist, self-perfection (one that inspired Nietzsche's elitist *Übermensch*) must therefore be shown to be consistent with democracy's egalitarian concern for good and justice for all. But Cavell (like Dewey and Putnam) wants more than mere consistency through compartmentalization. He wants the deep, essential integration of democracy and self-realization. In defending the conscious cultivation of distinctive self-perfection, his ambitious goal "is not simply to show that it is tolerable to the life of justice in a constitutional democracy but to show how it is essential to that life" (CH 56).

How, then? Put most briefly, perfectionism is "essential to the criticism of democracy from within" by providing the sort of caring, demanding, critical, self-improving individuals who can best guarantee that the institutions and practitioners of democracy will not rest content with the always imperfect justice and improvable good they provide. Cavell develops his argument through a critique of Rawls' seminal account of democracy as essentially a matter of institutional rules and procedures for administering justice. Praising Rawls' formulation of the general principles by which constitutional democracy can administer justice and criticize its failures "from within" its principled framework, Cavell nonetheless insists that perfectionism is *also* "essential to the criticism of democracy from within," and he challenges Rawls' claim that perfectionism is "inherently undemocratic or elitist"(CH 3).

Formulated in his distinctive writerly style, Cavell's arguments resist clear summary. Yet the main lines seem to be these: First, perfectionism is necessary because institutions and principles are only as strong, just, and effective as the individuals who animate, apply, and criticize them. Only perfectionism can build the "character to keep the democratic hope alive in the face of disappointment with it" (CH 56). This is precisely Dewey's argument why democracy must be practiced as a personal, individual way of life: "democratic *institutions* are no guarantee for the existence of democratic individuals ... [whereas] individuals who are democratic in thought and action are the sole final warrant for the existence and endurance of democratic institutions" (LW 14:92).

Secondly, to rely simply on institutional principles of justice allows us to become complacent about the injustices, brutalities, and waste of human opportunities that, given the complexities and scarcities of the world, are not excluded by mere compliance with the principles of justice. Cavell thus contests Rawls' idea that by correctly following these principles we could live "above reproach" (CH 18).[10] The perfectionist will never be satisfied with himself and the system as long as any injustice or misery exists. Reproaching himself and the system for not doing better, he will constantly struggle to better himself and others. Democracy, if it is to realize the best justice possible, needs this vigilance and supererogation.

Finally, Rawls sees perfectionism as a fixed teleological principle "directing society to arrange institutions and to define the duties and obligations of individuals so as to maximize the achievement of human excellence" in some particular set of valued domains.[11] But Emersonian perfectionism, Cavell argues, is no institutional principle promoting some fixed hierarchy of ends; it is rather an individual ethical injunction to strive to be better and do so by being always open to exploring the claims of different ends.

These critiques of Rawls' institutionalism again reflect Dewey's democratic ethics of the self, whose ideal of continual growth and self-perfection spurns complacency as intrinsically immoral and refuses the very notion of a fixed set of final ends that would set a limit to growth. Like Dewey, though clearly more inspired by Emerson, Cavell advocates a dynamic self that is directed at self-improvement and (through this) at the improvement of society. Constantly in the making, the self should always be striving towards a higher "unattained yet attainable self." "To recognize the unattainable self is ... a step in attaining it," but the process of striving is never completed: not because we never reach the next or higher self, but because in reaching it, we should always see yet a further, still higher self to reach for (CH 12).

Self-perfection, as "a process of moving to, and from, nexts," demands real courage. Not only must it overcome habit and anxious "resistance to internal change," but it must also face the unpleasant fact that we *need* radical improvement (CH 12, 16). For Cavell, this borders on self-loathing. "Emersonian Perfectionism requires that we become ashamed in a particular way of ourselves" so as to consecrate ourselves to our next selves and a better society. It involves "an expression of disgust with or a disdain for the present state of things so complete as to require not merely reform, but a call for a transformation of things, and before all a transformation of the self—a call that seems so self-absorbed and obscure as to make morality impossible." Replying to the apparent immorality of such self-perfecting self-absorption, Cavell questions: "what is the moral life apart from acting beyond the self and making oneself intelligible to those beyond it?" (CH 16, 46).

In linking self-transcendence with intelligibilty to others, Cavell deploys a Deweyan strategy for countering the radical opposition of self and society. The self must be seen as essentially dialogical and structured by the society it shares. Informed not only by society's shared language but also by the different voices it has heard and internalized, the self cannot fulfill and understand itself without regard for others. "Becoming intelligible to oneself may accordingly present itself as discovering which among the voices contending to express your nature are ones for you to own here, now" (CH xxxvi). Moreover, the self can define its own distinctiveness only by its relations of contrast and connection with others.

Hence perfectionism's preoccupation with self, its demand for "absolute responsibility of the self to itself," is not aimed at narcissistic isolation. It instead calls for "responsiblity of the self to itself, by way of others," "through the endless specification [of the self], by way of exemplification, in the world (of and with others)." Cavell calls this "the absolute responsibility of the self to make itself intelligible, without falsifying itself" (CH xxvii).

Such general arguments for the conceptual interdependence of self and society hardly dissolve all conflict between perfectionist cultivation of individualism and the claims of democratic community. They could not dispel Dewey's fear that democratic self-realization will only be stunted by taking one's own self (rather than one's environing community) as the conscious end-in-view. Yet by applying Dewey's own epistemological and aesthetic arguments, Cavell can make a strong case that democracy is excellently served by self-absorbed perfectionism. The key idea is that the struggle to perfect one's individuality and exemplify it in the social world will provide our democratic community with attractive models that recommend both why democracy is worth having and how it may be improved and enriched.

Epistemologically, perfectionism serves the democratic search for better life and greater justice by offering three related resources: an inspiring example of untiring meliorism, specific hypotheses about how best to live, and critique of such hypotheses. Perfectionism's relentless demand for self-improvement gives an exemplary standard and spur to improving the society in which the self is found. Not only does it build the "character to keep the democratic hope alive" in the face of disappointment, but it offers a potent way of recognizing the value of other selves by its privileging of the unattained, next self who is, as yet, another. Thus, "recognizing my differences from others [is] a function of my recognizing my differences from myself" (CH 53). If self-growth and intelligibility require acknowledging others, then self-perfection should promote social change toward a more democratic "human" order. Perfectionism means being:

> open to the further self, in oneself and in others, which means holding oneself in knowledge of the need for change; which means, being one who lives in promise, as a sign, or representative human, which in turn means expecting oneself to be, making oneself, intelligible as an inhabitant now also of a further realm ..., call this the realm of the human — and to show oneself prepared to recognize others as belonging there. (CH 125)

Cultivation of individualistic self-realization also serves democracy by providing the community with a wealth of different life-exemplars. The democratic community is involved in a search for better ways to live and to provide greater justice. By refusing to conform to conventional ways of living, but instead consciously cultivating one's individual distinction and exemplifying it in the world, perfectionists provide their fellow citizens with new models or experiments of good living whose value is tested through their lives, thus advancing democracy's "conversation of justice" (CH 24–25).[12]

Through his nonconformist, heightened sense of self, the perfectionist makes himself representative of a very particular way of life, developing his own special "partiality." There are always different ways of living that might be better, and our finitude means we can only live in some partial way. By presenting their distinctive lifestyles, perfectionists offer alternatives to conventional life that we might adapt and apply to our own conditions. Still better, they could inspire us "to let their foundings of partiality challenge us to find our own." Others thus stand for selves we have not yet recognized or achieved; they represent "our beyond" (CH 58, 126).

Finally, perfectionism offers the democratic community an immanent critique of its various visions of the good life. Each partial life of self-perfection constitutes an implicit critique not only of any universal claim of other perfectionist partialities, but *especially* of the necessity and value of conformity to the conventional. Such critique by exemplars of difference seems especially democratic because it works not by appeal to some absolute end or fixed standard that denies our freedom to choose the life we think more perfect. Instead the exemplar's critical force derives from its aesthetic appeal, its attraction over other ways of living.

The aim is not to refute the other's way of living, "but to manifest for the other another way" (CH 31).

The manner of persuasion is similarly aesthetic; here discursive "moral justifications come to an end and something is to be shown"— the superior appeal of such a life (especially in contrast to the misery that complacent principles of "good enough justice" still allow). Here, ethical "constraint names, in the place of the Kantian 'ought,' a form of attraction, the relation to the friend [another or further self]; and judgment is backed not by a standard (a moral law, a principle of justice) but fronted by the character of the judger" whose power is the attraction of the life and self he both displays and strives for (CH xxix–xxx, 124).

As aesthetics figures centrally in our assessment and adoption of the best ways to live, so it also affords an argument for encouraging individualistic self-cultivation in democracy. Besides a greater range of useful hypotheses for living, individualism offers self and society the pleasures of rich variety and distinctive difference: "separateness of position is to be allowed its satisfactions" (CH 25).

Though employing these very arguments for individual self-realization, Dewey still cautioned against its conscious cultivation, advocating instead that self-realization should be sought in selflessly attending to other things. Even Emerson made the same case for indirection in self-perfection. "I like not the man who is thinking how to be good, but the man thinking how to accomplish his work."[13] Yet Cavell may have an argument why this "indirect" strategy will not succeed. If the motor for self-perfection is self-critique that results in deep shame or self-loathing, then, *unless we examine ourselves closely and constantly*, this shame will not surface to constantly prod us toward perfection.

Cavell's argument why self-improvement requires self-absorption is presented as an absolute claim, as true for the ancients as for contemporaries. But even if historicized, it is cogent and perhaps even more convincing. For Dewey, who grew up with the Congregationalist ideal of selfless service and a deeply entrenched religious sense of guilt, the meliorative habit and sense of community may have seemed sufficiently strong to motivate self-perfection through social service. For seculars steeped in postmodern fragmentation and scepticism about progress, Cavell may be right that only intense concentration on oneself can generate a strong enough drive for continuous improvement.

But whether this drive must be fueled by shame and self-loathing is not clear. Narcissism and heroism, which run deep in the history of philosophical life, are also strong motives, even if egalitarian democrats may not want to face this. Indeed, we can see Cavell's perfectionism as a form of democratic heroism in which self-cultivation encourages us to ever greater efforts to respect the difference, claims, and suffering of others, even if these labors take the form of pursuit of our own further self who is represented in others as "our beyond."

VI

Cavell's reconciliation of self-cultivation and democracy is very ingenious: self-absorbed perfectionism entails respect for others because they are implied in the self's unattained but attainable further self. But will this strategy work? Does perfectionist self-cultivation really make us more democratic or is it, as Rorty thinks, indifferent to the question of democracy and therefore in need of relegation to the private sphere? Pure logic cannot supply the answer, nor does controlled experimentation seem a practical option here; so how indeed do we determine this issue? One is tempted to assess Cavell's theory by its own aesthetic standards of attraction, not simply as an abstract line of argument, but (as he puts it) by its "exemplification" in the philosopical life he leads. Has his own cultivation of individual perfection made him more democratic? Is Cavell an "exemplar" whose attraction constrains and inspires us to take a similar (though, given our own individuality, also a somewhat different) course of self-absorbed self-cultivation?

These questions clearly call for *ad hominem* arguments, which academic philosophy, as any freshman knows, has firmly outruled as invalid.[14] But if philosophy is viewed as recommending a way to live, such arguments cannot be dismissed; a philosopher's theory of living can surely be assessed also in terms of the actual life it inspires. But if pertinent, then how should *ad hominem* considerations be pursued? How available is a philosopher's actual life, and how far is it reasonable and moral to probe it? Do we need investigative reporters and private detectives to assess a philosophy of life?

Though he never directly raises such questions, Cavell's account of philosophical living suggests an answer to them. It is embodied in his advocacy of a tool of democratic self-perfection that he rightly criticizes Dewey for neglecting: the transformative activities of writing and reading. Compelling us to go beyond what we already are by expressing something new, writing drives us toward our unattained but attainable self. And, in so showing the importance of this other self, it helps us to appreciate the value of others. Conversely, reading compels us to consider thoughts we had not previously attained, thus inducing not only recognition of the other selves who wrote them, but also that of our own further self who, by embracing them, is enriched.

Cavell thus makes writing and reading the essence of the philosophical life of self-perfection. Speaking as much for himself as for his heroes Emerson and Thoreau, Cavell insists that the philosopher's "writing is part of his living, an instance of the life of philosophy"; "his writing is this life." Or, since writing and reading are simply "variations" of each other, we can say "the interplay of writing and reading is what he claims as his philosophy" (QO 10,18; CH 42).[15]

In highlighting philosophical textuality as a valuable means for democratic self-perfection, Cavell marks a real advance on Dewey. But even if we regard textual activity as important as more overt democratic action, we should not take it as an adequate substitute for the latter. Otherwise, Cavell's textualist advance on Dewey would be a grave regression. It may, in any case, reflect philosophy's retreat from more robust praxis. Cavell's emphasis on textual activity conveys (as it atones for) the admission that philosophy's true target is the ideal "city of words" (CH 7–8) rather than the direction of actual community life. Dewey was not ready to concede this, but his confidence in philosophy's public leadership is now much harder to share, though perhaps not quixotic in all domains.[16]

Construing democratic self-perfection as an essentially textual way of life might help answer the *ad hominem* questions raised above. It suggests both a criterion for assessing the attraction of a philosophical life and a way of limiting what in that life should be relevant for such assessment. If the philosopher's life is expressed primarily in his writing, then the attraction of that exemplified life must also be exemplified in that writing. So if the persuasiveness of a philosophy of life is in the attraction of the life lived, then this in turn is in the appeal of the life as written. No wonder Cavell has turned to "autobiographical exercises" as in *A Pitch of Philosophy*.

But there is danger of grave confusion here, because the notions of writing and its attraction have a very distinctive meaning for Cavell. Writing, for him, is not merely the formulation of texts and ideas but a deeply personal, ethical work of self-critique and self-transformation. It is (in Pierre Hadot's sense) a spiritual exercise or *askesis* on one's actual self.[17] If one's writings transcend one's self, it is only because they transcend it by moving toward a higher self toward which they also bring the actual, living self; it is not because they constitute a higher, merely textual *persona* that is only causally connected with the physically embodied person who writes.

Similarly, for Cavell, the attraction of writing cannot mean the easy charm of an appealing writing style, say, like that of William James. Otherwise, Cavell's philosophy would stand condemned by its own criterion. In contrast, the self-conscious difficulty of Cavell's writing aims not to flatter the reader's taste (or Cavell's own) but rather to challenge it and thus engage both self and reader more deeply so as to effect the aim of self-transformation.

If one challenged his "aversive" difficult style as an obstacle to democracy's egalitarian aims, Cavell could counter that an imposed easy style would be false to the struggle for self-knowledge and self-transcendence that is equally central to democracy's project. He might further argue that even apparently obscure and difficult texts (like Wittgenstein's) can reach a wide audience and be effective on various levels of understanding. Indeed, despite its uncompromising, often tortured style, Cavell's own work has enjoyed a wide reception outside academic philosophy.

The idea of simply perfecting and presenting oneself as a beautifully written text would be condemned by Cavell as a debased perfectionism. But such a vision of philosophical life has indeed been proposed, most strikingly in Alexander Nehamas's *Nietzsche: Life as Literature.* Here "Nietzsche himself" "is none other than the character [his] very texts constitute." His philosophical life has nothing to do "with the miserable little man who wrote them but with the philosopher who emerges through them, the magnificent character these texts constitute and manifest."[18] The whole life of philosophy, the philosopher's very substance, becomes a merely literary affair—no doubt a seductively flattering and cosy conclusion for academic philosophers after the linguistic turn, especially for those of us with literary pretensions.

But Nietzsche himself can be invoked against this. In attacking the modern neglect of philosophical living, he complains: "The only critique of a philosophy that is possible and that proves something, namely trying to see whether one can live in accordance with it, has never been taught at universities: all that has ever been taught is a critique of words by means of other words."[19] In scorning the academic textualism of the universities, Nietzsche reverts here to an ancient Hellenistic distinction between real philosophical living and mere philosophical words. The beauty of a life should be in the former, not merely in the latter.

Though Cavell's ethics of democracy is not reducible to a mere textual aestheticism, it leaves itself too vulnerable to such an interpretation through its extreme emphasis on writing and neglect of other important dimensions of democratic philosophical life. For isn't there more to knowing how to live than knowing how to write and read, even in the special, more demanding, perfectionist sense that Cavell gives these textual terms? If the philosophical life is really taken seriously — that is, with the full-blooded, more-than-verbal concreteness that life entails — we need to go not only beyond a fictive textual persona, but also beyond the ideal "city of words" and idealistic dimensions of self-transformation that Cavell emphasizes.

We want to know not only how attractively a philosophy of life was pursued and formulated in words, but also how attractively it was embodied in concrete deeds, in ethical and political praxis. Socrates' appeal to us derives not simply from his linguistic expression (for that is mostly Plato's) nor from his mere inner struggle for self-betterment, but largely from the heroic public actions of his exemplary life and death. If Dewey's philosophical life attracts us, this is not due to his expansive good will and meliorism as exemplified in the persistent reformulations of his often prolix prose; it is because his actual life embodied tireless democratic praxis.

An attractive ethics of democracy must be concretely lived as well as written. In distinguishing between mere professors of philosophy and true philosophers, Thoreau insists on this point:

> To be a philosopher is not merely to have subtle thoughts, nor even to found a school, but so to love wisdom as to live according to its dictates, a life of simplicity, independence, magnanimity, and trust. It is to solve some of the problems of life, not only theoretically, but practically.[20]

No one knows this better than Cavell, who first reclaimed Thoreau and Emerson precisely to criticize academic philosophy's retreat from the practical task of philosophical living. Yet by emphasizing philosophy as writing and reading, while saying nothing about other forms of self-perfection, Cavell does not do enough to prevent philosophy's reappropriation as a merely textual activity.

There are, of course, also problems in going beyond a philosopher's texts. If we assess a philosophy of life by its real-life embodiment, then philosophical criticism converges with biography. Heidegger's contemptible Nazi collaboration becomes relevant to his philosophy of authenticity, as do Foucault's bold experiments with drugs and S/M to his philosophy of transgression. Their writing on these topics does not suffice. What, then, is the range of biographical details that can be relevant? Any that can be shown relevant by a good critic who understands a philosopher by interpreting both writings and life in light of each other. Such philosophical criticism requires not only analytic power but historical skills and psychological insight.

If embodiment puts additional demands on the critic, then it is still more demanding on the philosopher, who must exemplify his way of life as attractively as he can: not only by exemplary writing and ethico-political praxis, but through the appeal of his own personal appearance and style. "The philosopher," Thoreau urges, should be "in advance of his age even in the outward form of his life" (W 270). The quest for attractive philosophical embodiment must therefore not neglect the philosopher's own body, whose shape and functioning express the nature and quality of his life:

> Every man is the builder of a temple, called his body, to the god he worships, after a style purely his own, nor can he get off by hammering marble instead. We are all sculptors and painters, and our material is our own flesh and blood and bones. (W 468)

What sort of body makes an attractive exemplar for a democratic philosophical life? This may seem a ridiculous question, but it simply extends Putnam and Cavell's concern with "how to live" to a crucial dimension of life they neglect. The soma is a site where we can really "change both our lives and the way we see our lives" (RP 200) by literally reshaping ourselves and our relationship to our bodies.[21]

Independent self-realization in this dimension can also contribute to the democratic discussion of how to live, by offering and testing new hypotheses about which somatic forms and practices are most rewarding and emancipatory.[22] The conformist oppression of our highly advertised standards of bodily aesthetics and functioning can thus be challenged. This remains an important task for philosophical critique through both words and embodied practice. Both are integral to the fullest life of philosophy.

Part II

ART, KNOWLEDGE, PRAXIS

4

Reason and Aesthetics between Modernity and Postmodernity

Habermas and Rorty

I

The past few centuries of secular Western thought present two main utopian strategies: the rule of reason with its measured, rationalizing improvement of life, and a libidinal aestheticism with its hedonistic *promesse du bonheur*. As the project of modernity (with its Enlightenment roots and rationalizing differentiation of cultural spheres) has been identified with reason, so the postmodern is contrastingly characterized as dominantly aesthetic. Though pragmatism may deploy these contrasting terms to make its points, it should not regard them as denoting dichotomous, inimical essences. The rational/aesthetic and modernity/postmodernity oppositions must not be taken too rashly. Modernity clearly has its aesthetic, while postmodernism has its reasons. As art typically displays a rationality of order, unity, and purpose, so reason reveals its own deep aesthetic dimension. For many of its central notions (coherence, balance, proportion, completeness, simplicity, fairness) not only have aesthetic connotations but, even when mechanically defined, require a kind of cultivated aesthetic perception or taste for their proper understanding and application.

A book advocating philosophy as the reasoned pursuit of aesthetic living cannot harbor an essential dualism between reason and aesthetics, reflected in an unbridgeable divide between the modern and postmodern. To explore and temper these oppositional notions, this chapter confronts the influential theories of Jürgen Habermas and Richard Rorty, around whom much of the debate has centered: the former championing the claims of reason and modernity, the latter representing the aesthetic and postmodern.

Despite their apparent disagreements, Habermas and Rorty agree in choosing philosophical narrative (rather than synchronic analysis) as the method for theorizing the postmodern. Both also ply the same central story line: the path from modernity to postmodernity is portrayed as the undermining of reason by the aesthetic. Rorty welcomes this aesthetic turn as liberating us from a stiflingly rigid, homogenizing, and ahistorical conception of reason; as instead encouraging the flexibility of creative imagination that seems better suited to our increasingly decentered contexts and rapidly changing times. Habermas, on the other hand, defends modernity by portraying postmodernism's aesthetic turn as an unnecessary, misguided, and subversive response to a false idea of reason — subject-centered reason. The *malheurs* of modernity can thus be remedied not by abandoning reason for the aesthetic but by replacing subject-centered reason with a communicative model of reason.

As Rorty and Habermas insist on the primacy of language, it is there that the reason/aesthetic debate is ultimately focused. Thus Habermas criticizes Rorty for "aestheticizing" language by privileging metaphor and rhetoric as semantically more central than truth and argument. This leads to a disastrous "leveling [of] the genre distinction between philosophy and literature" in which philosophy's long-standing commitment to truth and the rational consensus of problem-solving is replaced by the poetic quest for exciting new metaphors.[1] Rorty responds not only by questioning the foundationalist "universalism" implicit in Habermas's theory of communicative reason, but by challenging the very distinction "between rationality and irrationality" as an "obsolete and clumsy" piece of rhetoric. Even in its historicized Habermasian form, the ideal of reason represents a restrictive remnant of religion's need to supply a redeeming, unifying human essence, while what we need instead is to give free play to aesthetic "fantasy" and its enriching multiplicities. Opposing modernity's "Enlightenment hope" for rationalized society, Rorty advocates that "culture as a whole ... be 'poeticized.'"[2]

Through such polemics, Habermas and Rorty project a misleading dualism between reason and aesthetics that seems inconsistent with their own basic pragmatism. This troubling dualism can be undone by showing that its duelling theorists actually agree on more than they differ, though such agreement is concealed by the rhetoric of contrast so central to our habits of philosophical thinking and reinforced by the institutional frameworks in which theory takes place.[3] We should begin by seeing how the reason/aesthetic opposition arises in Habermas's and Rorty's narratives of postmodernism's aesthetic turn.

II

For Habermas, the story starts with Schiller's and Hegel's dissatisfaction with the tradition of subject-centered reason and its philosophy of reflection, a tradition that stems from Descartes and reaches its apotheosis in Kant. This concept of reason could not escape the self-referential dilemma of having to reflect critically on the subject's knowledge while basing such criticism wholly on the subject's own reason. Moreover, in focusing on the individual subject and thus neglecting the communicative dimension of human understanding, it heightened social fragmentation and prevented philosophy from fulfilling the role of promoting cultural unity, a role it had inherited from religion (PDM 19–22). Yet, for Habermas, reason—properly understood as communicative—constitutes "the absolute power of unification" (PDM 32). Philosophy's failure to grasp the idea of reason not in terms of subjectivity but in terms of communicative intersubjectivity—an idea implicit in Schiller's and the young Hegel's view of *art* "as the genuine embodiment of a communicative reason" and a noncoercive unifier—constitutes for Habermas the philosophical catastrophe of our epoch (PDM 48).

Blindness to this alternative model of reason has locked us in the relentless self-critique of subject-centered reason, so that we have become suspicious of reason altogether. To escape this divisive dialectic of Enlightenment—the self-critique of reason by its own immanent activity (complemented by its repressive self-control of the rational subject), Nietzsche turned instead to the aesthetic as "reason's absolute other" (PDM 94). Since Habermas affirms "the internal relationship between modernity and rationality," he sees Nietzsche's aestheticism as "the entry into postmodernity," and characterizes this aesthetic as an antirational, Dionysian "decentered subjectivity liberated from all constraints of cognition and purposive activity" (PDM 4, 94–96).

Of course, already in modernity's cultural economy of aesthetic autonomy (through the tripartite division of science, ethics–politics, and art), aesthetic experience was aimed at freeing subjectivity both from narrow self-centeredness and the constraints of scientific and moral-practical judgment. But such aesthetic freedom was essentially confined to the sphere of art. Hence aesthetic experience was not only directed by the rational discourse of art criticism, but also controlled in being framed by the regulative boundaries constituted by the corresponding autonomy of the more clearly reason-governed domains of science and morality. With Nietzschean postmodernism, however, the aesthetic no longer remains content with such rational limits. Displaying an irrational, limit-defying "anarchistic intention" of Dionysian will to power, it "reduces everything that is and should be to the aesthetic dimension," presenting itself as not only reason's other but its sovereign (PDM 95–96, 123).

Habermas's story thus contains two very different notions of the aesthetic, though often neglecting to distinguish between them. The first concerns the rational, compartmentalized, and disciplined domain of art. Embodying communicative reason, seeking artistic progress, and providing the pleasures of meaningful form, this classic aesthetic of modernity is, for Habermas, one of "aesthetic harmony" and "artistic truth" (PDM 207).[4] In contrast, what Habermas typically identifies as the aesthetic is an antirational drive of unconstrained hedonism and radical transgression, an aesthetic of "body-centered experiences of a decentered subjectivity," aimed at "limit-experiences" of "mystical" "ecstasy," producing "dizzying effects of … shock … [and] excitement without any proper object." As the dominating aesthetic in Habermas's polemic, it is demonized as "aesthetically inspired anarchism" and attacked as postmodernism's grave threat to modernity's project of progressive emancipation through reason (PDM 5, 306–310).

This aesthetic challenge is traced from Nietzsche to Georges Bataille's "aesthetically inspired" eroticism and then to Foucault's theory of biopower. It can also be seen in their idea of limit-experiences, which decenter the rationally controlled subject experientially, just as their genealogical critique decenters it theoretically (PDM 211–216, 221–93). Postmodern privileging of aesthetics over reason becomes, for Habermas, still clearer in Derrida's and Rorty's advocacy of "the primacy of rhetoric over logic," "world-disclosing" literary artistry over "problem-solving" argument, and metaphor over "normal" speech: all of this captured in their vision of philosophy as just a kind of writing (PDM 190–207). He also finds this dangerous aesthetic challenge in recent German philosophy. Most virulent in Heidegger's ecstatic appeal to an archaic disclosure of Being (an "ontologized art") through a poetic "thinking more rigorous than the conceptual," it can even be detected in a rational archmodernist like Adorno with his emphasis on the redemptive, nondiscursive truth of art's archaic "mimetic content" (PDM 104, 129, 136).

For Habermas, the antirational aesthetic derives its authority from the enormous power of aesthetic experience in modern times, particularly as it developed from romanticism to the modernist avant-garde. By seeming to surpass rationality (and overwhelm our self-possession), such experience seems to offer an alternative to reason and an escape from the self-centered critical self. Yet such potent aesthetic experience, he argues, is only the product of modernity's progress toward avant-garde art, and therefore depends on its rational discursive structures even while purporting to oppose and transcend reason. The aesthetic experiences employed by these antirational theorists "are due to the same process of differentiation [and rationalization] as science and morality" (PDM 339). Therefore, to appropriate aesthetic experience theoretically in order to escape or outflank rationality involves a performative contradiction. Moreover, to the extent that it negates the rationality embodied in modernity's artistic tradition, radical aesthetic experience loses all its meaning; "the contents get dispersed ... [and] an emancipatory effect does not follow." [5]

Though plausible as *ad hominem* arguments concerning the modernist taste of antirational champions of the aesthetic, these arguments fail to clinch the case for the primacy of reason. They wrongly presume that powerful aesthetic experience always needs modernity's rationalized, differentiated conception of art, that it never existed before nor is ever achievable outside the framework of modernity's aesthetics. This presumption not only unconvincingly excludes the passionate aesthetic experience of ancient Greece (so inspirational for Nietzsche), but that of African cultures where such experience is not prestructured by modernity's cultural divisions. [6]

Habermas, however, still has his master argument for the primacy of reason. There is no escaping reason, because there is no escaping language and because language is essentially and necessarily rational. Language is the medium through which we live; and it is unavoidably rational because there is "an internal connection between meaning and validity," i.e. between meaning and the rational, communicative assessment of truth claims and truth-related judgments (PDM 313–314).[7] Aligning himself with Peircean pragmatism, Habermas insists that this defense of communicative reason makes no appeal to a transcendent "pure reason that might don linguistic clothing only in the second place. Reason is by its very nature incarnated in contexts of communicative action and in structures of the lifeworld" (PDM 322).

But in viewing language as the essence of rationality and the ground of its primacy, Habermas must resist Derrida's and Rorty's deconstructive efforts to portray language as more fundamentally aesthetic, as more a matter of disseminating creativity, persuasive rhetoric, and world-making tropes than of logical validity. Their attempt to blur the distinctions between literature, literary criticism, and philosophy is likewise condemned as a strategy to undermine the primacy of reason by denying its rationalizing process of differentiation of disciplines, a differentiation Habermas sees as essential to the achievement and progress of those disciplines. "This aestheticizing of language," he claims, "is purchased with the twofold denial of the proper senses of normal and poetic discourse." Moreover, to deny all distinction "between the poetic world-disclosive function of language and its prosaic, innerworldly functions" obscures the crucial fact that it is ultimately on such normal "everyday communicative practice" that all "learning processes" (including those of poetic production) are based, and "in relation to which the world-disclosive force of ... language has in turn to prove its worth" (PDM 205).[8]

Habermas further argues that privileging the aesthetic language of innovative world-disclosure (paradigmatically expressed in "the esoteric work of art") fosters not only an "elitist contempt for discursive thought" but similar disrespect for the more ordinary and essential lifeworld practices of problem-solving and for the ordinary people engaged in them (PDM 186). By endorsing the primacy of communicative reason through the ordinary linguistic practices of the lifeworld, by enlisting pragmatism's stress on consensual practice and Anglo-American philosophy's linguistic turn, Habermas seeks to overcome the Nietzschean–postmodern aesthetic turn that pervades so much contemporary continental theory—not only in France but closer to home in Heidegger and Adorno.

III

Rorty also advocates the primacy of language, but no longer sees it as the incarnation of reason or the expression of a deep human essence. Instead language is taken primarily as an aesthetic tool for new creation and self-fashioning; we revise science, self, and society by redescription, by retelling their respective histories through different vocabularies. Philosophy should therefore also "turn against theory and toward narrative" (CIS xvi). Rorty's narrative of the path to postmodernity's "ironist culture" is one of progressive liberation from the rule of reason through the advocacy and appeal of the aesthetic. This tale is structured on a series of parallel binary oppositions that elaborate the central contrast of reason versus the aesthetic. The oppositions can be lined up as follows: truth/metaphor, necessity/contingency, universal/particular, public/private, philosophy/poetry, inference/narrative, logic/rhetoric, discovery/creation, foundations/apologetics, deep reality/surface appearances, metaphysicians/ironists, theorists/novelists. Freedom and progress are functions of reversing the repressive privilege of the former terms.

Hegel began the aesthetic revolt against philosophy by historicizing it as narrative in his *Phenomenology of Mind*. However, he lapsed by taking his narrative as the definitive story with his own philosophy as the ultimate conclusion. Nietzsche advanced the cause of freedom by highlighting the aesthetic, by advocating an uncompromising perspectivism, and by rejecting truth and metaphysics for creative interpretation and genealogical redescription. But despite Nietzsche's professed antimetaphysical perspectivism, there lurks a vestigial metaphysics and privileged perspective in his theory of the will to power.[9] Similarly, his antiauthoritarianism masks an autocratic injunction that the only worthy life is the sublime heroic one of the creative, striving *Übermensch*.

Heidegger, despite his attempt to overcome all metaphysics (including Nietzsche's), still falls victim to the same metaphysical impulse of universalizing his own vocabulary and interpretive redescriptions as *the* authoritative lexicon, narrative, and destiny of Western civilization. Derrida makes the same mistake by presenting his early notions of *différance* and "the myth of presence" as (respectively) the necessary root of all writing and the definitive interpretation of the entire history of metaphysics. Instead, he should recognize that these notions are nothing more than apt new ways to redescribe his own self and thought in relation to the past vocabularies and narratives on which he (like most of us philosophers) was raised.

This error of universalizing one's own preferred vocabulary and story as authoritative for the general public is, for Rorty, a pernicious remnant of the metaphysical claim of reason: the idea that private and public must be united through a rational grounding synthesis, the view that private ideals and beliefs are only truly valid if publicly validated, and that validity and legitimacy involve universalizability. Reason traditionally urged this standard of validity, just as metaphysics had the traditional goal of uniting our words and personal stories with something monumental, eternal and sublime: Truth, Reality, Power, Human Nature, History. But the aesthetic, for Rorty, is different. It can be satisfied with the particular and contingent, even the private, transitory, and fictional. For (to use another of Rorty's contrasting pairs), it can seek beauty rather than sublimity (CIS 105–106).

Freedom is thus better served by aesthetic writers who cherish particularity and personal linguistic invention than by philosophers who want to speak for all humanity in the name of universal reason or in terms of something else Big and Basic (like Power or *Dasein*). Such consciously aesthetic creators best realize Rorty's "liberal ironist" dream "to overcome authority without claiming authority": overcoming the authority of inherited narratives and vocabularies by creating a strikingly distinctive self and history in one's own terms, but doing so without claiming authority over the language and self-fashioning of others (CIS 105).[10] Proust (in contrast to Nietzsche and Heidegger) proves paradigmatic of the ironist's aesthetic ideal, "because he had no public ambitions" that his language would determine the true meaning of modern Europe. By unabashedly recounting personal stories rather than offering general theory, such an aesthete displays the humble irony and "the courage to give up the attempt to unite the private and the public, to stop trying to bring together a quest for private autonomy and an attempt at public resonance and utility" (CIS 118, 125).

The ironist aesthete can likewise escape the performative paradox that both Rorty and Habermas see as the prime stumbling block of postmodern philosophers: the problem of how to displace theory and reason without further theorizing and reasoning. The answer, for Rorty, is simply to circumvent theory's traditional claims of universal, essential truth by instead telling more personal stories for one's own individual emancipation; in short, to privatize philosophy.

Nominalist and historicist, postmodern irony "thinks nothing has an intrinsic nature, a real essence" (CIS 74). Though privileging language as constitutive of the self and lifeworld, Rorty rejects the idea of "language in general" as a substantive universal, as some "entity" or "unity" "intervening between self and reality" that constitutes the common core of human experience (CIS 13–15). For such an idea amounts to an essentialism about language that is no better (if indeed different) than an essentialism about reason. Instead Rorty advocates the idea of very particular, contingent, historicized linguistic practices. These are simply tools for coping with experience, and their highest function is not the Habermasian one of cooperative problem-solving to promote mutual understanding and consensus. Instead, this function is aesthetic: individual, original creation, to make things new, "to make something that never had been dreamed of before." The most crucial goal is innovative "self creation": refashioning and mastering oneself and one's structuring world "by inventing a new language" that redescribes these things in one's "own terms," "in words never used before," so as to escape from "inherited descriptions" and free oneself from the "horror of finding oneself to be only a copy or replica" (CIS 13, 27–29).

One likely objection to Rorty's aesthetic view of language as a tool for constant novelty and the expression of private individuality is that language requires some stable commonalities and consensus in order to be at all effective. Wittgenstein makes this point in his famous private-language argument, and Habermas similarly urges that language-games cannot work (hence sentences cannot "mean") without a linguistic community sharing to some extent the same vocabulary and "*the presupposition of intersubjectively identical ascriptions of meaning*" (PDM 198).

Rorty has two possible ways of meeting this objection. One is by adopting Donald Davidson's account of metaphoric meaning and his "passing theory" of language in order to argue that we need no stable shared rules for linguistic understanding. We can simply proceed on intuitive predictions of meaning based on current context and our previous habits of linguistic understanding. The rejoinder is that those habits would be undermined and unprojectible if language were fully aestheticized, privatized, and innovationally protean in Rorty's recommended way.

Rorty's preferred response is to separate a private from a public use of language. While the latter is fully shared to serve the needs of consensual social life, the private use need not be fully shared and indeed *should not be*, if the individual is to achieve autonomy. But this private rhetoric of self-creation can remain sufficiently anchored in shared public language so as to be comprehensible to others and thus avoid the problem of the private-language argument. Since effective communication and social functioning require some linguistic consensus and stability, Rorty admits that there can be no "culture whose public rhetoric is ironist.... Irony seems an inherently private matter" and necessarily "reactive," requiring "the contrast" of the public as a shared "inherited" base from which it can assert its novel difference, "something from which to be alienated." Here (as elsewhere) Rorty's entire project avowedly "turns on a firm distinction between the private and the public" (CIS 83, 87–88).

This sharp "public–private split" (CIS 85) involves not only separating the language of consensus from the language of creation. It also means separating the political realm of "social organization" from the aesthetic realm of individual autonomy (which he wrongly equates with unique, distinctive self-creation.)[11] Privileging the private and aesthetic as what gives meaning to life, Rorty advocates political liberalism as merely a means to provide the necessary stability and negative liberty for pursuit of our private aims, a framework for "letting its citizens be as privatistic, 'irrationalist,' and aestheticist as they please so long as they do ... no harm to others" (CIS xiv).

But, as already noted, Rorty's "firm distinction between the private and the public" is untenable, because the private self and the language it builds upon in self-creation are always already socially constituted and structured by a public field. Indeed, not only Rorty's particular privatized ethic of linguistic, aestheticist self-styling, but his whole notion of privatizing ethics clearly reflect the particular public and wider society that shape his thinking—the intellectual field and consumerist world of late-capitalist liberalism.[12]

Rorty's very idea of self-constitution and self-creation through language not only confutes his strong public/private dichotomy; it also suggests a lurking linguistic essentialism that differs from the one he repudiates, but seems even more pernicious. His view that the self is nothing but a linguistic web or set of narratives comes uncomfortably close to an essentialist view of human nature as exclusively linguistic. All that matters for selfhood and human being-in-the-world is language: "human beings are simply incarnated vocabularies"; it is simply "words which ... made us what we are." Thus Nietzsche is praised as one who "by describing himself in his own terms ... created himself," since he "created the only part of himself that mattered by constructing his own mind. To create one's mind is to create one's own language." For humans are "nothing more than sentential attitudes—nothing more than the presence or absence of dispositions toward the use of sentences phrased in some historically-conditioned vocabulary" (CIS 27, 88, 117).[13]

The only nonlinguistic element of experience that Rorty is willing to recognize is brute physical pain. But in contrast to the essentially linguistic *human* pain of "humiliation," it represents "the nonhuman, the nonlinguistic," what "ties us to the nonlanguage-using beasts." The power of such brute suffering even drives the antimetaphysical Rorty toward a seemingly metaphysical vision that pits human linguistic creation against a deeper, essentially cruel and inhuman ground-reality of "just power and pain ... to be found 'out there' " (CIS 40, 92, 94).

In arguing that man is essentially mind and that mind is essentially linguistic, Rorty not only violates his antiessentialism but endorses a mentalistic view of human nature against Nietzsche's own emphasis on the body's formative role and value. This linguistic mentalism and somatic neglect is particularly problematic in a philosopher intent on advancing the aesthetic, whose crucial connection with bodily senses and pleasures should be obvious, were it not for the rationalistic bias that has enthralled so much traditional aesthetic theory and still seems to ensnare Rorty's.

Rorty's aesthetic is thus hardly different from Habermas's. He exhibits none of that Dionysian aestheticism of Bataille or Foucault that Habermas condemns as postmodern. Nor does Rorty even affirm the more temperate forms of libidinal somatic aesthetics that I appreciate in certain forms of popular music and "body work."[14] He just likes to read books, and those he likes (notably Proust, Nabakov, Orwell, and Kundera) all belong to the refined modern canon of serious art rather than to wacky Dadaism, anarchistic postmodernism, or the hedonic works of popular culture. Moreover, he recommends his chosen forms of art not for the wild ecstacies they produce but because they may "help us become autonomous ... [and] less cruel" (CIS 141).

In short, Rorty's aestheticism is rationally melioristic, advocating art to improve the lifeworld by making the individual stronger in himself and more tolerant of others. How different is this from Habermas's strategy for continuing modernity's project of progress while overcoming its cultural fragmentation? Both strategies seek to appropriate the achievements of our progressive, specialized high-art tradition by translating its contents, through expert interpretive criticism, into the language and experience of our lifeworld.

IV

To sum up, Habermas and Rorty see postmodernism as privileging the aesthetic over the Enlightenment tradition of reason, and both supply historico-philosophical narratives to explain this aesthetic turn. Moreover, both cherish the modernist aesthetic tradition of high art in its more formally disciplined and rational forms, prizing it for its useful contributions to the lifeworld. Finally, both identify this lifeworld with language, which thus becomes the essence of human nature and the battleground over which aesthetics and reason struggle for dominance. Here at last, in their contrasting privileging of the linguistic centrality of these terms, Rorty and Habermas exhibit real difference.

But how momentous is it? Habermas clearly affirms language's important aesthetic dimensions: not simply "the world-creating capacity of language," its special "poetic-world-disclosive function," but also an "aesthetic-expressive" dimension that he recognizes in every speech act (PDM 313, 315). Conversely, Rorty readily admits the usefulness of the rational/irrational distinction within "the interior of a language game" and particularly within the domain of "public rhetoric"—which Habermas of course would call "public reason" (CIS 47, 87).

Rorty loves to shock old-fashioned rationalists by advocating aesthetic primacy even in "the language of theoretical science," which he sees (like Mary Hesse) as "irreducibly metaphorical." Metaphor "is essential to scientific progress," because its innovative aesthetic imagination provides the necessary means to escape the entrenched vocabularies of old scientific paradigms, thus paving the way for more productive new theories (EHO 166; ORT 162). But Habermas also recognizes that "the specialized languages of science and technology ... live off the illuminating power of metaphorical tropes." He simply insists that these "rhetorical elements" are eventually submitted to argumentative and experimental disciplines of consensus-oriented discourse in the process of theory justification and in being "enlisted for the special purposes of problem-solving" (PDM 209; cf. PT 205). So if Rorty portrays the history of scientific progress "as the history of metaphor" (CIS 16), Habermas is simply objecting that this is not the whole story.

Yet Rorty clearly admits this too. In defending Habermas against Lyotard's postmodern vision of science as pure innovational paralogy, Rorty recognizes the useful regulative role of "normal science," arguing that science no more aims "at piling paralogy on paralogy" than politics "aims at piling revolution on revolution" (EHO 166). Likewise, though preferring to highlight science's revolutionary moment as more interesting and inspiringly heroic through its creative difference, Rorty nonetheless shows great respect for normal science's language of consensus. Celebrating it as the expression of "unforced agreement" through the discussion of wide-ranging "suggestions and arguments," he recommends it as an exemplary "model of human solidarity" (ORT 39). Finally, even the privileged aesthetic moment of novel difference must in some way gain validation through public discourse and its normative (albeit revisable) justificational procedures. This convergence of "private" fantasy with shared public language and the community's needs is recognized even by Rorty as what distinguishes "genius" from mad "eccentricty or perversity" (CIS 37).

The limits of Rortian aesthetic sovereignty become even clearer when we turn to the realm of politics and the public sphere. *There*, as we saw, the "public rhetoric" of consensus must prevail; there we don't want idiosyncratic metaphors but shared norms, common categories, stable procedures and consistent rules of argument. There, even universalism is affirmed—not in the Habermasian sense of a foundational "idealizing presupposition of communicative action" (PDM 206), but as the goal of an ever wider, more inclusive community of reasonable, tolerant liberals. The aesthetic and its individualism dominate only in the private sphere, though this is the sphere that Rorty privileges in contrast to Habermas's championing of the public.

We see here another reason why the public/private split is so important to Rorty. It performs his postmodern remapping of modernity's tripartite schema of science, art, and the ethico-political into a dualism of *public* discourse based on normalcy and consensus versus a *private* discursive sphere aimed at radical innovation and individual fulfillment. If normal science and politics can be fit into the former, personal ethics joins art in the latter and becomes aestheticized.

But Rorty's postmodern mapping remains modern and Habermasian in compartmentalizing the aesthetic from the political and normal scientific, even if the aesthetic now includes the ethics of taste in lifestyles. On the other hand, Habermas's ideal of communicative reason is procedural and liberal enough to accept differences of taste in art and aesthetic lifestyles, as long as these differences do not endanger the essential social norms of the public sphere. So if they both insist on the primacy of language and share a taste for aesthetic modernism and liberal politics, why does the Rorty–Habermas debate seem so urgent to us philosophers?

Their question of privileging aesthetics or reason—the private or public—concerns our very conception of philosophy and our self-image as philosophers. For Rorty, philosophy gets aestheticized with ethics and is relegated to the private realm. It becomes an art of living one's own life with greater autonomy and fulfillment, and perhaps inspiring others to do likewise. But it should never pretend to determine general norms for improving the direction of science or the public sphere. For Habermas, in contrast, reason's primacy over the aesthetic means keeping philosophy firmly with science in the public domain of consensus and knowledge. Philosophy remains the unifying discipline of the public sphere, integrating and legitimating its scientific, social, and even aesthetic norms. If no longer the authoritarian arbiter of culture, it remains the crucial "stand-in [Platzhalter] and interpreter," "the guardian of reason."[15]

While Habermas presents himself as philosopher of the *polis*, Rorty more often assumes the modest role of campus philosopher, recreating himself through books and inspiring colleagues and students to do the same.[16] It is easy to condemn the retreat from unificational public philosophy to individual aesthetics, particularly from the perspective of European cultures like France and Germany, where organic national publics are still thought to exist and philosophers may still have a visible role in determining their political culture. But current American society neither presents such a *polis* nor grants the philosopher the role of guiding it and securing its unity. In such conditions, which may soon become the conditions of a confederated Europe, one might reasonably concentrate philosophy on what it may do best: help the individual lead a better life. Just as Habermas's fear of noncompartmentalized aesthetics may reflect the horrid national memory of aestheticized Nazism, so Rorty's aesthetic turn may reflect not mere personal taste but recognition of the philosopher's rather limited role in American politics and culture.

Two points, however, must be recalled from chapter two. Between the center court of the national *polis* and one's private aesthetic theater, there remains for American philosophers a wide realm for effective political engagement. Besides, political action can be recommended also for its personal aesthetic rewards of self-enrichment through the satisfactions of solidarity and collaborative struggle. Conversely (as I argue in chapter five), the aesthetic power of an artwork or a life can be deeply enhanced by its political engagement, even if such aesthetico-political cocktails can have a dangerously blinding power that necessitates an always vigilant philosophical critique. Forcing philosophy to choose narrowly between public reason and private aesthetics therefore makes no sense.

V

In trying to ease the Rorty–Habermas, aesthetic-reason oppositions, I hope to have tempered the opposition between the modern and postmodern. Postmodernity — aesthetically, politically, philosophically, and economically — should be conceived as largely continuous with its modern roots, though conspicuously lacking in modernity's faith in progress, compartmentalization, and in the purity, universality, and adequacy of reason.[17] Postmodernism's critique of reason can thus be seen as a continuation of modernity's, while its advocacy of the aesthetic helps highlight dimensions of experience that modern reason could not adequately handle through strategies of compartmentalization and marginalization. The postmodern implosion of aesthetics into ethics and politics shows that modernity's rationalizing differentiation of culture into separate spheres has not been entirely successful.

Rorty's aestheticization of the ethical is a symptom of this postmodern reaction. But his aesthetic remains too constrained by the modern rationalist tradition: not simply in its taste and confinement to the private sphere, but also through its exclusive concern for language, its denial of the somatic which is *alogon* in the sense of nondiscursivity, though not necessarily in the sense of rabid Dionysian excess. The conflation of these two senses, in thinkers like Bataille, Deleuze, and Foucault, comes only by coupling the idea of somatic aesthetics with the avant-garde ideology of radical transgression. One task for postmodern inquiry is to test the limits of reason by probing this nonlinguistic aesthetic realm, which though devoid of discursive rationality is not devoid of intelligent direction. Pervading the experience of our everyday lifeworld but also the activities of expert culture, such nondiscursive *aisthesis* presents a domain whose ameliorative care could enhance our science and politics, not just our ethics and aesthetics. I develop this notion of *somaesthetics* in chapter six, but a sense of its philosophical difficulty (even of its alleged perverse impossibility) should be faced already here.

All theoretical attempts to free the aesthetic from rationalist discursive dominion run against the power of tradition. The very concept of "aesthetics" was introduced by philosophers (originally by Baumgarten, a Leibnizian rationalist) precisely to rationalize the nonlogical dimension of aesthetic experience. Aesthetics of the nondiscursive must also face the dialectical dilemma that to discourse about the "other of reason" or "other of language" is already to inscribe that other within the ambit of reason and language. Habermas sees this as his trump card of performative contradiction against reason's critique by its other, while Rorty's equation of aesthetics with language only suggests a parallel reinforcing argument.

But surely one value of the aesthetic, through the intense pleasures and often overwhelming power of aesthetic experience, is to make us forget for a moment about language and reason, allowing us to revel, however briefly, in nondiscursive sensual joy. This crucial sensual dimension is sadly neglected by Rorty because of his global linguisticism. As its denial makes his aestheticism joylessly eviscerate, his contrasting emphasis on pain is still more discouraging. Despite his emancipatory progress, Rorty remains the product of a puritan America. Ignoring somatic satisfactions, his aesthetic program is one-sidedly driven by the restless, relentless production of new vocabularies and narrative identities. It is more a toiling poetics, a theory of industrious verbal making, than an aesthetic of embodied delight.

Of course, as Foucault reminds us, the body is not free from the imprint of society's rationalizing practices. But it remains (as he also recognized) a promising place where discursive reason meets its limits, encounters its other, and can be given a therapeutic shock towards redirection. Nor should we heed the objection that somatic aesthetics is impossible because such experience is too subjective and individualistic. We share our bodies and bodily pleasures as much as we share our minds, and they are surely as public as our thoughts.

There remains the ultimate paradox that the very attempt to theorize the body as something outside our linguistic structures self-refutingly inscribes it in those structures. As T. S. Eliot's Sweeney complained, "I gotta use words when I talk to you." In one sense, this is a trivial sophism, but in another a deep truth. Discourse about the somatic is not enough, as even Socrates realized in advocating and practicing dance for his philosophical life.[18] To understand the body as the "nondiscursive other," we have to stop pushing words and start moving limbs: stop talking and start dancing. Perhaps I should *say* no more. Though confined to discursivity, my next two chapters hope at least to point farther, through rap's dancing aesthetic and the reconstruction of somatic experience.

5

ART IN ACTION, ART INFRACTION

Goodman, Rap, Pragmatism
(New Reality Mix)

I

How can art assume a more active, practical role in our lives? Since the dominant cultural ideology sharply separates art from the serious praxis of life, this question suggests infraction. If philosophy is to be conceived not simply as a life-practice but as an *aesthetic* life-practice, then the traditional opposition of practical/aesthetic must be transgressed. Pragmatism, I have argued, provides the best philosophy for challenging not only this opposition, but also other misguided dichotomies which subtend it (e.g. art/reality, art/knowledge, art/popular culture).[1]

Pursuing the better integration of art and life, this chapter combines two very different forms of pragmatist aesthetics: the respected aesthetic theory of Harvard philosopher Nelson Goodman and the much condemned artistic practice of hip-hop or rap music. After sketching five pragmatist themes through which Goodman prefigures and reinforces rap, I hope to show how rap's practice illuminates and correctively supplements his theory.[2]

II

Pluralism

The first pragmatist theme is radical pluralism. For Goodman this involves the recognition of multiple "worlds" through recognizing the validity of multiple points of view, multiple histories, or, in sum, multiple world-representations. William James and John Dewey had earlier affirmed a more moderate pluralism in opposing the popular Hegelian monism of their day and objecting to its constraining vision of a single, totalized "block universe." They insisted on the validity of different ways of viewing or representing the world as a function of our different contexts and purposes in dealing with it.

Adopting this plurality of valid world-representations, Goodman makes the further Peircean point, that, because all thought is symbolic or representational, there is no way to conceive of the world apart from its world-representations. Hence there is no place for a firm distinction between world and world-representation. Nor is there any real substance in talking about the one world which stands outside its different but correct representations. The one real world thus dissolves into a multiplicity of world-representations, or more simply (given the untenability of the world/world-representation distinction) multiple worlds.

Goodman's principal argument for the multiplicity of worlds is the impossibility of combining conflicting world-representations into a single world-picture. For accepting such contradiction within one world means accepting the validity of "all statements whatsoever," since, by the propositional logic of material implication, all statements "follow from any contradiction" (WWM 110). To accommodate conflicting but acceptable world-versions, we need to admit different worlds where they can be accepted. As contradiction cannot exist within one world, it is rather relegated to differences between worlds, just as the schizoid deals with contradictions of personal emotion and desire by adopting different personalities.

Radical pragmatism will question whether this formalist strategy of relegation really helps resolve contradictions in a substantive way. They often simply return, in equally troubling form, as "wars between worlds." Similarly, pluralism may challenge the principle that "everything follows logically from a contradiction" as being itself only one point of view and thus true only for certain logicized world-versions; so that there may be other world-representations where contradiction can be tolerated within a world. Goodman must admit that in giving this overriding priority to the principle of noncontradiction he is embracing a particular (and particularly logical) world-representation. But the possibility of alternative positions need not vitiate the belief that his is the best. Pluralism is consistent with preference and fierce advocacy, as rap's rivalries and multiple styles manifest.

Art and Cognition

Goodman's pragmatism also prefigures rap in his Deweyan opposition to the traditional compartmentalization that radically divides art from science and philosophy. Opposing the entrenched Kantian aesthetic of formalist autonomy, Goodman rejects the idea of "autonomous aesthetic objects" valued merely for the pleasure of their form (OMM 6). Instead he claims the underlying unity of the scientific and the aesthetic.

In challenging the traditional art/science opposition (along with its supporting dualisms of emotion/cognition, form/content, pleasure/truth), Goodman continues Dewey's strategy of replacing dichotomies by continuities and integrating the aesthetic into life's manifold pursuits. Dewey insists not only that art involves hard thinking and cognitive discovery, but that "science ... is an art" which, like philosophy, can provide its practitioners real aesthetic experience.[3] Goodman is even more outspoken about the fundamental unity of art and science through "their common cognitive function." So important is this unity that aesthetics, along with philosophy of science, "should be conceived as an integral part of metaphysics and epistemology," while aesthetic value gets subsumed "under cognitive excellence" (OMM 148; WWM 102; LA 259).[4]

If philosophy, science, and art share the role of enlarging understanding by creating insightfully satisfying world-versions, then perhaps the scientist or philosopher should be something of an artist, and vice versa. The fundamental unity of these apparently different roles becomes a crucial theme of hip-hop, whose rappers claim at once to be poets and philosophers. Goodman's own work seeks such a synthesis of philosophy and art, portraying his highly stylized prose style as neither mere external decoration nor attention-getting gimmick, but rather "part and parcel of the philosophy presented and worlds made."[5] His desired hybrid status as philosopher-artist is equally evident in his multimedia creation *Hockey Seen*, as much an inquiry into the interaction of different perceptual, cultural, and referential modalities as it is a "simple" work of art (OMM 69–70, 193).

Dynamic Function

Goodman's pragmatism joins Dewey's in challenging the standard identification of art with its material objects. Such reification fosters the fetishization and commodification of art, whose oppressive distortions impoverish contemporary aesthetic experience. Condemning this unhealthy attitude as "the museum conception of art," Dewey inveighed against its compartmentalizing elitism, while linking its history to the woes of nationalist imperialism and rootless, ruthless international capitalism. Goodman provides a more detailed, constructive critique of museums (that is less political though no less caustic), attacking their excessive preoccupation with sacralizing works of genius rather than educating the public in artistic appreciation necessary for making artworks *work* in the lives of ordinary people.[6]

For Dewey and Goodman, what matters in art is not the object but how it functions in experience. Dewey's challenge to the fetishization of art's objects was to redefine art in terms of dynamic experience and process. Goodman's complementary strategy is to redefine the very question "what is art?" into the question "when is art?" The real aesthetic issue is not what properties an object permanently has but how it temporally (even if ephemerally) functions in organizing and symbolizing experience (WWM 69–70; OMM 142–45, 182). This emphasis on art's temporal functioning and dynamic process, which scorns the sanctity of the fixed artistic object, is enormously important to the time-conscious, deconstructive art of rap. It also compensates for Goodman's intense preoccupation with defining the specific identity of particular artworks, an analytic philosophical concern that both reflects and reinforces the traditional myth of their sanctity and fixity.[7]

Popular Art

Pragmatist aesthetics denies the rigid division of aesthetic legitimacy typically drawn between high and popular art. On this matter I have tried to go farther than Dewey or Goodman, not only by showing popular art's aesthetic potential and past contributions to our high-art tradition, but by exposing the historical mutability and questionable principles of the high/low distinction.[8] Still, the Dewey-Goodman critique of traditional museum elitism inspired my efforts, and Goodman's

own attempt to "rub out the hard line between the elite and the popular" (OMM 193) goes well beyond his case for democratizing the museum; it informs his actual artistic-philosophic practice.

More striking here than his *Hockey Seen* (which remains a high-art
multimedia work about hockey) is Goodman's use of comic Woody
Allen's philosophic wit to support his own philosophical arguments
(WWM 96). This serious yet humorous use of popular art purveying
philosophy blurs the lines not only between high and popular culture; it
also unites the roles of philosophy and art, linking philosophers with
critically insightful comics. It suggests that Goodman sees himself, like
"Professor Allen," as an artist-philosopher or philosopher-artist whose
ability to entertain is inseparable from his insight and instruction. This
ideal of the philosopher-artist is championed with still greater exuber-
ance by BDP rapper KRS-One, whose album title proclaims the goal
of "Edutainment" and whose artistic moniker stands for "Knowledge
Reigns Supreme Over Nearly Everyone."[9]

Meliorative Change and Hope

But how can one dare oppose such time-honored dogmas as the disinterested autonomy of art, its contrast to science and philosophy, its reification into fetishized objects, and its elitist separation from popular art?
Is there any philosophical basis for the cheeky defiance of established
doctrine which Goodman shares with hip-hop culture? It could be
pragmatism, a philosophy characterized by its future-looking attitude
and valorization of change.

Though respecting the productive power of the past (through the
efficacious force of entrenched habits, practices, and institutions),[10]
pragmatism nonetheless locates authority not in past givens but in consequences for the present and future. Recognizing the temporal change
and plasticity of our world and tools of understanding, pragmatism insists on not accepting them *as they've been* but on making them better.
William James thus defines pragmatism as "the attitude of looking away
from first things, principles, 'categories,' supposed necessities; and of
looking towards last things, fruits, consequences, and facts." For pragmatism, the goal of knowledge is not to *copy* existing reality but to
transform it to provide better experience. Even the facts themselves

(partly through the ways they are determined and represented) are not foundationally fixed but instead made and remade by human inquiry.[11]

If our facts are fabricated and our concepts can be similarly reconstructed and improved, then we need not show excessive respect for the accepted wisdom of the past, though much of it will continue (through force of habit and utility) to exercise a strong, often valuable influence on our thinking. This meliorism and time-conscious, future-looking hope lies behind Goodman's often brash infractions of the views of common sense ("that repository of ancient error") and his contrasting advocacy of Carnapian rational reconstruction and of imaginative, multiple world-making.[12]

Melioristic hope is also what engendered the aesthetic infractions of rap, born in America's black ghettos as an art of stolen musical fractions, composed by appropriating bits of previous musical events to create an excitingly new sound. Emancipatory hope through self-confident artistic achievement, conscious-raising knowledge, and the joyful power of musically inspired social struggle: this was clearly rap's defining message when I first wrote about it at the start of the nineties.[13] By mid-decade, rap's positive infractions have been so obscured by its media-hyped image of monstrous gangsterism that we must recall its history, aesthetic, and progressive purpose in order to regrasp its rich socio-cultural potential and its import for the notion of philosophical life. Hence the following rap remix for the new realities.

III

Aesthetic Techniques and Infractions

Artistic appropriation is the historical source of hip-hop sound and (despite an increased use of live music) remains a central aesthetic technique and message. The music stems from "sampling," i.e. selecting and combining parts of prerecorded songs to produce a new soundtrack. This soundtrack, produced by the DJ on multiple turntables, constitutes the musical background for the rap lyrics. These in turn frequently praise the DJ's virtuousity in sampling and synthesizing the appropriated music, but are most often devoted to boasting of the lyrical rhyming power and skillfully phrased delivery of the rapper himself (called the

MC). While the rapper's vaunting self-praise often highlights his sexual desirability, fame, and material success, these signs of status are all presented as secondary to and derivative from his verbal power. Even the image of hard-core invincibility centers here—mind, mouth, and microphone being typically touted as the rapper's most trusted lethal weapons.[14]

This valorization of language should not surprise us, because sociological and anthropological studies clearly show that verbal virtuosity is highly appreciated in black ghetto life. The assertion of superior social status through verbal prowess (rather than brute physical strength or violence) remains a deeply entrenched black tradition that goes back to the griots in West Africa and was long sustained in the New World through traditional verbal contests or games such as "signifying" or "the dozens." Conscious of this heritage, rappers such as Guru proudly claim, "Deeply rooted is my rhymin'/Like ancient African griots/Precise is my timin'."[15]

Like its stylized boasting language, rap's other most salient feature—its dominant funky beat—can be traced back to African roots, to jungle rhythms later developed in exile and adopted by rock and disco before being reappropriated by rap DJs in North America's black urban centers. Despite these African roots, rap music is unquestionably a diasporic product, emerging only through the disco era of the mid-seventies in the grim ghettos of New York, first in the Bronx and then Harlem and Brooklyn, and not releasing its first records until 1979.

While appropriating disco sounds and techniques, rap undermined and transformed them—much as jazz (an earlier and previously scorned black art of appropriation) had done with the melodies of popular songs. Proudly linking itself to the now respected art of jazz, rap also sampled frequently from its tracks (and later collaborated with its musicians). But in contrast to jazz appropriations, rap's sampling did not take mere melodies or musical phrases—that is, abstract musical patterns that can be differently played in different performances and thus have the ontological status of "type" entities. Instead, rap snatched concrete sound-events, prerecorded "token" performances of such musical patterns. Thus, unlike jazz, its borrowing and transfiguration did not demand skill in playing musical instruments, but rather in manipulating records and other forms of audio technology.

As jazz's technique of improvisation challenged the idea of an art-work's fixed identity, so rap's appropriative sampling poses peculiar problems for defining the musical work, especially from Goodman's perspective. In contrast to what he calls the "autographic" arts of paint-ing and sculpture, Goodman considers music "allographic." This means that the different authentic instances of the same musical work are defined entirely in terms of a defining notational score, irrespective of their history of production. Whatever musical event complies with that score by playing the notes it designates (or would designate if the work is not yet scored) counts as a fully authentic instance of the work. How-ever, if rap is explicitly an appropriative art whose works are based on sampling certain recorded performances, then a performance or sound-track produced independently by ordinary musicians (even if it fit the score and was auditorily indistinguishable from what the DJ produces) would not count as an authentic instance of the given rap, since it did not involve that rap's sampling or indeed any sampling whatever. Defin-ing the identity or authenticity of the rap work would then require, as in autographic art, a certain history of production.

Since Goodman regards music as the paradigm of allographic art, how should he treat rap's musical art which courts the autographic? One solution would be simply denying that rap is musical art, as many aesthetic bigots insist. A better alternative is treating rap as not *purely* musical, but as a mixed art: not only a mixture of music and words (both, for Goodman, allographic), but also of (autographic) style in tone, timing, and texture of vocal delivery, and of (autographic) virtu-ousity in manipulating the technological equipment from which the genre derived.[16]

This view gains support from hip-hop history. Rap originated from the techniques of cutting and blending which DJs in traditional discos had developed to make smooth transitions between one record and the next. Dissatisfied with the tame sound of disco and commercial pop, self-styled DJs in the Bronx reapplied this technique of cutting to con-centrate and augment those parts of the records which could provide for livelier dancing.

From the basic technique of cutting between sampled records, hip-hop developed three other formal devices which contribute signifi-cantly to its sound and aesthetic: "scratch mixing," "punch phrasing," and simple scratching. The first is simply overlaying or mixing sounds from one record to those of another already playing. Punch phrasing is a refinement of such mixing, where the DJ moves the needle back and forth over a specific phrase of chords or drum slaps of a record so as to add a powerful percussive effect to the sound of the other record already playing on another turntable. The third device is a wilder, far more rapid back and forth scratching of the record, too fast for the recorded music to be recognized but productive of a dramatic scratching sound which has its own intense musical quality and crazed beat. The skillful application of these three techniques is vividly evident in the rap classic "The Adventures of Grandmaster Flash on the Wheels of Steel," which I like to play at this juncture to make these points when I lecture.

Complementing these diverse appropriative techniques is rap's variety of appropriated content. Not only sampling from a wide range of popular music, it feeds eclectically on TV theme songs, advertising jingles, classical music, and the electronic music of arcade games. It even appropriates nonmusical content: police sirens, gunshots, baby-cries, bits of media news reports, fragments of political speeches (most notably of Martin Luther King and Malcolm X), and snatches of TV or movie dialogues (e.g. Grandmaster Flash's use of *Family Affair* in his above-cited hit, or 2 Live Crew's "Me So Horny" sample from Kubrick's film *Full Metal Jacket*). Though DJs sometimes concealed (for fear of competition) the exact records they were sampling, there was never an attempt to hide the fact that they were working from prerecorded sounds rather than composing their own original music. On the contrary, they openly celebrated their method of sampling. What is the aesthetic significance of this proud art of appropriation?

First, it challenges the traditional ideal of originality and uniqueness that long enslaved our conception of art. Though artists had always borrowed from each other's works, the romantic ideology of genius obscured this fact, posing a sharp distinction between original creation and derivative borrowing. Rap marks a deliberate infraction of this dichotomy, creatively deploying and thematizing its appropriation to show that borrowing and creation are not at all incompatible. It further recalls that even the most original artwork is always a product of older materials, the novel text always a tissue of familiar words and earlier echoes.

Originality thus loses its absolute status and is more freely reconceived to include the transfiguring reappropriation and recycling of the old; so creative energy can be liberated to play with familiar creations without fear of denying its own artistry by not producing a totally original work. Goodman, who critiques our one-sided preoccupation with originary genius, makes a related point. Art demands not only the creative production or "execution" of new works but also their creative "implementation," which is needed for "making a work work" in variant contexts of reception (OMM 143). Yet rap goes further than Goodman in blurring the very distinction between execution and implementation, between producing and reproducing music. By simultaneously celebrating their borrowing and their originality, rap undermines any dichotomy between creation and appropriation, between making works and remaking them in making them work better. Transfigurative appropriation can take the form of art.

Rap's sampling is also an infraction of art's traditional ideal of unity. Since Aristotle, aestheticians typically viewed the artwork as an organic whole so perfectly unified that any tampering with its parts would damage the whole. Later ideologies of romanticism and "art for art's sake" reinforced the notion that works of art are sacred ends in themselves, whose integrity we should respect and never violate. In contrast to this austere aesthetic of rigid unity and devotional worship, rap's cutting and sampling offers the pluralistic pleasures of deconstructive and reconstructive art—the thrilling beauty of dismembering (and rapping over) old works to create new ones, dismantling the prepackaged and wearily familiar into something stimulatingly different that often achieves a complex, fragile unity of its own.

But rap does this without the pretense that its own work is ever inviolable, that the artistic process is ever final, that there is ever a product which should be so fetishized as to prohibit appropriative transfiguration. Instead, its sampling implies that an artwork's integrity as object should never outweigh the possibilities for continuing creation through use of that object. Appropriating and remixing its favorite tracks, rap thus suggests the Deweyan message that art is more essentially process than finished product, the Goodmanian message that art is a question of dynamic temporal functioning rather than static being. This is a welcome message in our culture whose drive to reify and commodify all artistic expression is so strong that rap itself is victimized by this commercializing tendency, even while protesting it.

In defying the fetishized integrity of artworks, rap also challenges the traditional demands for monumental permanence and universality—that an artwork should be forever and for everyone. Though it may claim some unforgettable "classics" (e.g. Grandmaster Flash's "The Message" and Public Enemy's "Don't Believe The Hype"), rap highlights the artwork's temporality not only by its sampling and remixing, but by thematizing the work's temporal context in the self-referential dating of its lyrics. Declarations of date (like BDP's "Fresh for '88, you suckers!", "Fresh for '89, you suckers!", "Fresh for 1995, you suckers!") suggest the likelihood of datedness in future years.[17] But in rap's pragmatist aesthetic, transience does not entail worthlessness. The temporality of a work's "freshness" or power does not preclude the reality of its value; no more than the ephemeral freshness of cream renders its sweet taste unreal.

Recognizing that it can't please everyone, rap does not even try, thematizing specific contexts of place and public as well as time. Neighborhood identity has always been important: not only engendering stylistic differences in sound and lyrics, but contributing to aggressive duelling between West and East coast rappers that threatens hip-hop solidarity. What now rocks Compton may bomb in Brooklyn or miss in Marseille.[18] Rap's impressive international success depends on neither a standard sound nor a monolithic message—the target issues, cultural allusions, and even musical mix often differ sharply in different nations. It instead bespeaks the imbrications and affinities of contemporary contexts of cosmopolitan diasporic cultures, and also the productive flexibility of rap's form. By highlighting changing contexts, rap underscores the pragmatist point that art's meaning and value are defined more by contextual functioning than by the fixed art object.

The transient contextuality of rap's works does not preclude the genre's proud survival, just as the mortality of each individual does not mean the death of our species. Nor should we forget that transfigurative sampling not only supercedes old works with new creations but also dialectically recalls and so preserves the sampled works in lived experience. Through the rich intertextuality thereby produced, rap is not a mere junk-pile of throw-away sounds but an aural museum, one particularly devoted to the works of its own tradition.[19]

Praxis and Knowledge

As rap's eclectic sampling questions conventional ideals of aesthetic purity and integrity, so its militant insistence on the deeply political dimension of culture challenges one of modernity's most crucial dogmas: aesthetic autonomy. Having disenchanted religion's unified world-order, the modern project of enlightened progress through rationalized specialization has carved the world of human endeavor into three separate spheres of secular culture: science, art, and ethical-political praxis, each governed by its own inner logic of theoretical, aesthetic, or moral-practical judgment. This tripartite division was powerfully reflected and reinforced by Kant's critical analysis of human thinking in terms of pure reason, practical reason, and aesthetic judgment.

In this division of cultural spheres, art was distinguished from science as not being truly concerned with knowledge, because its aesthetic judgment was essentially nonconceptual and subjective. Art was also sharply differentiated from the practical activity of ethics and politics, which involves real interests and appetitive will (as well as logical reasoning). Instead, art was consigned to a disinterested, imaginative realm that Schiller affirmed as play and semblance but logical positivism later dismissed as mere emotive meaning.

As pragmatism *pursues in theory*, so hip-hop *performs in practice* the defiant infraction of this trivializing compartmentalization. More than any other genre, rap forcefully demonstrates art's important political dimensions, socio-ethical stakes, and practical consequences. With its antiestablishment message and public, rap quickly earned the acute critical attention of institutions not typically associated with art's "free" realm of semblance. Police, law courts, and government officials have long been busy with its censorship and surveillance. Politicians of the highest rank have publicly condemned rap, not merely for fomenting divisive racial enmity and anti-American thinking but for destroying the nation's social fabric through the celebration of crime and gangster values.[20]

Rap's power for praxis is indeed recognized, but only by demonizing it as the incarnation and cause of all inner-city evils. This is achieved by blindly conflating *all* rap with the much publicized genre of "gangsta rap," whose notorious works are often not only morally detestable (in tending to glorify greed, sexism, and ruthlessly violent crime) but also brutally unimaginative and commercially preprogrammed. Though the conflation is obviously false (there being not only nongangsta rap but also militantly *anti*gangsta rap), it grows ever more strongly entrenched by serving a potent constellation of political and economic interests.

Making rap the general scapegoat for black criminality, the gangsta image provides a symbolic target that can unite very different political groups of often conflicting agendas, while at the same time obscuring the real socio-economic and political causes of ghetto poverty and violence. Moreover, since this image panders (in both ghetto and suburb) to juvenile instincts of rebellion through vicarious criminality (including the purchase of a "criminal" yet eminently legal commodity), the gangsta–rap connection proves economically most lucrative. Experience shows that public condemnations and threats of censorship provide the greatest marketing hype, while the news media—always interested in facile sensationalism—likewise prefer to focus on rap's more spectacular criminal image than on its everyday positive uses: in developing linguistic skills, in communicating cultural tradition and history while raising political consciousness and ethnic pride, in offering a symbolic yet powerfully audible form of protest, in providing fruitful new means of employment and wealth for the ghetto community.[21] Seduced by media sensationalism, even academic rap criticism has become increasingly fixed on the gangsta issues, though not always in one-sided condemnation.[22]

"When everything is bad," notes Adorno, "it must be good to know the worst."[23] Let gangsta rap form the focus for such archpessimism. Pragmatist aesthetics is instead melioristic: recognizing rap's flaws and consequent *need* for improvement, but equally recognizing that it *deserves* meliorative care because of its proved potential for aesthetic merit and social praxis. Meliorism means looking also at the good in rap, in order to build on it and broaden its dominion.

One of rap's founding and still most central genres is self-consciously devoted to the integration of art with the pursuit of knowledge in the aim of ethical growth and socio-political emancipation. So let me concentrate here on this genre of "knowledge rap" (or "message rap") and its positive infraction of aesthetic purism and disinterestedness. In this genre (already signaled by Grandmaster Flash's "The Message" and "Message II (Survival)" of 1982), rappers insist that their role as artists and poets is inseparable from their role as insightful inquirers into reality and teachers of truth, particularly those aspects of reality and truth which get neglected or distorted by establishment history books, institutional religion, and contemporary news coverage.

KRS-One, for example, presents himself not simply as "a teacher and artist, startin' new concepts at their hardest," but preeminently as a *philosopher*, a scientific purveyor of truth in such raps as "My Philosophy," "R.E.A.L.I.T.Y.," and "The Truth."[24] Seeing his art as philosophy, he even signs his albums "KRS-One Metaphysican" and advocates (both on and off vinyl) a naturalistic, historicist metaphysics to support the radically militant critical humanism of his ethics and politics. As he raps in "The Real Holy Place," the sacred focus of progressive faith should be not a supernatural god, but the spiritual potential of the embodied mind that can question accepted dogmas and so change reality. "The real holy place is mental" yet embodied; for reality is "mental-physical, metaphysical," though not divisively dualistic, foundationally fixed, or extrahistorical.

On this basis of historicist naturalism with its faith in critical intelligence, KRS-One can develop his toughly critical humanism that rejects the supernatural opiates and fixities of traditional religions. Since reality is largely made and unmade through the struggles of human history, KRS-One urges a combination of critical revisionist history and revolutionary practice.

> You gotta know your history
> Or they'll tell you that God is a mystery
> And that when you're born, you're born in sin.
> They're only sayin' you can't win,
> You can't succeed, you can't advance....
> Well I ain't hearin' that lesson.
> 'Cause one thing I know
> Is that the truth can always be questioned....
> Keep that Bible on the shelf
> God helps those that help themself.

In contrast to quiescent Christianity ("no answers, ... [but] hand clappers and a whole lot of dancers"), Christ's historical role as a revolutionary teacher is stressed and linked to KRS-One's own self-image as teacher of progressive revolution. Since establishment media and education likewise breed uncritical quiescence, they too are frequently targeted for critique. Opposing the media's whitewashing lies, stereotypes, and escapist entertainment, he elsewhere proudly claims:

> I'm tryin' not to escape, but hit the problem head on
> By bringin' out the truth in a song....
> It's simple; BDP will teach reality
> No beatin' around the bush, straight up;
> Just like the "P" is free
> So now you know a poet's job is never done.
> But I'm never overworked, 'cause I'm still number one.[25]

Of course, the realities and truths that hip-hop reveals are not the transcendental, eternal verities of traditional philosophy, but the mutable yet coercive facts and patterns of the material socio-historical world. But this emphasis on the temporally changing and malleable nature of the real (reflected in rap's frequent time-tags and its popular idiom of knowing "what time it is"[26]) represents a very tenable metaphysical position defended by pragmatists like James, Dewey, and Goodman. Rap philosophers continue the pragmatist tradition not merely in their metaphysics of material, historical flux, but in their noncompartmentalized aesthetics that highlights cognitive function and embodied process in the pursuit of productive practical reform.

Identifying himself as a "knowledge seeker" and "soldier of truth [to] protect the lives of our youth," New York rapper Guru advocates (in his "New Reality Style") "a mind revolution" aimed not simply at facing the problematic new realities already in place but more importantly at creating new *positive* realities: "a mind revolution [for] redefining our purpose, organizing and utilizing our resources to gain focus so that we can produce positive change." A central part of this program is "stressing the importance of the family ... and showin' more respect for one another."[27] This requires combating the negativity of gangsta rappers: not only by warning them to "watch what you say" and exposing the bloated falseness of their "weak talk" and their danger as "role models for youth," but also by offering a more positive examplar of "*real* hip-hop": "A sense of purpose is fillin' me./To display credibility and show responsibility" ("Watch What You Say").

In embracing functional praxis as part of art's meaning and value, rap provides a needed corrective to Goodman's imperfect pragmatism. For though stressing the cognitive-aesthetic connection, Goodman reverts to the old aesthetic/practical opposition that "the aesthetic attitude disowns practical aims" and confines itself (like science) to pure "disinterested inquiry" (LA 242).[28] Joining Dewey's affirmation of art's productively practical interests, rappers also endorse his view that science be likewise directed by life's proper needs and values. France's premier rapper MC Solaar (who peppers his philosophical messages with allusions to Descartes, Rousseau, Nietzsche, and even Lacan) urges this point in "La concubine de l'hémoglobine." Attacking science's prostitution to a destructively greedy military industry, he insists that technological advancement must not be taken for real progress and is dangerously unconscious of its own abuses: "Science sans conscience égale la science de l'inconscience./Elle se fout du progrès mais souhaite la progression/De tous les processus qui mènent à l'élimination."[29]

Knowledge rap serves a variety of messages and practical ends. Many are explicitly devoted to raising African-American political consciousness and cultural pride, often through revisionary historical narratives ranging from biblical history to the history of African-American music. Other songs try to inculcate family values, work ethics, and neighborly respect by presenting ideals of sensitive caring and stability, while critiquing the stereotype ghetto life of drugs, violence, promiscuity, and sexism celebrated by gangsta rap. This is true not only for soft, commercial "candy-rap" like Arrested Development's *3 Years, 5 Months, and 2 Days in the Life of*, but also for positive hard-core rappers like KRS-One and Guru. A whole subgenre of knowledge rap aims at stopping the violence in the hip-hop scene itself and can be traced from KRS-One's 1988 hit "Stop the Violence" through to Guru's (1995) "Watch What You Say."

Even rap that employs a criminally violent or gangsta style (the two must be distinguished since criminality can be purely political) often aims at educating its public toward values quite remote from crime, precisely by luridly depicting its dangers. Functioning as street-smart moral fables, such songs offer cautionary narratives and practical advice on the seductions of crime, drugs, sex, and money.[30] Unfortunately, the vivid depiction of such seductions can instead reinforce them. Hence knowledge rappers like Guru insist on an unmistakably clear message of positive guidance. "So many misconceptions/So many evil deceptions/I come to bring direction./For I am the Lifesaver," he raps, directing his public toward the positivities of self-disciplined self-improvement and respect for others while attacking the evils of violence, greed, and despair.

Rap as a Philosophical Life

Knowledge rap's most crucial message is that the resources for self-improvement and better living can be found in the proper practice of rap itself. So urgent is this message that its argument can be literally read off Guru's *Jazzmatazz II* song titles. Rap here is a means of "Looking Through the Darkness," "Defining Purpose," and "Maintaining Focus," thus serving as a "Medicine," "Revelation," and "Lifesaver" for "Lost Souls," and as the best "Choice of Weapons" for "Living in This World." Hip-hop does more than "educate and elevate your mind." By "turning the anger and frustration straight into energy" (of poetry, music, and dance), it helps "maintain self-control" and "channel rage," providing joyful "stress-relief [through] the hip-hop beats" while communicating the therapeutic light of this very message: "I rock from East New York to the suburbs./ The light keeper, knowledge seeker,/ I switch the stress that's on my mind into the voice that rocks your speaker."[31]

Rap is thus urged as a superior, symbolic form of combat that can overcome not only criminal violence, but also the poverty that spawns it. Pragmatically alive to capitalist reality, rappers have always recognized the economic power of their art, once again portrayed as a poetic alternative to crime (the idea aptly captured in the very title of Ice-T's early "Rhyme Pays"). But money, though undeniably central and thematized, is only a tool in knowledge rap's fuller quest for improved existence. ("The game is money, but what about inner wealth/ The mental, the spiritual, and physical health." "It's not about a salary, it's all about reality.")[32]

Much more than a means of livelihood, rap loudly recommends itself as a complete art of living, a comprehensive way of life designated globally by the term "hip-hop culture" and including not only rap music but breakdancing, graffiti, and a distinctive style of dress, speech, gesture, and more—a style that is as easily recognizable as misunderstood. This pragmatic message makes rap particularly attractive to youth who, malcontent with establishment ethos, are seeking an alternative cultural style to help them shape their lives aesthetically. Rap's rich diversity also allows the individual to exercise personal creative taste while remaining within a distinctive taste-community. That hip-hop's distinctive style requires neither affluence nor an Ivy-league diploma makes it still more appealing, while proving that aesthetic self-stylization is not a project confined to an economic or intellectual elite. For its deepest devotees, rap thus becomes an all absorbing, comprehensive art of life — in the vernacular, *a philosophy*.

Stoicism, Epicureanism, and Cynicism were such philosophies in the ancient world, winning their followers less for their technical doctrines of metaphysics and logic than for the different styles of living they prescribed and practiced. Such lived philosophies covered not only matters of mind, but also bodily practice, often specifying particular modes of exercise, diet, or even dress that might improve mental and moral functioning. The case is similar in Asian traditions.[33] Considered in this context, KRS-One's advocacy of style and vegetarianism in "My Philosophy" is not an outrageous irrelevance but a reminder of philosophical forms disenfranchised by Western modernity but still implicitly demanded by the many who are seeking a better, more attractive way to live.[34]

In such philosophies, instruction was as much by the teacher's lived example as by words of formulated doctrine. Hence knowledge rap's pragmatic insistence on the actual *practice* of its theory, the importance of being a good "role model" by living up to a positive musical message. "Quand je dis, je fais, pratique ma théorie," raps MC Solaar, for (in the Wu-Tang Clan's words), the MC should "be livin' proof, to kick the truth, to the young black youth."[35] Recognizing his responsibility as exemplar ("eyes are watchin' me, every single step I take"), Guru thematizes the need for self-mastery, especially in eschewing crime and resisting the sexual temptations of groupies ("Young Ladies"). This lived exemplarity of the philosophical teacher is also stressed by KRS-One. He too links sexual self-control with the quest for self-perfection through self-knowledge, concluding his 1995 album with the refrain "Monogamy — nothing else, but health, wealth, and knowledge of myself," followed by an exemplary act of tribute to his long-time wife: surrendering to her the mike so she can have the very last word in the album.[36]

Ameliorative self-mastery for better living is indeed what knowledge rappers want most to be imitated—not the mimicking of their clothes or the worship of their persons. "Please don't worship Sister Souljah," she herself raps, "Take what is useful and prove your belief/In the ideas and values through your own deeds." The goal is not conformist copying but what MC Solaar calls "la recherche de la perfection" through one's "sens critique." Confirming rap's commitment to the ancient philosophical message of disciplined care for the self, Guru urges: "Realize that the key is for each to master his own destiny/Deal with reality and keep a tight focus/'Cause there's a lot we gotta cope with."[37]

Conquering one's own negativity is thus the first step to conquering it in the world. Though clearly committed to active political engagement, rap philosophers reformulate the classic argument traceable from Socrates through Cynicism and Stoicism to the self-perfectionism of Wittgenstein, Cavell, and the later Foucault: that the transformational perfection of society can be achieved only (though not exclusively) through the ameliorative self-mastery of its individual constitutive members. As New York rapper Jeru the Damaja argues, the social body like the human organism is a collective whose individual parts must take care to perform their own special functions: "That's why each person is supposed to get with their own individual self. Because the way you destroy any negativity in the world is to destroy it first within yourself."[38]

In treating rap as philosophy, I am sure to face the charge of falsely imposing my own philosophical meanings on its alleged mindless content. Do rappers themselves see their art as a life-philosophy of comprehensive stylization? Guru's "Hip-Hop as a Way of Life" (rhythmically delivered in unrhymed earnestness over a jazz-inspired background) is an unequivocally clear affirmation, worth citing at length with no interposed gloss.

> Yo, hip-hop is a way of life. It ain't a fad; it ain't a trend. Not for those who are true to it. It's reflected in our style, in our walk, and in our stance, in our dress and in our attitudes. Hip-hop has a history, an origin, and a set of principles, including rules and regulations that a lot of kids overlook nowadays.... Over the years hip-hop has evolved to represent what is happening now, the reality of street life. Rap is the oral expression of this, the tool, the literature. Hip-hop is the lifestyle, the philosophy, even the religion, if I may.... Although the music and lifestyle is now propagandized by the media, and is now exploited by business, it will still remain for some of us as the raw essence of life. Peace.[39]

Though long stifled by modernity's academic ideal of philosophy as impersonal theory, the notion of philosophy as an embodied, comprehensive art of living retains a popular power by serving an undeniable existential need. Rap philosophers like KRS-One, Guru, and MC Solaar join the likes of Thoreau and Foucault in trying to revive this venerable practice. Here, rap challenges not only modernity's compartmental aesthetics but its very conception of philosophy.

Modernity's purism of aesthetic autonomy had another limiting side.[40] Just as the aesthetic was distinguished from the more rational realms of knowledge and action, it was also sharply separated from the more sensate and appetitive gratifications of embodied human nature — aesthetic pleasure instead was confined to distanced, disinterested contemplation of formal properties. Hip-hop repudiates such purity. It wants to be appreciated fully through energetic movement and impassioned dance, not immobile, dispassionate contemplation. Queen Latifah, for example, insistently commands her listeners, "I order you to dance for me." For, as Ice-T explains, the rapper "won't be happy till the dancers are wet with sweat" and wildly "possessed" by the beat, as indeed the captivating rapper should himself be possessed so as to rock his audience with his God-given gift of rhyme.[41]

IV

Contradictions and Judicious Vacillation

Is this emphasis on passionate movement inconsistent with rap's cognitive role as philosophy? If we are bodily possessed by the beat, how can we process the often subtle, complex meanings of rap's texts?[42] Pragmatism provides at least two kinds of answers. The first challenges the whole mind/body opposition on which the apparent inconsistency rests. Bodily movement and impassioned feeling are not the enemies of cognition, but often necessary aids to it. Cognition includes more than what is conveyed by propositional content; and nonpropositional forms of cognition can often create the context necessary for properly understanding certain claims of propositional knowledge. Dancing and thinking are not incompatible activities, and Nietzsche, in advocating the notion of a dancing philosopher, was not recommending a philosopher who would not think.[43]

Though this response helps resolve inconsistency between rap's claims for embodied ecstacy and intellectual reflection, there still remain other troubling contradictions for hip-hop. Most striking are its equivocal take on violence (as often celebrated in gangsta rap as denounced in the "Stop the Violence" tradition) and its concern for liberation yet its frequent use of a viciously sexist "pimpin' style." Rap's view of the ghetto is equally conflicted: affirming its rugged, hard-knocks training and artistic inspiration, while fiercely depicting its miserable woes. Though proud of its core identity as ghetto music, rap also aims its "penetration to the heart of the nation" (Ice-T) so as "to teach the bourgeois" (Public Enemy). There is, moreover, rap's ambivalent relation toward technology and the mass-media (which it both condemns and supports); its attitude toward capitalist wealth and commercialism is similarly divided. Rappers often extol their own achievement of consumerist luxury while condemning its uncritical quest as dangerously wrong for their ghetto audience. In the same way, underground rappers at once denigrate commercialism as an artistic and political sell-out, but celebrate their own commercial success, often regarding it as indicative of their artistic power.[44]

Such contradictions are not merely a product of rap's rich plurality of styles. They are expressive of more fundamental contradictions in the socio-cultural fields of ghetto life (where one must fight for peace) and so-called noncommercial art (both in and outside the ghetto). Such art must in some way be commercially effective in order to survive. High art's once "hidden" economy (already diagnosed by Dewey in the thirties) has become increasingly manifest, not simply through critical research but through the transformations and crises of the art market.[45]

In African-American culture, there is surely a connection between independent expression and economic achievement that would impel even noncommercial rappers to tout their commercial success and property. As slaves were converted from free men to property, their way to regain independence was to achieve sufficient property of their own so as to buy their manumission (as in the traditional liberation narrative of Frederick Douglass). Having long been denied a voice because they were property, African-Americans could reasonably conclude that only the economic power of property can ensure full expression. For underground rappers, then, commercial success and its luxury trappings may function essentially as signs of an economic independence that enables free artistic and political expression, and that is conversely further enabled by such expression.[46]

Unlike Dewey, Goodman does not provide socio-cultural explanations of the contradictions in our world. That is not the world of his philosophy. Instead he offers a general strategy for handling the conflicts of pluralism that is neither dissolution, resolution, nor synthesis of the conflicting points of view. He hails it as "a policy common in daily life and impressively endorsed by science: namely, judicious vacillation. After all, we shift point of view and frame of reference for motion frequently from sun to earth to train to plane, and so on. The physicist flits back and forth between a world of waves and a world of particles as suits his purpose" (OMM 32).

In the same way, the underground rapper will vacillate between talk of his ghetto hunger and of his Gucci luxury, condemnation of his media censorship and celebration of his media success—in different contexts and for different purposes of legitimation. Sometimes he adopts the gangsta and pimpin' styles so as to convince his listeners that he knows the hard-core ghetto realities of sex, violence, and drugs. Other times, to highlight hip-hop's utopian message, he instead embraces the style of philosopher of peace. But even here a violent tone can suddenly return in order to insist that ideals of peace and love are not mere products of weakness but instead demand tough strength and struggle.[47] The MC (*and* the rap fan) can likewise vacillate between intellectual study of the lyrics and wild dancing to the beat—often a complex message in its own right.

The trick, however, in all these cases, is to preserve enough coherence between contextual points of view so that their plurality enriches rather than annuls each other, enabling rather than merely confusing the human subject who alternatively adopts them.[48] Such practical coherence, implied in the very notion of *judicious* vacillation, does not entail the existence of a supercontext where all conflicting contexts are made to cohere through resolution of all their tensions. Nor does the notion of judicious vacillation imply that a general formula for coherent combination can be articulated in advance. Achieving coherence becomes a challenging part of that difficult genre of aesthetic living which aims at pushing the values of pluralistic richness and complexity toward the very limits of unity.

Goodman himself applies the strategy of judicious vacillation in negotiating the conflictual field of Anglo-American aesthetics. There are two divergent personae in Goodman as philosopher of art: the analyst and the pragmatist. Goodman acquired his logical tools and stature through analysis, which dominated American philosophy and structured his *Languages of Art*. The book's two central projects are extremely analytic in both method and spirit: strictly distinguishing between allographic and autographic arts, and rigidly defining the identity of particular artworks in such a precise manner that not a single wrong note or letter could be tolerated. Such projects of constrictive control, which suggest the "anal" side of analytic philosophy, are very different from the free-wheeling multiple world-making and irrealism of Goodman's later writings, though they are never repudiated.

The analytic persona maintains a presence in these later writings (in their logicism about contradiction and nominalism, and in their referential account of meaning). But the major thrust is clearly pragmatist: to undermine false dichotomies and overcome compartmental limits, to transform our practices not just to analyse them.[49] This is the pragmatist aesthetician preaching positive infraction. Here, to remix our title in hip-hop style, "Goodman rap pragmatism."

Part III

EMBODIMENT AND ETHNICITY

6

SOMATIC EXPERIENCE

Foundation or Reconstruction?

I

Pragmatism, as I conceive it after Dewey, is antifoundationalist, breaking with philosophy's traditional quest to guarantee our knowledge by basing it on fixed, unquestionable grounds. These were long sought in self-evident first principles, primal essences, necessary categories, and privileged, primary certainties: in notions like the *cogito*, the Kantian categories, sense-data, and the a priori laws of thought. Such indubitable foundations, Dewey argued, are neither available nor required for human knowledge and social practices.

In freeing philosophy from its search for foundations, Dewey hoped to enlist it for practical reform, directing its critical acumen and imaginative energy to the resolution of concrete social and cultural problems. Since these could be hardened through the ideology of past philosophies, new philosophical thinking is needed to help resolve them: by making room for new solutions that do not fit with established ways of thinking. Philosophy should be transformational instead of foundational. Rather than a metascience for grounding our current cognitive and cultural activities, it should be cultural criticism that aims to reconstruct our practices and institutions so as to improve the experienced quality of our lives. Improved experience, not originary truth, is the ultimate philosophical goal and criterion.

Experience is surely the heart of Dewey's philosophy. Paradoxically, it is also where his disciple Richard Rorty thinks Dewey's philosophy is most vulnerable and dangerous, since foundationally retrograde. With characteristic bluntness (and noting Dewey's own doubts), Rorty argues that "Dewey should have dropped the term 'experience'" rather than making it the center of his philosophy.[1] Pragmatism must replace this central notion with that of language and insist on a radical discontinuity between linguistic and sublinguistic behavior which the notion of experience can only blur. Since the value of "experience" represents the major divide between Deweyan (and Jamesian) pragmatism and the postlinguistic-turn pragmatism advocated by Rorty and others, the question of Dewey's use and abuse of this concept is crucial.[2]

This chapter probes the extent of Dewey's experiential foundationalism to see whether, *pace* Rorty, the idea of experience still has a vital role to play in pragmatism. I think it does; and much of its value lies even in that notion of experience—immediate, nondiscursive experience—which seems most vulnerable to charges of foundationalism. Since the most salient locus of nondiscursive immediacy is bodily feeling, somatic experience will become the focus.

My claim is that in emphasizing nondiscursive experience and its cognitive role, Dewey was on to something valuable that he unfortunately confused and devalued by treating it as the guarantor and ground of inquiry. Repudiating this nondiscursive dimension, Rorty seeks to discredit it by identifying it with an already discredited foundationalism, with which it is, in fact, most typically linked. My goal is to separate the non-discursive from the foundational better than Dewey did, so as to avoid not just Rorty's charges of foundationalism but others that seem more convincing. We should start, then, by sketching Dewey's use of nondiscursive experience and its Rortian critique.

II

One of Dewey's major goals in deploying his concept of experience was to advance a "naturalistic humanism" that could overcome the traditional dualisms of metaphysics and epistemology, dualisms that stemmed from the primal dualism of mind and matter. Given this dualism and secular culture's acceptance of the scientific materialist world-picture, the metaphysical question was how to find room in objective reality for the spiritual phenomena of consciousness, knowledge, and value without trying to justify them as "superimposed" from a superior, extra-natural world and without trying to reduce them to purely mechanistic networks of neurophysiology. There was also the epistemological question, at least as old as Descartes, of how material reality could be known by a mind defined as its radical other.

Dewey's naturalistic thesis of continuity and emergence answered both these questions. Inspired by Darwin, it argued that the higher human expressions of life emerge naturally from more simple organic forms through increasingly greater organization and more discriminating behavior. Mind was not an outside observer of the natural world but an emergent part of it; knowledge and value were not transcendental imports but emerging products (and tools) of natural interactions. Experience, Dewey thought, was the best general notion to bridge these different but continuous dimensions of nature. Since "experience" could cover both *what* was experienced and the specific *how* of experiencing, it could span the object/subject split which spurs epistemology; and since it could also be attributed to lower animals, it could bridge the gap between discursive mental life and cruder forms of existence. To affirm such continuity is surely one (but not the best) reason why Dewey insists that experience be conceived more widely than its standard philosophical construal as conscious, intellectual experience:

> When intellectual experience and its material are taken to be primary, the cord that binds experience to nature is cut. That the physiological organism with its structures, whether in man or in the lower animals, is concerned with making adaptations and uses of material in the interest of maintenance of the life process, cannot be denied. The brain and nervous system are primarily organs of action-undergoing; biologically,... primary experience is of a corresponding type. Hence, unless there is breach of historic and natural continuity, cognitive experience must originate within that of a noncognitive sort. And unless we start from knowing as a factor in action and undergoing, we are inevitably committed to the intrusion of an extra-natural, if not supernatural, agency and principle. (EN 29–30)

Rorty cites this passage in repudiating its notion of experience. Though sympathetic to Dewey's naturalism and critique of dualisms, he argues that experience is not only unnecessary for realizing Dewey's aims, but also renders them suspect by contamination with foundationalist confusions and myths: confusions of justifying knowledge through appeal to original causes and to myths of an immediate given. Experience is unnecessary because its target of dualism can be overcome through other means:

> Dewey ... confuses two ways of revolting against philosophical dualisms. The first way is to point out that the dualism is imposed by a tradition for specific cultural reasons, but has now outlived its usefulness. This is the Hegelian way—the way Dewey adopts in "An Empirical Study of Empiricisms." The second is to describe the phenomenon in a nondualistic way which emphasizes "continuity between lower and higher processes." This is the Lockean way—the way which led Locke to assimilate all mental acts to raw feels, thus paving the way for Humean skepticism. (DM 82)

Dewey's notion of experience, Rorty argues, serves the Lockean way of foundationalist epistemology by blurring the line between cognitive and noncognitive existence so that the latter can ground the former. Rather than eliminating "epistemological problems by eliminating the assumption that justification must repose on something other than social practices and human needs," Dewey tries "to solve" them by finding "'continuities' between nervous systems and people, or between 'experience' and 'nature.'" But "one does not need to justify our claim to know that, say, a given action was the best we could take by noting that the brain is an 'organ of action-undergoing'"(DM 82).

We should surely not try to justify specific knowledge-claims by mere appeal to the causal conditions of knowing. But Rorty never shows that Dewey commits this confusion in asserting the continuity of cognitive and noncognitive experience. To make his case Rorty cites Dewey's view that language gives meaning to more primitive qualities of organic experience, thus objectifying them in conscious, definite feelings.

> This "objectification" is not a miraculous ejection from the organism or soul into external things, nor an illusory attribution of psychical entities to physical things. The qualities never were "in" the organism; they always were qualities of interactions in which both extra-organic things and organisms partake. (EN 198–99).

Rorty then rightly critiques this notion of experience's "qualities of interaction" for simply dodging the standard questions of dualistic epistemology, e.g. "Is my *interaction* with this table brown, rather than, as I had previously thought, the *table* being brown?"(DM 83).

But this ambiguous use of experience with its failure to resolve the debate between idealism and realism surely does not amount to using noncognitive experience as justificational evidence for our conscious cognitive claims. In asserting the general continuity of cognitive and noncognitive experience, Dewey is *not* claiming that the latter functions cognitively as a criterion for the truth of the former. In fact, on the very page Rorty cites, Dewey denies this by asserting that primitive noncognitive experience is simply *had* but not *known*, and that its qualities cannot be known until "with language they are discriminated and ... 'objectified'" (EN 98).[3] Since not even known as "had," immediate experience is unavailable for use as evidence to support specific knowledge claims.

Indeed, in insisting that only language constitutes qualities as objects of knowledge, Dewey has already taken the linguistic turn which requires that the realm of cognitive justification be entirely linguistic. This suggests that Dewey's claims for nonlinguistic experience are ultimately motivated by something other than the quest for epistemological foundations, a suggestion I later develop in terms of aesthetics and somatics.

The closest Dewey comes to foundationalism in *Experience and Nature* is to suggest that though any particular knowledge claim may be questioned, we can't take global scepticism seriously because we are linked to the world in a primal way before the question of knowledge-claims can even arise. For even the formulation of sceptical doubts presupposes a behavioral background and use of world materials, organs, and language. There can be no total, unbridgeable gulf between subject and object (or mind and world), for both are only constituted as distinct terms through experiential interaction.

Rorty himself employs the same kind of antisceptical strategy through his preferred notion of language. Rather than a continuum of experience (extending from the precognitive hence presceptical), we have a continuum of linguistic behavior ranging from merely practical, noncognitive use to the making and justification of knowledge-claims. Since we can have no sense of the world apart from how it is used, determined, and known through language, there is no wedge for a radical scepticism that language is completely out of touch with the world. Here the subject/object dualism is dissolved not in the common solvent of experience but in the network of language as a social practice through which particular minds and particular objects are constituted as individuals.

Rorty is right that language works much better than experience for such epistemological purposes, since language is a clearer notion and epistemology is a distinctively linguistic enterprise. But this does not mean that noncognitive experience is intrinsically a foundational notion, while language is intrinsically immune to such uses. Protocol sentences have been used foundationally, and even the Wittgensteinian linguistic line that I share with Rorty is open to such misconstrual.

Consider Wittgenstein's claim that justifications must come to an end and the way he typically ends them by invoking the fact that "*this language-game is played*," that this is how we were taught to use words and to live our "forms of life."[4] While Wittgenstein was seeking therapy from philosophy's quest for ultimate foundations, his remarks are easily read instead as substituting empiricism's myth of the given with an allegedly nonmythical *linguistic* given. The huge project of analytic metaphysics through philosophy of language constitutes such a foundationalist reading.

Even if the notion of immediate, nonlinguistic experience does not *entail* foundationalism, philosophy has most often used it for this purpose. Dewey himself does not always resist such temptations. Let us see precisely where he succumbs and whether immediate experience can be stripped of Dewey's foundationalist use and still be philosophically important. If not, Rorty is right that pragmatism should renounce it.

III

Dewey's most thorough accounts of how immediate experience relates to knowledge occur in his essay "Qualitative Thought" (1930) and in his culminating treatise *Logic: The Theory of Inquiry* (1938).[5] Here, as elsewhere, he firmly eschews the standard foundationalist strategy of using the qualities of immediate experience as indubitable, incorrigible evidence for particular claims of knowledge. They could not possibly have such a role because they are simply *had* rather than *known*, and would have to be linguistically reconstructed in order to serve as a justificational ground for truth.

But Dewey courts a different, more subtle variety of foundationalism when he argues that experience of immediate, nondiscursive quality not only underlies but must guide all discursive thought. Here immediate experience is invoked not to justify particular truth-claims but to ground the coherence of *any* thinking from which such claims emerge. Dewey claims that even if immediate experience is unknowable and ineffable, its existence and functioning can be recognized by introspection and, moreover, can be inferred as necessary in all our thinking. For it performs (as I count them) five logical functions needed for thought which, Dewey maintains, are otherwise not provided.

Opposing the atomism of traditional empiricism, Dewey's argument for experiential foundations rests on the good holist premise that "we never experience nor form judgments about objects and events in isolation, but only in connection with a contextual whole. This latter is called a 'situation'" (L 72).

1. But if all thinking is contextual, what determines the relevant context or situation? What makes it the single context it is, and gives it the unity, structure, and limits necessary for providing thought with an effective framework? Dewey's answer is *immediately experienced quality*: "a situation is a whole in virtue of its immediately pervasive quality" (L 73). It is "held together, in spite of its internal complexity, by the fact that it is dominated and characterized throughout by a single quality," "constituted by a pervasive and internally integrative quality" (Q 97). "The pervasively qualitative is not only that which binds all constituents into a whole but it is also unique; it constitutes in each situation an *individual* situation, indivisible and unduplicable" (L 74).

2. In constituting the situation, this immediate quality also controls the distinction of objects or terms that thinking later identifies and employs as parts of the situation (e.g. whether we notice a sound sequence as one message or two, or instead disregard it as background noise). Hence, for Dewey, "a universe of experience is a precondition of a universe of discourse. Without its controlling presence, there is no way to determine the relevancy, weight, or coherence of any designated distinction or relation" (L 74).[6] Yet this controlling immediate quality lies below the level of thematized consciousness and language. It "surrounds

and regulates the universe of discourse but never appears as such within the latter" (L 74); and when we bring it into speech and awareness we are transforming it into an object of a new situation defined by its own immediate and ineffable unifying quality.

3. Immediate quality also provides a sense of what is adequate in judgment, what level of detail, complexity, or precision is sufficient to render the contextual judgment valid. Is the earth really round? Is running good for your health? Does water boil at 100 degrees centigrade? We can always make our judgments more detailed and precise. "But enough," as Dewey says, "is always enough, and the underlying quality is itself the test of the 'enough' for any particular case" (Q 108).

4. A fourth function of immediate quality is to determine the basic sense or direction of the situation and to sustain it over time, despite the confusing general flood of experience. Although the quality is nondiscursively "dumb," it has "a movement or transition in some direction" which provides the needed sense of unity and continuity in ongoing inquiry (Q 107). "This quality enables us to keep thinking about one problem without our having constantly to stop to ask ourselves what is it after all that we are thinking about." This "unique quality" is "the thread" or "directive clue" that "not only evokes the particular inquiry engaged in but that exercises control over its special procedures. Otherwise, one procedure in inquiry would be as likely to occur and to be as effective as any other" (Q 99; L 109).[7]

5. Finally, Dewey argues that immediate experience's integrative quality is the only adequate way to explain the association of ideas. The standard explanations of physical contiguity and similarity are insufficient to make the link, because "there is an indefinite number of particulars contiguous to one another in space and time" and because everything, in some respect, is similar to everything else. Mere spatiotemporal proximity and similarity cannot explain, for example, why I associate an empty nest with a bird I never saw rather than with "the multitudinous leaves and twigs which are more frequently and more obviously juxtaposed" to the nest (Q 111). And why should mere similarity and contiguity lead my thought from this hammer to a nail rather than to another, identical hammer in the store?

Something else is needed to make the connections of associative thinking. For Dewey this can only be the ineffable quality of immediate experience which binds through its sense of relevance: "What alternative remains save that the quality of a situation as a whole operates to produce a functional connection?" Association must be "an intellectual connection" produced through "an underlying quality which operates to control the connection of objects thought of"; "there must be relevancy of both ideas to a situation defined by unity of quality" (Q 111).

Had Dewey simply claimed that immediate quality sometimes grounds or directs our thinking, his position would be more convincing. Unfortunately, however, such quality is claimed as "the background, the point of departure, and the regulative principle in all thinking," determining *in every particular situation* the coherence of thought, the structure of discourse, and the measure of adequacy in judgment (Q 116; L 74). Moreover, it does all this without being a distinct object of awareness or term of discourse. We can never really analyze it, because doing so transforms it into something else. Yet, Dewey argues, we know it must exist and function as described; for if it did not, coherent thought would be impossible. Here Dewey's radical empiricism forsakes him for a foundational metaphysics of presence justified by transcendental argument.

Why accept this ineffable experiential foundationalism, if Dewey himself provides the means to avoid it? Thought and action, he elsewhere argues, are governed by the habits, purposes, and needs of the organism, and by the specific saliencies of the situation (as shaped by the organism's habits, purposes, and needs). Such factors, which typically function unreflectively, can perform all the five necessary tasks for which immediate qualitative experience was invoked as thought's indispensable foundational guide.

Unity of situation is provided by the practical unity of purpose and the continuity and direction of habit.[8] Purpose binds together the situational elements enlisted in its pursuit, and habit already implies an internal organization of activity which projects itself on further organization. Habit and purpose not only shape our distinctions of objects and relations within the situation, but guide our judgments of their relevance and importance.[9]

Habit and purpose can also give the situation its sustained direction. Since "all habit has *continuity*" and is "projective" by its very nature, our thinking habits naturally continue their directional course and tend to resist interruption or distraction (HN 31, 168). Purpose also "gives unity and continuity" of action, its "end-in-view" calling forth a series of coordinated means to reach it.[10] These factors, rather than a mysterious qualitative presence, are what bind and control the successive steps of inquiry.

Purpose also better explains what is adequate in judgment; hence Dewey, even while claiming immediate quality as the criterion of adequacy, reverts to purpose: "Any proposition that serves the purpose for which it is made is logically adequate" (Q 108). Finally, habit and purpose can explain our association of ideas without invoking a mysterious ineffable quality to link them. "When I think of a hammer," Dewey asks, "why is the idea of nail so likely to follow?"(Q 111). The obvious answer is not the qualitative glue of immediate experience, but the entrenched habit of their functional association for practical purposes of building. Dewey's argument for the necessity of immediate experience as the guiding ground for all thinking is thus as unconvincing as it is inimical to his antifoundationalist agenda.

IV

Why then does Dewey affirm nondiscursive experience as an epistemological foundation? His deep motive was not to provide such foundations but to celebrate the importance of nondiscursive immediacy. Its importance was first of all *aesthetic*, central to the realm of experienced value. He always insisted that our most intense and vivid values are those of on-the-pulse experienced quality and affect, not the abstractions of discursive truth. For Dewey, aesthetic satisfaction takes privilege over science, which is simply "a handmaiden" providing the conditions for achieving such satisfaction more frequently, stably, and fully (EN 269). Yet he further saw that nondiscursive somatic experience also played an important role in cognition and action. Proprioceptive discriminations beneath the level of thematized consciousness structure our perceptual field, just as unformulated feelings ("expansions, elations, and dejections") influence our behavior and orient our thinking (EN 227).

Wanting to celebrate the importance of this nondiscursive experience, Dewey did so in the way philosophers typically emphasize things they consider essential—by erecting it as a theoretical foundation. This

was a bad confusion of what was (or should have been) his true aim—
to establish and improve the quality of immediate experience as a practical end and useful tool. Dewey wanted philosophers to see that
nondiscursive experience could be used to enrich knowledge, not just
the "felt" quality of living. That such experience had no value for philosophy's favorite cognitive goal of epistemological justification did not
mean that it has no other cognitive value. A better measured sense of
breathing could promote a calmer, better measured process of thought;
an ineffable flush of energetic excitation could spur one to think beyond habitual limits.

Though traditionally focused on discursive reason, philosophy's presumed task of giving a full account of human reality required recognition of the role of nondiscursive experience.[11] Moreover, if pragmatism
sought not simply to explain but to improve reality, the value of nondiscursive experience became still more important as a project to be realized; and its crucial but much neglected locus was the body.[12]

A major inspiration here was F. Matthias Alexander, the renowned
body therapist and founder of "Alexander Technique," whose influence
on Dewey has not been adequately recognized.[13] Long a devoted student of Alexander (not simply of his texts but of his somatic exercises),
Dewey wrote encomiastic introductions to three of his books, defending Alexander's work against sceptical reviewers and praising it as having
"demonstrated a new scientific principle with respect to the control of
human behavior, as important as any principle which has ever been discovered in the domain of external nature."[14]

Alexander argued that many of the physical and mental ills that we
suffer in the modern world result from disharmony between our more
advanced intellectual behavior and our more basic bodily functions.
While the efforts of millennia were devoted to developing the intellect,
bodily functioning—long scorned as belonging to the base realm of
flesh and unchangeable instinct—has been left to entrenched habits
and instincts inherited from ancient times when the body worked under different conditions. Contemporary civilized conditions are unsuited
to the inherited forms of somatic expression and moreover subject us
unconsciously to new customs and regimes of body control (like Foucauldian disciplines of biopower). The result "is the larger number of
physical disorders which inflict themselves exclusively upon civilized

man [e.g. lower-back syndrome], and the large number of neuroses which express themselves in intellectual and moral maladies."[15] Yet no serious inquiry had been devoted to develop somatic functioning so as to make it not only better coordinated and more suited to the contemporary world, but also to render it an effective stimulus for improving that world to satisfy human needs of psychosomatic fulfillment.

Alexander therefore urged a reeducation of our somatic functioning which required a reeducation for somatic awareness, a new attention to bodily experiences which have so far gone unattended and thus unimproved. More importantly, he offered a concrete method of such reeducation. Its key was to extend "conscious control" over bodily actions formerly abandoned to unconscious habit by focusing heightened awareness on previously unnoticed and unattended somatic experience. *Conscious* somatic control is increasingly necessary in today's rapidly changing world, where old and slowly, unconsciously formed physical habits become ever more quickly outmoded and unfit. This insistence on *thinking* through the body, so as to achieve more conscious control and more acute perception of its condition, clearly distinguishes Alexander's approach from standard forms of calisthenics and body building. In fact, he vehemently attacked them for dealing only with externals by means of brute drill rather than bringing greater sensitivity and quality to inner experience by means of heightened consciousness (MSI 13–28).

Dewey's emphasis on immediate nondiscursive experience and its continuity with higher intellectual activity is better understood in this Alexandrian context: not as foundational epistemology but as a panegyric to the somatic in the face of centuries of denigrating philosophical scorn. In his 1918 introduction to Alexander's *Man's Supreme Inheritance*, seven years before advancing his theory of experiential and mind-body continuity in *Experience and Nature* (in which Alexander's work is twice invoked and his terminology appropriated), Dewey writes:

> Men are afraid, without even being aware of their fear, to recognize the most wonderful of all the structures of the vast universe—the human body. They have been led to think that a serious notice and regard would somehow involve disloyalty to man's higher life. The discussions of Mr. Alexander breathe reverence for this wonderful instrument of our life, life mental and moral as well as that life which somewhat meaninglessly we call bodily. When such a religious attitude toward the body becomes

more general, we shall have an atmosphere favorable to securing the conscious control which is urged. (ISI 351)

Recognizing that body-functioning influences the mind, Alexander likewise grasped the mind's potential for the body. His project was to improve somatic (and consequently mental) functioning by using the mind, employing a method of "constructive conscious control" directed by the individual on her body.[16] Our bad bodily habits (e.g. bad posture or poorly coordinated movement) are usually performed without thinking and are taken for granted. Moreover, when we *do* focus on them, they seem right because they are familiar as our habits. When asked to stand or move differently we may be unable to, not because we are anatomically impaired but simply because we cannot yet feel ourselves into an alternative way.

To improve our bodily habits and psychosomatic integration we need to bring our somatic functioning and its attendant feelings into greater consciousness, so we can learn both to detect subtly different modalities of posture and movement, and to assess the quality of their coordination and their attendant affectivity. Without detecting these modalities we could never learn how to perform different somatic actions that could be developed into better habits; without qualitative appreciation we would not learn which somatic behavior should be rendered habitual so as to provide a better background of unconscious psychosomatic functioning.

For example, we need to become conscious both of how to hold the head in different positions and of which position gives us the best "felt" quality and ease of breathing in order to select this position over others for a new habituation. But having been reconstructed through this concentrated attention, the now improved habit can well be returned to its unreflective character in order to allow consciousness to concentrate on other tasks.

Such an improved habit, even if it functions unconsciously, can also enhance our conscious thought, since better breathing can mean better awareness and more steady concentration. We must recall, however, that conscious attention was required to improve this unconscious functioning; and so, by the way, is language—as the means for designating body parts, movements, and feelings on which we are instructed to concentrate. The interdependent continuity of mind and body is reflected in the similar continuity of conscious thinking and the nondiscursive background which orients thought, an often unconscious somatic background which can however be brought into consciousness.[17]

We can now understand what Dewey's experiential foundationalism was concerned with, and how it erred. He was wrong to think that an unconscious, nondiscursive immediate quality was the necessary grounding guide or regulatory criterion of all our thinking, though he was right to insist that nondiscursive background experience influences our conscious thought. Rather than such unnoticed quality being the unifying guide of all conscious thought, it is the noticing of such quality that can help give our thinking greater unity and better feeling, by improving thought's nondiscursive experiential background and better integrating the psychosomatic and the intellectual. Dewey's mistake is not in emphasizing the unifying quality of experience, but only in seeing it as an antecedent foundation rather than an *end* and *means* of reconstruction.

Through the Alexandrian perspective we can also see the limits of Rorty's critique. *Pace* Rorty, the crucial pragmatic aim of Dewey's philosophy of experience is not the metaphysical goal "of obtaining continuity between us and the brutes" by our "sharing something called 'experience'—something not the same as consciousness or thought but, something of which consciousness or thought are more complex and developed forms." Nor is it the epistemological goal of ensuring that our perceptions are not "'out of touch' with nature" because both belong to the unity of experience (DHD 58–59).[18] Instead, Dewey's prime purpose was (and surely should have been) the aesthetic and practical aim of improving experience by making it the focus of our inquiry: to enrich and harmonize our experience, for example, by affirming and enhancing the continuity between soma and psyche, between nondiscursive experience and conscious thought. The aim, as he presents it in advocating Alexander Technique, is "to integrate into harmonious coordination our animal inheritance and our distinctively human capacities of intelligence" (RR 355).

So even if Rorty is right that experience cannot solve the theoretical problems of metaphysical and epistemological continuity, this does not nullify the point of Dewey's philosophy of experience. For this philosophy (in its most useful construal) is not so much aimed at proving theoretical continuity but instead at enhancing continuity *in practice*, at healing the painfully (though often unconsciously) experienced fragmentation of human life. This, he believed, could be achieved only by recognizing the immediate dimension of somatic experience, a recognition which he occasionally misconstrued in foundational terms.

V

But what does it mean for philosophy to recognize this somatic dimension? Simply to say that it exists, even as a necessary feature of human existence, seems an empty gesture. The importance of nondiscursive experience in actual living does not entail that it is *philosophically* important. And how could it be, if philosophy as traditionally practiced can apparently do nothing with it except misuse it discursively for foundationalist fantasies? Somatic and nondiscursive experience, so central to the pragmatist thought of Dewey and James, are therefore abandoned by today's leading pragmatists as philosophically useless and troublesome notions. Indeed, as Rorty puts it, we should drop the whole notion of experience and instead insist that language exhausts the realm of philosophy, following Peirce's cue that "my language is the sum total of myself" (DHD 55).[19]

Though appreciative of the linguistic turn, I fear its totalizing tendencies and refuse to abandon pragmatism's traditional concern with the somatic and nondiscursive (which even Peirce recognized in his notion of "Firstness"). Before burying the body or simply textualizing it, we need to assess more critically philosophy's resistance to nondiscursive experience. Such resistance is based not only on arguments but on deeply entrenched biases that work, most effectively, beneath the level of conscious thought.

The reason Rorty most frequently gives for banishing nondiscursive experience from the domain of philosophy is that it involves us in the foundationalist "myth of the given." In our search to base knowledge on something immune to error, we retreat to a brute experiential immediacy whose nondiscursivity makes it even immune to linguistic error. But this appeal to a nondiscursive given is mythical, because such experience can function as justificational evidence only if it is rendered discursive.

This critique of the myth of the given seems impeccable. But it does not follow that philosophy should never concern itself with the nondiscursive. Drawing this conclusion means assuming that philosophy's only possible use for nondiscursive experience is in justificational epistemology, and that assumption is neither self-evident nor argued for. Finding more fruitful ways for philosophy to treat the nondiscursive remains a vital task for pragmatism. Prefigured in Dewey's confused advocacy of immediate experience, it is today more urgently demanded by our culture's increasing devotion to techniques of somatic transformation yet continuing failure to give them adequate philosophical study.[20]

This somatic option is implicitly denied by Rorty's second argument for banishing the nonlinguistic: that introducing somatic experience into philosophical practice undermines philosophy's distinctive role and logical space by confusing between causes and reasons. This argument again concerns the myth of the given. For in this myth, nondiscursive bodily sensation—which may be the antecedent *cause* of knowing something (e.g. a burning sensation resulting in awareness that the plate is hot)—is falsely taken for a *reason* that justifies such knowledge, a reason that seems irrefutable by its brute immediacy. But nondiscursive experience cannot, as such, play a role in the language-game of epistemological justification, whose regimentation has always been philosophy's distinctive task. Such experience may be "a causal condition for knowledge but not a *ground* for knowledge."[21]

Since philosophy is concerned with the rational justification of our beliefs, not their psychological or physiological causes, it should therefore resist trafficking with things like somatic experience which belong to the nondiscursive domain of causes; it should remain within "the logical space of reasons." For "nothing is to be gained ... by running together the vocabularies in which we describe the causal antecedents of knowledge with those in which we offer justifications of our claims to knowledge" (PMN 182; DM 81).

Nothing gained, that is, for epistemology, from whose standpoint Rorty attacks the nondiscursive. But why should philosophy be confined to its standard role of justifying by reasons rather than modifying through causes, of merely legitimating beliefs and practices rather than creating or transforming them? Such justificational limits seem particularly foreign to pragmatism, and Rorty himself boldly rejects them when he comes to his own central philosophical topic—language.

Here Rorty advocates a philosophy of causation rather than legitimation. The aim is to create new vocabularies and transform our ways of speaking, not to ground those already in place.[22] He even insists on blurring the very distinction he elsewhere strictly defended: "once we raise the question of how we get from one vocabulary to another, from one dominant metaphoric to another, the distinction between reasons and causes begins to lose utility," for here there is insufficient common ground to provide decisive *reasons* for this change (CIS 48).

Building on Rorty's own example, we can argue: if philosophy takes for its pragmatist goal not the grounding of knowledge but the production of better lived experience, then it need not be confined to the realm of discursive truth and the language-games of their justification. Philosophy can aim more directly at the practical end of improving experience by advocating and embodying practices which achieve this. And if the practice of linguistic invention provides one such tool, why can't the practice of somatic disciplines focusing on nondiscursive experience provide a complementary other?

This option is never admitted, however, because philosophy's dominant ideology of textualism represses the nonlinguistic. This ideology, common to analytic and continental philosophy, insists that language exhausts the scope of experience, since whatever lies outside of language cannot be thought or given content. Hence Sellars claims that "*all* awareness ... is a linguistic affair"; Gadamer stresses "the essential linguisticality of all human experience of the world"; Rorty asserts that we humans are "nothing more than sentential attitudes"; and Derrida declares that there cannot be a "*hors-texte*," "a reality ... whose content could take place, could have taken place outside of language."[23]

Textualist ideology has been extremely helpful in dissuading philosophy from misguided quests for absolute foundations outside our contingent linguistic and social practices. But in making this therapeutic point by stressing what Rorty terms the "the ubiquity of language,"[24] textualism also encourages an unhealthy idealism that identifies human being-in-the world with linguistic activity and so tends to neglect or overly textualize nondiscursive somatic experience. As "the contemporary counterpart of [nineteenth-century] idealism," textualism displays idealism's disdain for materiality, hence for the corporeal. Seeking to secure a realm of spirituality after natural science had displaced religion's authority and despiritualized the world, idealism focused on mental consciousness and inherited, by and large, the dominant Christian impulse to depreciate the body.[25] After Freud's disenchantment of consciousness, language has become the new representative of the spiritual in contrast to corporeal nondiscursivity. The whole project of policing the borders between "the logical space of reasons" and the realm of "physical causes" so as to confine philosophy to the former is just one more assertion of the old dualism of separating the concerns of the superior soul from the corruption of the material body; study of the latter is thus consigned not to the human but to the natural sciences.

Textualism's resistance to the nondiscursive soma goes well beyond its modern idealist heritage. Such resistance is built into the old Platonic project of philosophy as a saliently linguistic discipline devoted to the *logos*. The *alogon* was at once the nonlinguistic and the irrational. Two factors thus tend to repress philosophy's treatment of the nondiscursive.

The first is simply structural censorship by the philosophical field through disciplinary inertia. Despite a fine heritage of materialist thinkers, philosophy's long dominance by idealist logocentrism and its entrenched practice as a linguistic form have structured the discipline in a way that excludes serious focus on the nondiscursive.[26] There is no allocation for it in Western philosophical space, no subdiscipline of "philosophy of body" to complement philosophy of mind (as hatha yoga serves the more spiritual raja yoga in Indian thought). The result is that nondiscursive somatic experience is either ignored—relegated to other fields like psychology or neuroscience—or instead subsumed under clearly discursive projects, such as epistemological justification or genealogical accounts of "reading the body" as a social text on which a society's practices of formative power are inscribed.

The second implicit ground for ignoring the nondiscursive involves what might be called *the disciplinary fallacy*: the idea that whatever a discipline ignores (or does not treat seriously) cannot be important for that discipline. Such reasoning precludes disciplinary growth and would have denied chemistry's importance for botany or the central role of the unconscious for psychology. This fallacy is especially dangerous in philosophy, which sees itself both as a specialized profession (concerning technical, strictly regimented questions) and also as a basic, time-honored human enterprise of universal significance and scope. Through the former self-conception it materially reproduces itself as a professional institution, while the latter affords it a charismatic aura of deep relevance and wisdom (often lacking in its actual institutional expression) that helps legitimate its institutional reproduction. By the professional conception (especially as understood through textualism), nondiscursive somatic experience has no place in philosophy. But by the general conception, if it has no place, then it cannot be important for understanding human experience; hence no new place should be made for it. The upshot of this equivocation is that philosophy is right to shirk the nondiscursive as unimportant, because its very doing so proves this unimportance.

The disciplinary fallacy seems persuasive because it expresses a good pragmatic point. An individual discipline can't do everything, so it should therefore concentrate on doing what it does best and avoid doing what it can't do. Since philosophy is strongly centered on language and seems ill-equipped to handle the somatic and nondiscursive, it should not try to treat them. For what, after all can philosophy do with these notions, except embroil itself, as even Dewey did, in foundationalist regressions? This question presents a major task for somatic philosophy that I cannot discharge here. Let me at least briefly suggest three ways that philosophy can productively engage nondiscursive somatic experience.

First and most simply, philosophy can argue for the importance of such experience (as Merleau-Ponty did far better than Dewey) so that it will not be merely acknowledged to exist but will be more vigorously explored as a legitimate object of research and of personal cultivation. Overcoming its *parti pris* against the nonlinguistic, philosophy can lend support and analytic skills to scientific inquiries into the nondiscursive features of human experience (e.g. Daniel Stern's ground-breaking work on the prelinguistic understanding of infants).[27] It might even launch its own inquiries into the role of nonverbal experience in aesthetics, ethics and other domains.

Secondly, contemporary popular culture displays an intense preoccupation with the body. Apart from the proliferation of gyms and centers for aerobics, massage, and body building, there is a growing number of somatic therapies which promise not merely relief from physical ailments but improved psychosomatic integration, or, more simply, better harmony of lived experience. Since the work of Alexander, we have been offered Rolfing, Bioenergetics, Eutony, Feldenkrais Method, and

Ideokinesis, to name just a few. There is also the greatly heightened interest in older practices like yoga and t'ai–chi ch'üan. We philosophers are prone to dismiss these things as New Age quackery or simply ignore them as none of our business.

But Dewey's attention to Alexander should give us pause. If philosophy sees itself most broadly as culture criticism, then somatics is an increasingly significant dimension of our culture that is ripe for philosophical critique. Philosophy here can have the role of critically examining such body practices and their attendant ideologies to see what sense they make, what good or harm they do, and whether they could profit from a better formulation of aims and methods.[28] It might helpfully disentangle useful technique from misguided theory so as to make these practices more convincing and effective.

Finally, the most radical and interesting way for philosophy to engage somatics is to integrate such bodily disciplines into the very practice of philosophy. This means practicing philosophy not simply as a discursive genre, a form of writing, but as a discipline of embodied life. One's philosophical work, one's search for truth and wisdom, would not be pursued only through texts but also through somatic exploration and experiment. By acute attention to the body and its nonverbal messages, by the practice of body disciplines which heighten somatic awareness and transform how one feels and functions, one discovers and expands self-knowledge by remaking one's self. This quest for self-knowledge and self-transformation can constitute a philosophical life of increasing embodied enrichment that has irresistible aesthetic appeal.

Though alien to today's academy, the idea of philosophy as an embodied, aesthetically engaging way of life was central to the *logos*-loving Greeks and Romans. It was also shared by Emerson and Thoreau, who affirmed that philosophy "is admirable to profess because it was once admirable to live," and that "life is not [mere] dialectics.... Intellectual tasting of life will not supersede muscular activity."[29]

Such a vision of philosophy as a thoughtfully disciplined, somatically centered way of life was powerfully revived by Foucault in his very last lectures at the Collège de France (in 1984), inspired in large part by the example of Diogenes the Cynic. "The *bios philosophicos*," Foucault explains of Diogenes, "is the animality of being human, taken up as a challenge, practiced as an exercise—and thrown in the face of others as a scandal."[30] But the somatically focused, aesthetically potent philosophical life need not be as scandalous as Foucault preferred to see it. Thoreau's exercises in simple living, labor, and purity of diet—or Dewey's explorations through Alexander Technique (to which he attributed his improved capacities for attention and awareness, and even his longevity)—present alternative models of embodied philosophical life that may prove equally informative, transformative, and aesthetically enriching, though of course less dramatically spectacular than either Diogenes' exhibitionist primitivism or Foucault's experiments in drugs and S/M.

Philosophy needs to pay more critical attention to the variety of somatic practices through which we can pursue our quest for self-knowledge and self-creation, for beauty, potency, and pleasure, for the reconstruction of immediate experience into improved living. The philosophical discipline that would treat this embodied pursuit could be called "somaesthetics." Experience, in this somatic sense, should belong to the practice of philosophy.

7

NEXT YEAR IN JERUSALEM?

Jewish Identity and the Myth of Return

"L'authenticité juive consiste à se choisir *comme juif*, c'est à dire à réaliser sa condition juive. Le Juif authentique abandonne le mythe de l'homme universel: il se connait et se veut dans l'histoire comme créature historique et damnée; il a cessé de se fuir et d'avoir honte des siens."[1]

—Jean-Paul Sartre

I

If the central issue of philosophy is how one should live, then how should this "one" be construed? Not as mere mind, for we found a distinctly somatic side of philosophical life. The embodied self is also socially and culturally situated. Far from the expression of universal Reason or Man, the philosopher is now recognized as a differentially embodied, gendered, and ethnic individual. Such lived differences should surely make a difference to philosophy.[2]

I conclude with a chapter on ethnicity, not simply as a gesture to such issues of difference, but because Jewish ethnicity has been a determining factor in my own philosophical life. It explains why I first learned philosophy as an immigrant in Jerusalem and later returned to teach it in the United States. It even explains why I now write these words in Berlin, revising an earlier draft composed in New York City. If philosophy is a life-practice of self-examination and self-creation in the quest to live better, a book that only examined the life-questions of others would be incomplete, perhaps even dishonest. The question of

Jewish identity raises issues of my own identity as I struggle to understand and reconstruct it.

How, then, should one live as a Jew? We don't need a Socrates to tell us that this depends on how Jewish identity is to be defined. Nor do we need a lexicographer to witness its rival definitions. Jewish identity (like more clearly honorific concepts as "justice," "democracy," or "art") is essentially contested; it has, in fact, long been the focus of intense debate and struggle in the legislature and courts of Israel. Any attempted neutral definition will be virtually void of content. Given the many different ways of being Jewish, how should one realize one's Jewish identity?

Part of the answer to this question surely depends on the contingencies of personal background and context. To use a notion of William James, some choices of Jewish self-realization are not "live options" for every Jew. The son of the Admor of Sedogora cannot express his Jewishness in the manner of a Woody Allen or an atheist kibbutznik. Conversely, despite some exceptional, dramatic conversions to religious orthodoxy, it is not a live option for secularly reared American Jews to realize their Jewish identity through orthodox religious life. Indeed, to express one's Jewishness primarily through religious practice of any sort is not an attractive option for secular Jews. The more central religion becomes, the less the label "secular" seems appropriate. Nor is the notion of participation in "the Jewish community" very appealing, because it is always somehow tied to the synagogue and thus by extension to religion. What meaningful mode of Jewish self-expression remains for the secular Jew in the secular (yet clearly Christian) culture of America except to regale himself with Jewish "soul food" and Jewish jokes? Since this can satisfy only superficial appetites, the perplexed, hungering, secular Jewish spirit has often turned to Israel.[3]

During the sixties and early seventies (when it seemed a promisingly progressive socialist state and in other ways a more hopeful, united, and just society than today), Israel looked like the best chance for secular Jewish fulfillment. For secular Jews in the Diaspora, it offered a unique opportunity for radical and romantic redefinition, a way of being meaningfully Jewish without being religious and with the welcome bonus of no longer belonging to an ethnic minority. *Aliyah* (i.e. immigration, literally "ascent," to Israel) became the preferred project for those seeking to "find themselves" as individuals and as Jews. "Next year in Jerusalem" (the concluding prayer of every Passover) was transformed from a mythic dream of return into a concrete immigration proposal for forging a firm new self in a promised land, a permanent home to cure the restless rootlessness of the ever wandering Jew.

This chapter explains why the promise proved illusory, why Zionism and immigration to Israel cannot be a simple solution to the problem of secular Jewish identity, and how the myth of return should be reinterpreted in the more flexible spirit of postmodernity. Since I shall speak partly from personal experience, I should face the charge that this should have no place in philosophical discourse.

II

"What matter who's speaking?" asks Foucault in challenging the author's position as determiner of meaning.[4] But in the contestatory discursive field of Jewish identity and Zionism, locating authorial standpoint is essential; and the injunction to declare where you are coming from can be taken in a literal, geographical sense. If only to attain a critically reflective level of thought, one should clearly avow one's perspective through some account of one's own Jewish background. Why then my reluctance? Are autobiographical remarks tastelessly out of place in a philosophical essay? Why should the personal be philosophically taboo, even in an essay dealing with ethnicity and personal identity?

This taboo of the personal and contingent reflects philosophy's deep-rooted prejudice for universality and necessity. Inquiring into personal identity, it seeks a necessary core on which all individual selfhood must be based, an essential ground of particular personhood in something like an embodied mind or soul. Philosophy's traditional assumption was that there must be some necessary principle determining human identity. Behind it lurked the deeper presumption that if identity were a matter of contingency rather than ontological or rational necessity, then something deep and sublime would disappear from personhood, and self-dignity would be lost.[5]

Once we recognize the self as socially constituted rather than ontologically given, its contingent nature becomes manifest. Shaped by different societies that are themselves the (changing) products of historical contingencies, the social self must be a contingent product. However, such contingency is not tantamount to wild randomness and so does not preclude the regularities and consensus on which social life is based (see chapter two). Trying to ground the self on something deeper than the social will not escape contingency. Our most private thoughts and wishes are still structured by a given language, i.e. a contingent sociohistorical product. Any private self alleged to lie beneath public language and consciousness seems no less contingent, portrayed by Freud as a web woven from chance occurrences and perceptions. Even our basic bodily actions rely on habits and neural pathways whose variable routing depends on the contingencies of our experience rather than necessary instinct.[6]

If the self is a contingent product, its proper understanding should take these contingencies seriously. Inquiry into its identity should thus allow an autobiographical moment long repressed in philosophy, though no doubt motivating much of it. Philosophers can overcome this repression of self without losing their power to speak to others. Consider the evidence of Kierkegaard and Nietzsche, if not, more recently, of Derrida and Cavell.

A second strong theme of current identity theory joins contingency in supporting a more personal approach: self-constitution through self-narrative. Central to the quest of radical self-creation advocated by Foucault and Rorty, it also structures the more traditional, socially bound ideal of self advocated by Charles Taylor and Alasdair MacIntyre.[7] If we help determine who we are by the stories we tell of ourselves, then one is surely entitled to theorize issues of the self in one's own voice and from one's own experience. Further, if philosophy is a personal life-practice devoted to self-improvement through self-understanding, then certain details of one's life surely become relevant for analysis. Which details, precisely? That, of course, is also contingent, determinable only through concrete philosophical interpretation, though certain details (like gender and ethnicity) seem more apt to be significant than others (say, social security number or mother's maiden name).

Of course, my personal study of Jewish identity will not be valid for every Jew, let alone every human being. But neither is most so-called universal ethics, even if it be more than the disguised autobiography Nietzsche alleged. Though my study speaks best to those vexed with similar difficulties of Jewish self-understanding and self-definition, some of its lessons also apply to other ethnicities and especially other minority "Others," particularly those who share with Jews a complex, diasporic identity.[8] Here, then, is the minimal story-line from which these lessons are developed.

I was born in Philadelphia to a middle-class, Jewish American family that was neither religiously observant (prayer being confined to the High Holidays) nor politically Zionist (its Jewish activities being focused on the American Jewish community). As a youth, my strong secular and rebellious instincts led to expulsion from Hebrew school. But not very much later, at the age of sixteen, I found myself in Israel, since that same spirit of rebellion (reinforced by the spirit of the late sixties) made me leave home and country. Israel promised the excitement of self-definition through an exotic Jewish-socialist adventure, and also offered a warm, welcoming sense of belonging to an organic, supportive community. This welcome was further expressed in attractive material terms of financial aid and university scholarships through the Jewish Agency. No less seductive was the striking natural and human beauty of Israel. I remained there for almost twenty years: studying and teaching in its universities; serving as an officer in its army; populating it with three children; making it my new home and country.

In fulfilling the Zionist imperative of *aliyah* to Israel, I certainly became clearer and more comfortable about being Jewish. More precisely, I found a way of being Jewish that I could be clear and comfortable about—the life of a secular Jewish Israeli. As a Jew, I was automatically naturalized through the "Law of Return," the most fundamental statute of the State of Israel, which guarantees the rights of citizenship to all Jews returning to their ancient homeland. Of course, in a literal sense, neither I nor any other immigrants so naturalized were really returning to Israel, having never been there before. When I first arrived, it was only my homeland in a very mythical, questionable sense. Truly to return there I would have to go elsewhere, thus suggesting the deep conceptual link between return and departure. My eventual Israeli departure involved a return to my more literal American homeland.

In 1985 I came back to Philadelphia for a year's visiting appointment at Temple University; a complex constellation of personal and institutional factors led me to give up my tenured position in Israel in order to extend my stay in the States. For the Israeli census bureau, I became no longer an immigrant but an emigré; from the Zionist perspective, no longer one of the redeemed ascenders to full Jewish national identity (*olim*) but one of the fallen (*yordim*) who lives in what is termed "exile" (*golah*).[9] My own sense of self is far more complex and equivocal. Having forged my manhood, Israel remains a deep part of me, and the home of my three children. Often I dream of resettling there and reenacting the myth of return that seems so central to Jewish identity. But such a return, in contrast to my official *aliyah*, will be a real return as well as a mythic one, for I will have already been there before.

III

Identity and Narrative

Three points of philosophical interest emerge from my story. The first is that our notions of personal identity and agency depend on narrative. We can define the self only in terms of a narrative about it. Defining it purely in terms of its actions will not work, for the very meaning (or proper description) of any action is not atomistically given in itself, but is a function of the narrative context in which it appears. This is why even a conservative thinker like MacIntyre insists on "a concept of self whose unity resides in the unity of a narrative."[10] No other unity can ground it that does not itself rely on narrative unity, since even the barest stories of bodily and mental continuity do.

Earlier chapters have treated the problem of narrative unity—problems of integrating the self's conflicting roles and stories into narrative coherence, of unifying multiple transformations of character into a coherent sense of self. My Jewish question raises another problem with narrative as constituting the self's unity—call it "the underdetermination of self by narrative." For any open series of narrative events, given an indeterminate future in terms of which these events can be interpreted and also given the future revisability of past narrative interpretations, there will always be more than one narrative that can fit the facts of the individual. This plurality of comprehensive self-narratives raises the possibility of living as more than one self. More acutely, the actual awareness of very divergent futures, hence divergent narratives, not only shakes one's fixed sense of self-identity but denies any univocal sense of the meaning of any action.

For example, I can see myself as having returned to my American home after a youthful exploration of an essentially foreign culture, or I can see my current stay in America (as I had originally planned it) as an excursion for professional development so I could better serve a less developed Israeli society to which I shall return. The very meaning of my actions, the definition of myself as agent, changes significantly according to the story told: Is my involvement in American life a central, permanent project or merely a temporary convenience until I return to Israel? It's not merely that I don't know the answer with Cartesian certainty because I don't know the future. The point is rather the clear and painfully divided consciousness of simultaneously living two radically divergent self-defining narratives, because both are quite probable and there is no way of knowing which is the true one. For there is no true one. How, then, can I know how to realize my Jewish identity unless I know who I am? But how can I know who I am unless I know how I will (or won't) realize my Jewish identity?

If the self is constituted by narrative and there is no one true narrative, then there is no one true self. This does not mean that any self-narrative is as good as any other; some are clearly better not only for explaining past action but for projectively fashioning better selves. Moreover, on the primitive logical level, a single self must be presupposed as the referent needed to talk at all about self-narrative (and especially divergent self-narratives). But this minimal, logical notion of self as "subject for predication" has no real substance. It neither assures a substantive, coherent self nor precludes the existence of multiple selves identified with the same logical subject for predication. The substantive integrity of the self, the coherent fullness of a life, cannot be guaranteed by the referential identity of logic; it remains a task for the art of living.[11]

With respect to my Jewish question, such integrity remains problematic and I experience myself as a rather multiple self. To put it crudely, there is an Israeli self (with an American background or penumbra) whose Jewish identity is strongly and clearly defined through Israeli national culture. But there is also a (recently reclaimed) American self (with an Israeli shadow), whose Jewish identity is mostly neglected, expressed only indirectly through its Israeli background when that occasionally gets foregrounded in my American life. In short, though *aliyah* has made me more sure of my Jewish identity, it has not resolved my problem of being a secular American Jew; it has only circumvented it by allowing Jewishness to be expressed through Israeliness.

Israel/Golah Tensions

In fact, *aliyah* has made it much harder to see myself as an American Jew and relate to that community. Through my Israeli eyes, American Jewish experience always seems somehow false or superficial. Attending Yom Kippur services at a progressive synagogue in order to express my solidarity with the American Jewry I should feel closest to, I was strangely alienated by the use of English rather than Hebrew as the main language of prayer. Though I'm not religious, my lived experience of Hebrew and its national liturgical use (familiar even to secular Israelis through public education, mass media, and official ceremonies—too often military burials) made the translated prayers sound hollow and inauthentic. Still worse, tradition-rich and poetically powerful phrases like *Avinu, Malkenu* ("Our Father, Our King") were feebly transformed into the likes of "Our Parent, Our Sovereign" to suit current American sensibility about gendered language, a sensibility I appreciate in English. (Does this mean my Israeli self is more sexist than its American counterpart? I think it is, though this in no way invalidates my sense of the translation's inauthenticity.)

That American Jews share my love of Israel should provide a way to identify myself with them. But since their grasp of Israel seems foreign and shallow, their attempts to bring me into the American Jewish community through appeal to my Israeliness tend to put me off. Israeli experience forming an obstacle to American Jewish identity is not my personal aberration. Israeli *yordim* are known for *not* assimilating into the American Jewish community, preferring to form their own. The only apparent exceptions appear to be the "professional Israelis" engaged in Jewish education or Jewish community "business." But they tend to be more religious rather than secular; their motives for interaction with American Jewry tend to be professional rather than social; and the interaction is indeed confined mainly to professional frameworks.

Hence the second lesson I draw from my history: achieving (secular) Jewish identity through Israel is largely incompatible with fulfillment as an American Jew. The reason is not a subsuming incompatibility between Israeli and American nationality, for I never felt such strong conflicts in being binational. The problem is rather that the concept of Jewish identity is overdetermined and its two major determinants—nationality and religion—are in deep tension. This conflict is painfully obvious in the continuing strife between national and religious interests that stridently divides Israeli society as a whole; so there is no surprise to find it reflected in the individual Jew.[12]

According to Israeli author A. B. Yehoshua, the fundamental tension between national and religious definitions of Jewish identity provides the prime reason why life in *golah* has been so attractive, even though it "was the source of the most terrible disasters to befall the Jewish people" and remains today a dreadful "neurotic condition."[13] Though originally imposed on the Jewish people, exile became the preferred choice for its survival by blunting the conflict that, since biblical times, threatened to divide and destroy it. In exile there was no need to resolve unequivocally the religious/national debate, to determine whether the Jewish nation had to be observant worshipers of the Jewish religion. For there was no organized state to provide the apparatus to enforce such a decision. "The Jewish framework in the *golah* is essentially voluntary. The Jew is, in essence, free to direct the fervor of his Judaism in any way he desires," and (I may add) is also free to have no fervor at all. "The *golah* freed the national and religious systems from the need to disavow each other," not only because it made definitive conflict-resolution unenforceable but because it made all such conflict unwelcome and unwise. Jewish unity was needed to face the threat of a politically stronger, typically hostile host nation, so "disputes over the content of Jewish identity were of secondary importance" (E 24–25).

Though recognizing *golah*'s attractions and deep roots in Jewish history, Yehoshua condemns it as a "neurotic, painful, and compulsive choice," a pathetic state of "schizophrenia." Insisting that Jewish identity should be realized univocally by national life in Israel, Yehoshua hopes "to eliminate the *golah* as a viable possibility" for Jewish life (E 22, 31, 33). To achieve these ends, Israel should assert a haughty attitude of independence from *golah*, urging the necessity of *aliyah* and refusing to legitimate *golah* either by gratefully accepting its financial support or by taking pride in its achievements.

Yehoshua's case for Zionism relies on three insufficiently examined oppositions. First, *golah* is necessarily perceived by all "authentic" Jewish thinking as an "abnormal," deficient, and fallen situation, as opposed to the redemption of "sovereign, normal life in *Eretz Yisrael*." Hence the neurotic tension of *golah*—though spiritually we repudiate it, practically we seek to preserve it (E 22–23). Second, while rightly castigating the religious Israeli philosopher Yishayahu Leibowitz for thinking that Jews do things (e.g. eat, dress, copulate) essentially "differently from other peoples," Yehoshua posits, without argument, his own differentiating essentialism: "The essence of our life in Israel is different from that of *golah* life, and the differences should not be obscured" (E 26, 34).

Such essence and defining differences are, however, never clearly articulated. No wonder. For there is no definable essence of the complex divisive multiculturalism of Israeli life, nor of the very varied Jewish lifestyles in the many different countries constituting *golah* or Diaspora. Yet the alleged root of presumed essential difference forms Yehoshua's crucial third premise. Life in Israel is one of independence, while exile is neurotic bondage. "Zionism is a process of self-liberation from the fears of independence," and *golah* represents the refusal of the Jews to accept independence and normalcy (E 28).

Together these premises generate a radical Zionism aimed at linear progress toward fixed unity and definitive closure with the final return of all Jews to Israel. Questioning these premises through postmodern strategies, I seek a better, more flexible model for Zionism's ideal of return. To do so, I turn to the third point raised by my biographical sketch: the conceptual interdependency of *aliyah* and *golah* that undermines a total privileging of the former.[14]

Israel/Golah Dependence

By the logic of complementarity,[15] there can be no return without departure, hence no *aliyah* without *golah*. This is no triviality. If *aliyah* is an essential myth for Jewish identity, then not only the presence of *golah* but actual life in the Diaspora are preconditions of *aliyah*'s enactment and remain crucial to its meaning. The notion of origin or homeland can have no sense without the contrasting ideas of sequel and foreign parts; national homecoming means nothing without some absence or departure from that land.

Jewish tradition, however, links *aliyah* and *golah* in ways far richer than mere conceptual interdependence through differential definition. The idea that Jewish identity is realized in *aliyah*—in a movement from *golah* to Israel—serves as the founding, formative myth of the Jewish people. Remember that Abraham, the very first Jew, was born outside of Israel and that his *aliyah* to Israel was central to his covenant with God to father the Jewish nation. Yet Abraham also quickly became the first *yored*, leaving for Egypt when there was famine, though later returning again to Israel. This pattern was repeated with Jacob and his sons. Only in Egyptian *golah* did the Hebrews become a numerous (albeit enslaved) people, achieving demographically, if not yet politically, the status of a nation.

Only through exile, as the Exodus story further shows, did the Jews achieve real nationhood and establish their religion. The Law was given to them in the wilderness of Sinai, where they also wandered for forty years to gain sufficient national unity to enter Israel. Moses, founder of the Jewish religion and redeemer of its enslaved people, performed all his work in *golah* and never reached the Promised Land. Significantly, the most important national-religious holidays of Sukkot, Passover, and Shavuot (as distinguished from the purely religious ones like Rosh Hashanah and Yom Kippur) deal with Jewish experience in *golah* wilderness rather than Israel proper, and are designated as the three holidays of pilgrimage (*aliyah*) to Jerusalem or Zion.

From the beginning, then, *golah* forms the necessary ground that enables Jewish self-realization through *aliyah*. Already evident in early biblical times, its role in defining Jewish life and building the Jewish spirit became increasingly dominant through the two-thousand-year exile. Even Yehoshua recognizes "how closely woven the *golah* is to the essence of a Jew," though he insists that this condition is "abnormal" and "neurotic" (E 16). But in terms of Jewish history, *golah* remains more the rule than the abnormal exception, and its role has been clearly more than pragmatic survival, contributing richly to Jewish religion and culture. It cannot be dismissed as inauthentic, for it is precisely what structures the authenticity of *aliyah*.

Yehoshua's premise of essential cultural difference is equally indefensible. Israeli life clearly differs from life in other places (most countries, after all, are obviously different). But apart from Hebrew language and an intense military-security consciousness through a strong environing Arab presence, perhaps the only "essential" difference between secular Jewish life in Israel and the States is the nationally enforced, oppressive religious authority that Israel imposes and that Yehoshua himself would like to undermine.[16]

Whether Israel could (or should) achieve a secular culture independent both of Jewish tradition and foreign cultures is a vexed issue in its history of cultural politics. We need not rehearse this debate to challenge Yehoshua's presumption of a pure Israeli culture essentially different from and privileged over other forms of Jewish life. It suffices to recall that secular Israeli culture was always largely shaped by foreign influence. Its folk songs and dances derive largely from traditions that immigrants imported from *golah*, particularly from Eastern Europe and Arab cultures. Its high art also clearly developed from European sources (e.g. the Moscow theater and Parisian painting). Today's Israeli culture increasingly absorbs and apes America's culture, not only in the arts and mass media but in the consumer culture of everday life. For most secular Israelis, America represents not only the paradigm of quality goods but the very ideal of the good life.

Thus, paradoxically, assimilation into secular Israeli culture means living like an American. Israeli academics are no exception. To get tenure in Israel, one must publish in English and with journals and publishers housed mainly in the United States. Israeli scholars pursue professional prestige by trying to land a job in America for their sabbatical year (almost never spent at home). The quest for America is so rife and strong that it spawned a joke about a coveted new degree to follow the B.A., M.A., and Ph.D. It's a G.T.A., and stands for "Going to America." I lived this assimilation paradox myself, religiously watching "Dallas" in Tel Aviv because it was the Israeli thing to do, though hardly glancing at it when visiting the States. Ironically, the search for a short-term job in America that resulted in my apparent *yeridah* was prompted primarily by Israeli peer pressure. My most admired colleagues were also seeking American jobs for their sabbaticals, and I felt the need to emulate and measure myself against them.

The thrust of these remarks should be obvious. Israeli life is so completely pervaded by American and other foreign culture that no appeal can be made to an authentic Israeli essence that can stand autonomous of *golah* and make the latter gratuitous or inauthentic for Jewish life. But neither can American culture claim pure autonomy, being a motley hybrid of different national cultures arising from successive waves of immigration (sometimes imposed through slavery). If American culture pervades Israel, we should not forget that America's own multicultural mix includes the hora and the *yored*.[17]

Such cultural blurring undermines radical Zionism's argument from difference, which is why Yehoshua strikes out against *golah*'s growing absorption of Israeli culture, insisting that we keep a firm distance and division between them.

> Recently Israel has become a too-familiar presence in the *golah*, especially in the United States. Paradoxically, it is no longer necessary to immigrate to Israel, and it is possible to acquire scraps of significant Israeli reality in the *golah* itself. The aura of distance and mystery surrounding Israel has become blurred.... We must at all costs reestablish a certain feeling of alienation between the *golah* and Israel—a controlled disengagement. (E 32)

The many American Jews (and expatriate Israelis) who regularly vacation in Israel, and the legions of Israelis who descend upon America, show that no controlled disengagement is possible. Israel and *golah* are not only conceptually interdependent, they culturally interpenetrate each other.

Defenders of Israeli essentialism might claim that *golah*'s attraction is not through its penetration of Israeli culture but precisely by the lure of its foreignness. Not only laughably false, this cannot explain why Israelis prefer America to places more culturally remote.[18] But it does suggest an important insight. Self-knowledge and self-expansion, so crucial to self-realization, typically involve exploration into the unfamiliar. Israelis often come to a cultural self-understanding only by defining themselves against foreign lands and people. The voyage out to the unknown, the exploratory quest of the alien, is a central myth of self-discovery that is embedded into the myth of return. But this is no argument against the importance of *golah*. Quite the contrary. As a necessary moment in *aliyah*'s myth of return, *golah* remains essential to Jewish identity, even when Zionistically defined.

How could one defend Yehoshua's third premise, that Israel alone realizes "the things for which we [Jews] are fighting: freedom and independence" (E 34)? Its long, oppressive occupation of conquered Arab territories hardly makes it a model of freedom. Even its Jewish population is harshly constrained and beleaguered: not only in terms of punitive taxes, threats to security, and military curbs on one's liberty, but, far more shockingly, with respect to religious freedom for Jews. There is no such freedom: religious orthodoxy enjoys unchallengeable authority. Marriages and divorces by Reform or Conservative rabbis are not recognized; and, for Jews, there is no procedure for civil marriage and divorce. Nor do they have a choice about burial services or alternative funeral arrangements. In contrast, American Jews have such religious freedoms, but more importantly can also enjoy a freedom *from* religion, which in Israel is unthinkable. Moving from personal to national life, we see that Israel's own freedom is severely constrained by economic, political, and military dependencies on *golah*. (The Gulf War made this very clear). Perhaps multinational capitalism has everywhere eroded the very idea of full national autonomy. But no such general arguments are needed to challenge the claim of Israel as the only place where Jews are really free.

IV

Rejecting Yehoshua's repudiation of *golah* does not entail rejecting *aliyah* as the best way for a secular Jew to realize her Jewish identity. *Golah* is central to Jewish identity partly because *aliyah* is, since it gives *aliyah* its precondition and point. If Jewish identity is best realized through *aliyah*, and if self-realization is not performed by a single act but by a whole life of activity, then an intriguing possibility arises: a life of continued Jewish self-expression and self-realization through cycles of *yeridah* and *aliyah*, departure and return to Israel.

Many Israelis practice this option, though not always consciously or programmatically; and there are good reasons to endorse it. First, it incorporates the historically central *golah* as a necessary and contributory moment in the determination of Jewish identity, thus allowing for a richer notion of Jewishness than Yehoshua's rigid Zionism will tolerate. Second, its circular structure provides for flexibility and openness that are helpful in dealing with life's contingencies. Rather than making *aliyah* "a once and for all" affair (where any temporary turning back means a despicable fall), recognition of the cyclical movement of departure and return enables us to integrate the periods of Israeli and *golah* living that fate may thrust on us, to weave them into a coherent narrative of continued Jewish commitment.

It thus allows for the narrative construction of a reasonably unified, stable Jewish self who repeatedly moves between *golah* and Israel, where each phase enriches the developing self that emerges from it. Adapting this circular view of *aliyah*, we are not forced to condemn a life divided between Israel and the States as inevitably a see-sawing schizoid split between redeemed Israeli and fallen *yored*. Nor must we handle the alternative phases through a strictly compartmentalizing strategy of judicious vacillation between contradictory identities that must be kept apart. These oppositional moments can instead be seen as deeply interpenetrated by narrative unification and experiential funding, just as Israeli and *golah* culture can be seen as interpenetrated by each other. This circular narrative of Jewish identity provides perhaps the richest form of self-unity that postmodern experience allows—an open, flexible narrative unity embracing a multiplicity of subnarratives that allows (like the overarching narrative itself) divergent interpretations and future reconstructions.

For this reason, the life of a "cyclical" Israeli seems an especially good way to realize Jewish identity. But this entails no general injunction that Jews make *aliyah*. The question, "How does one realize one's Jewish identity?" gets its practical force from the presumption that this is something one *should* realize. But we might just as well ask, "Why should one bother to realize one's Jewish identity at all?" This question is not easily answered.

We can hardly argue that one's Jewish identity be realized so as to be true to one's essential self, if there is no such essential self to be true to. Even if there were, why would Jewishness be a necessary part of it? And if being born Jewish is a mere contingency, why make it a central project of one's life? We may feel compelled to live out certain contingencies of birth that seem particularly hard to avoid or transform (say, contingencies of race and sex). But even if we classify Jewishness with these stubborn features, the question "why live Jewish?" remains. For there is a huge difference between living with a contingency and making it a project for self-realization.

One common but misguided argument for Jewish self-realization invokes what could be called "the Hitler principle": Though your Jewishness be insignificant to you, it is essential to anti-Semites; and you should therefore see yourself and live your life according to their benighted outlook, since, in the (albeit unlikely) possibility that they again take power, it could become the determining outlook. But surely one's choice of life should be guided by realities, probabilities, and hopes rather than unlikely fears. One should not live madly because of the possibility that madmen will come to rule the world.

A better argument for realizing one's contingent Jewishness emerges from the postmodern affirmation of contingency and narrative plasticity. If the self is a contingent product, we have no choice but to build our lives on contingencies, while recognizing that there are different degrees of contingency, some of which set fairly firm limits to the plasticity of self-narrative. The secret of successful living is not to escape our contingencies but to construct them into an appealing form, a story we can embrace as our own.

This sense of transforming imposed contingency into meaningful creation is the source of *aliyah*'s great appeal to secular Jews like myself. One's Jewishness, originally experienced as a senseless imposition of *filiation* through the accident of having Jewish parents, becomes transfigured through *aliyah* into a conscious, meaningful choice of *affiliation* with a long-struggling people and continuing national project that one can now claim as one's own. One's own self-narrative and hence one's self become greatly enriched by being embedded into this larger, historically momentous story. Such richness is further enhanced by the Jews' tradition of relying on narrative to sustain and recreate their shared identity, as evident, for example, in the ritual Passover narrative.

The power of this model of self-creation still does not imply the need for *aliyah*. First, secular Jewishness can be made meaningful by linking it to other rich Jewish traditions. Take, for example, the celebrated tradition of the international Jewish intellectual, paradoxically characterized by Isaac Deutscher as "the non-Jewish Jew."[19] Including the likes of Marx, Freud, Benjamin, Adorno, and Hannah Arendt, this model of Jewish identity has enchanted Gentiles and Jews alike. Its fascination prompted me to explore its practice first in Paris and now in Berlin—as much in their streets, through experiments of living difference, as in their libraries.

Secondly, secular Jews have contingencies other than Jewishness on which to build aesthetic life-narratives. Jewish birth may be thrust out of the picture by other contingent features whose greater importance is the product of still other contingencies. Only an extreme "unity fetishist" would require an adequate life-narrative to contain and fully integrate every contingent feature of the self.

Aesthetic unity is, in fact, easier achieved by ignoring some features, sacrificing potential richness precisely to insure unity against the threat of confusion through congeries of contingency. Such is the minimalist ethic of integrity advocated by Epicurus and Stoics like Epictetus. It provides a sharp contrast to modernity's more familiar (Faustian-Nietzschean) ideal of maximal richness whose complex tensions are bound in a far more difficult, strenuous, and dangerously fragile unity. Too often we ignore the aesthetic motives and merits of the minimalist "simple" life by calling it ascetic. But asceticism and aestheticism are not contradictory, as the Greeks recognized in their dictum that "Beauty is difficult."

If self-realization need not embrace all the self's contingencies, then some Jews may choose to make nothing of their Jewishness without violating their integrity by denying it. Being born a Jew can (under certain circumstances) remain an unredeemed fact that is neither explicitly rejected nor endorsed, but is simply not incorporated into one's life project. This is the phenomenon of assimilation. Even if ethnicity enriches, there is no aesthetic imperative for one born Jewish to make himself a Jewish work of art.

Finally, there is no absolute imperative to direct one's life by aesthetic imperatives at all. At the end of a book that advocates philosophy as a life-practice of aesthetic self-realization through disciplined self-critique and self-creation, this point may seem strangely out of place. But it is all the more necessary. Aesthetic self-creation is a fine project, *if* one wants to pursue it and is privileged to have the means to do so. There is, however, no absolute obligation to do so. Whatever the aesthetic imperatives, the freedom to live as one chooses (even if this means living inartistically) overrides them. One also has the right to be unhappy. The argument for happiness is not its obligational necessity but its experienced beauty.[20] That, too, may be the best reason and reward for a life of philosophy.

NOTES

Notes to Introduction

1. The quotation is from *Walden*'s first chapter in Henry David Thoreau, *The Portable Thoreau* (New York: Viking, 1969), 270.

2. See Epictetus, *The Handbook* (Indianapolis: Hackett, 1983), 28; Seneca, *Letters From a Stoic* (London: Penguin, 1969), 160, 171, 207; Montaigne, *The Complete Essays of Montaigne* (Stanford: Stanford University Press, 1992), 124 (quoting Cicero), and 850–51; and Diogenes Laertius, *Lives of Eminent Philosophers* (Cambridge: Harvard University Press, 1991), vol. 1, 17.

3. As a typical instance of this pervasive attitude, take the opening remarks of a recent book by Colin McGinn, *Mental Content* (Oxford: Blackwell, 1989), vi: "Philosophy is a wonderful subject but it does not make a human life.... There is something heartless about it, and withering too. Too much of it is not good for a person."

4. Some exemplary exceptions are featured in the following chapters. Others include Pierre Hadot, *Philosophy as a Way of Life* (Oxford: Blackwell, 1995), which includes an introduction by Arnold Davidson; and Martha Nussbaum, in her *The Therapy of Desire* (Princeton: Princeton University Press, 1994).

5. See Michel Foucault, *Technologies of the Self* (Amherst: University of Massachusetts Press, 1988), 27–30.

6. See the writings of Epicurus in Diogenes Laertius, vol. 2, 611–615, 651, 667–71.

7. The philosophical impact of modern science is only one reason for the decline of the idea of philosophy as a special way of life. An earlier and complementary reason was Christianity's absorption of the philosophical life's ideals of spiritual *askesis* and self-improvement, coupled with medieval Scholasticism's subordination of philosophy to theology, where it served as merely a conceptual, theoretical tool for the latter. As Hadot describes this process: "Theology became conscious of its autonomy *qua* supreme science, while philosophy was emptied of its spiritual exercises which, from now on, were relegated to Christian mysticism and ethics. Reduced to the rank of a 'handmaid of theology,' philosophy's role was henceforth to furnish theology with conceptual—and hence purely theoretical—material. When, in the modern age, philosophy regained its autonomy, it still retained many features inherited from this medieval conception. In particular, it maintained its purely theoretical character." See Pierre Hadot, *Philosophy as a Way of Life*, 107–108.

8. Montaigne, 380.

9. Richard Shusterman, *Pragmatist Aesthetics: Living Beauty, Rethinking Art* (Oxford: Blackwell, 1992). See especially the book's final chapter on "Postmodern Ethics and the Art of Living."

10. The Greeks in fact did not even employ our modern concept of "aesthetics," which was coined in the eighteenth century. But this does not mean that in describing Greek ethics as an aesthetics of existence, Foucault and others are committing anachronistic howlers. For there is adequate continuity with the ancient notions of beauty and art to make the term "aesthetic" applicable.

11. See Michel Foucault, "On the Genealogy of Ethics: An Overview of Work in Progress," in P. Rabinow, ed., *The Foucault Reader* (New York: Pantheon, 1984), 347.

12. Though some may question Foucault's pragmatist character, Rorty notably argues for him "as an up-to-date version of John Dewey" without Dewey's moral optimism. See Richard Rorty, "Moral identity and private autonomy: The case of Foucault," in *Essays on Heidegger and Others* (Cambridge: Cambridge University Press, 1991), 198; and "Method, Social Science, and Social Hope" in *Consequences of Pragmatism* (Minneapolis: University of Minnesota Press, 1982), 203–208.

13. In this connection, I commend the empirical approach of Ben-Ami Scharfstein, *The Philosophers: Their Lives and the Nature of Their Thought* (New

York: Oxford University Press, 1980), which includes short biographical sketches of twenty important philosophers. Unfortunately, it is often too tendentious and simplistic in seeking to explain very different and complicated philosophical positions as decisively determined by very similar problems of childhood experience (particularly relations with parents).

14. For further elaboration of these themes, see my "Art in a Box," in Mark Rollins, ed., *Danto and His Critics* (Oxford: Blackwell, 1993), 161–74; and "Breaking Out of the White Cube," my interview with Suzi Gablik, in her *Conversations Before the End of Time* (New York: Thames and Hudson, 1995), 247–65.

15. The idea that the United States is an anomalous third that violates the binary Israel/Diaspora classification has been argued by a number of recent American Jews. For one blunt example: "There are three areas of Jewish identity today: Israel, the Diaspora, and the United States." See Harold Bloom, "A Speculation Upon American Jewish Culture," *Judaism* 123 (Summer 1982), 268.

16. The Jewish question remains practical and existential for non-Jews as well, though in a somewhat different sense: i.e., what should one make of the Jewishness of the other (spouse, child, sibling, friend, lover, colleague, neighbor, enemy, fellow citizen) in the construction of one's life (which includes one's politics)? This question of the Jewish other emerges, of course, for Jews as well, forming the essential background for their individual realizations of Jewish identity.

Notes to Chapter One

1. On the difference between Socrates and *Plato's* Socrates, see Gregory Vlastos, *Socrates: Ironist and Moral Philosopher* (Ithaca: Cornell University Press, 1991). The former "is exclusively a moral philosopher" who, though forever seeking knowledge, "keeps avowing that he has none," while the latter has substantive theories about almost every philosophical domain and is confident that they are correct (47–49).

2. Plato's arguments against the writing of philosophy include the following: it makes the mind weak by undermining the cultivation of memory; it bloats men with empty conceit of their wisdom, which without memory is shallow and unabiding; it is epistemologically inadequate, because, orphaned from the voice of its author which could explain or defend it, it cannot speak to answer interrogation and is helplessly exposed to misinterpretation; finally, the written word is metaphysically inferior, a lifeless image of oral communication that is consequently two removes from "the word of thought graven in the mind." See *Phaedrus* 274b–78c.

3. The books referred to here include: Brian McGuinness, *Wittgenstein: A Life. Young Ludwig 1989–1921* (London: Duckworth, 1988); Ray Monk, *Ludwig Wittgenstein: The Duty of Genius* (London: Penguin, 1990); Robert Westbrook, *John Dewey and American Democracy* (Ithaca: Cornell University Press, 1991); Steven Rockefeller, *John Dewey: Religious Faith and Democratic Humanism* (New York: Columbia University Press, 1991); Alan Ryan, *John Dewey and the High Tide of American Liberalism* (New York: Norton, 1995); Didier Eribon, *Michel Foucault* (Cambridge: Harvard University Press, 1991); James Miller, *The Passion of Michel Foucault* (New York: Simon and Schuster, 1993); and David Macey, *The Lives of Michel Foucault* (New York: Pantheon, 1993). The books of Westbrook, Monk, McGuinness, Miller, and Eribon have been the most useful in writing this essay, and references to them will appear parenthetically in my text with the respective abbreviations: We, Mo, Mc, Mi, Er. My account of Wittgenstein's life also relies on the brief biographical studies of Malcolm and von Wright, in Norman Malcolm, *Wittgenstein: A Memoir* (Oxford: Oxford University Press, 1958, 2nd. ed. 1985), henceforth Ma; and Rush Rhees (ed.), *Recollections of Wittgenstein* (Oxford: Oxford University Press, 1984); and Paul Engelmann, *Letters from Ludwig Wittgenstein, with a Memoir* (Oxford: Blackwell, 1967). I also learned from Alan Janik and Stephen Toulmin, *Wittgenstein's Vienna* (New York: Simon and Schuster, 1973) and from the controversial account of William W. Bartley III, *Wittgenstein* (La Salle: Open Court, 1985), that focuses especially on Wittgenstein's Austrian experience and homosexuality.

For Dewey's texts I use the complete edition of his works, published by Southern Illinois University Press and divided into separately numbered volumes of *The Early Works* (EW), *The Middle Works* (MW) and *The Later Works* (LW). Some of his more important books are referred to more specifically: *Art and Experience* (Carbondale: Southern Illinois Universty Press, 1987), AE; *Ethics* (Carbondale: Southern Illinois University Press, 1985), E; *Experience and Nature* (Carbondale: Southern Illinois University Press, 1981), EN.

The Wittgenstein texts I cite are abbreviated as follows: *Tractatus Logico-Philosophicus* (London: Routledge, 1966), T; *Philosophical Investigations* (Oxford: Blackwell, 1968), PI; "A Lecture On Ethics", *Philosophical Review*, 74 (1965), 3–12, LE; *Notebooks 1914–1916*, 2nd. ed. (Chicago: University of Chicago Press, 1979), N; *Lectures and Conversations on Aesthetics, Psychology, and Religious Belief* (Oxford: Blackwell, 1970), LC; and *Culture and Value* (Oxford: Blackwell, 1980), CV.

I use the following abbreviations for the Foucault texts I cite: *The Archaeology of Knowledge* (New York: Harper, 1972), AK; *Power/Knowledge* (New

York: Pantheon, 1977), PK; *Remarks on Marx* (New York: Semiotext(e), 1991), RM; *The Foucault Reader* (New York: Vintage, 1984), FR; *Death and the Labyrinth* (New York: Doubleday, 1986), DL; *Language, Counter-Memory, Practice* (Ithaca: Cornell University Press, 1977), LCP; *The History of Sexuality*, vol. 1 (New York: Vintage, 1980), HS; vol. 2, *The Use of Pleasure* (New York: Vintage, 1985), UP; vol. 3, *Care of the Self* (New York: Random House, 1986), CS; *Politics, Philosophy, Culture* (New York: Routledge, 1988), PPC; *Foucault Live* (New York: Semiotext(e), 1989), FL; *Technologies of the Self* (Amherst: University of Massachusetts Press, 1988), TS; *The Final Foucault* (Cambridge: MIT Press, 1988), FF.

With the works of Foucault and Wittgenstein, I sometimes prefer to use my own translations to the published English versions, whose page references will nonetheless be given.

4. Dewey elsewhere chides academic philosophy for ignoring Plato's concern for genuine practical and social problems and thus turning him into an artificially abstract thinker—"the original university professor" (LW 5: 517).

5. Wittgenstein was in fact born and baptised into the Catholic faith; not only his parents but his grandparents were Christians, though three of the four came from Jewish descent. His two paternal grandparents were born Jewish and converted to Protestantism before they were married.

6. I prefer this translation of *"Lebt wohl!"* to the vague "Fare well!" that appears in the standard English translation by Peter Winch. A similar injunction (though in the grammatically singular form) of "Live happy!" (*"Lebe glücklich!"*) can be found earlier in his notebook of 1916 (N 75).

7. See also Wittgenstein's remark: "If one does not *will* to know himself, one's writing is a form of deceit." Here the italics are in Wittgenstein's manuscript, cited in Rhees, 174.

8. In interviews, Foucault repeatedly described his books as "fragments from an autobiography," that deal with his "personal problems." "Each of my books is part of my own biography." A writer's "major work is, in the end, himself," "the work [that includes] the whole life as well as the text." (See TS 11 and other interviews cited in Macey, xii–xiii).

9. There were, of course, pre-Socratic philosophers who led striking, influential lives. But Socrates' exemplary philosophical method and martydom made him the founder of philosophy, as we know it, and the essential prototype of philosophical life as developed through antiquity and beyond. For a study of this development, see Pierre Hadot, *Exercices spirituels et philosophie antique* (Paris: Études Augustiniennes, 1987), translated with other materials by Arnold Davidson, and published as *Philosophy as a Way of Life* (Oxford: Blackwell, 1995).

10. Other salient models (e.g. virtue, wisdom, or reasoned harmony with the cosmos) are assimilable into the medical or aesthetic model. The medical model was especially popular among the Stoics, but the Stoic Marcus Aurelius also deployed aesthetic models of beauty and art for successful philosophical living in his *Meditations* (London: Penguin, 1964), 67, 165–66, 188. So did Epicurus and Plotinus; see *The Epicurus Reader* (Indianapolis: Hackett, 1994), 52, and Plotinus, *Ennead* I, 6:9: 8–26: "If you do not yet see your own beauty, do as the sculptor does with a statue which must become beautiful: he removes one part, scrapes another, makes one area smooth, and cleans the other, until he causes the beautiful face in the statue to appear. In the same way, you too must remove everything that is superfluous, straighten that which is crooked, and purify all that is dark until you make it brilliant. Never stop sculpting your own statue, until the divine splendor of virtue shines in you.... For it is only an eye such as this that can look on the great Beauty."

   For an extensive, advisory study of the medical model, see Martha Nussbaum's fine book, *The Therapy of Desire* (Princeton: Princeton University Press, 1994), which takes "as its central guiding motif the analogy between philosophy and medicine as arts of life" (6). Pierre Hadot's earlier ground-breaking work also emphasizes the model of therapy. My book prefers to develop the aesthetic model (as it relates to contemporary times), though the two models are not inconsistent but complementary and overlapping. Hadot opposes the aesthetic model because he identifies it too narrowly with dandyism and artificial posing or adornment (no doubt because of Foucault). But, as I show below, this falsely equates all aesthetics with the aesthetics of opulence, novelty, and artifice. Aesthetics can also be minimal and ascetic; and Plotinus's image of sculpting the self (cited above and in Hadot, 100), expresses precisely such an aesthetic of ascetically purified beauty.

11. The citations are from W.D. Rouse's translation, *The Great Dialogues of Plato* (New York: Mentor, 1956), 103, 105, 106.

12. This tradition receives more detailed critique in chapters 4 and 5 below; and in my *Pragmatist Aesthetics* (Oxford: Blackwell, 1992).

13. This phrase comes from Nietzsche's subtitle to *Ecce Home*, "How one becomes what one is." The notion of artfully creating oneself can also be found in nineteenth-century American thinkers like Emerson (who greatly influenced Nietzsche) and Thoreau. The latter writes: "It is something to be able to paint a particular picture, or to carve a statue, and so to make a few objects beautiful; but it is far more glorious to carve and paint the very atmosphere and medium through which we look, which morally we can

do.... Every man is tasked to make his life, even in its details, worthy of the contemplation of his most elevated and critical hour." See Henry David Thoreau, *Walden* in *The Portable Thoreau* (New York: Viking, 1969, 343).

14. Describing his *Tractatus Logico-Philosophicus* to his Austrian friends, Wittgenstein writes: "The book's point is an ethical one." See Engelmann, 143–44.

15. One genre simply involves the pursuit and delectation of aesthetic pleasures. But this is not what these philosophers are recommending as aesthetic living. Their goal is not aesthetic consumption but aesthetic creation, the shaping of one's life into an admirable aesthetic form, a work of art. For an analysis of three different models of aesthetic life, see the chapter "Postmodern Ethics and the Art of Living," in my *Pragmatist Aesthetics*.

16. Foucault knew that our term "aesthetic" did not exist in antiquity but was rather coined and established in modernity through those very tendencies which came to separate art and the aesthetic from the practice of life. However, this does not mean that the term cannot be meaningfully used to characterize premodern (or postmodern) experiences of art and beauty. For my arguments to defend this claim against its critics, see *Pragmatist Aesthetics*, ch. 2.

17. See the Foucault interview, published as "The Social Triumph of the Sexual Will," *Christopher Street*, 64 (1982), 38 (cited in Mi 316); and RM 121–22. Baudelaire claims the dandy's ideal is "simply to become subjectively conscious of being uniquely himself, and unlike anyone else." "When I have inspired universal horror and disgust, I shall have conquered solitude." Charles Baudelaire, *Intimate Journals* (London: Panther, 1969), 21–22.

18. The phrase comes from Foucault's secondary doctoral thesis (*thèse complementaire*), *Introduction à l'anthropologie de Kant*, vol. 1, 125.

19. Another cause may be a displaced religious ascetism, inspired by the influence of Augustine and Tolstoy, and by Kierkegaard's injunction for care and unrest. The two causes can easily be related by seeing genius as a modernist expression for the divine. The quest for genius therefore becomes essentially a quest for, and sacrifice to, God.

20. He writes, for example: "Amongst Jews 'genius' is found only in the holy man. Even the greatest of Jewish thinkers is no more than talented. (Myself for instance.) I think there is some truth in my idea that I only think reproductively. I don't believe I ever *invented* a line of thinking, I have always taken one over from someone else. I have simply seized on it with enthusiasm for my work of clarification" (CV 18–19).

21. From Wittgenstein's letter to Paul Engelmann, 41. Though Wittgenstein never sought the role of public celebrity, he was very concerned about

protecting the originality of his views from plagiarism and misuse, for such attempts "stung [his] vanity" (Ma 49–50).

22. For the record, Foucault's father Paul-Michel (whom Foucault was named after, though he dropped the "Paul" in rebellion) was a wealthy surgeon of great reputation in the Poitiers region where he practiced. Wittgenstein's father Karl was "one of the wealthiest men in the [Austro-Hungarian] empire, and the leading figure in its iron and steel industry" (Mo 7).

23. See the testimony of Lytton Strachey and Leonard Woolf in H. Holroyd, *Lytton Strachey: A Biography* (London: Penguin, 1971), 199, and the related remark (201) that "Still slim in those days, Moore seemed indeed not of this miserable planet, but a prophet nourished with wisdom and goodness from some far-off mysterious source, enhaloed with transcendental illumination." Elsewhere his teachings are described as being "branded into the consciousness of his students by a variety of startling forensic devices (opening wide his eyes, raising his eyebrows, sticking out his tongue, wagging his head in the negative so violently that his hair shook)." See G. Spater and I. Parsons, *A Marriage of True Minds: An Intimate Portrait of Leonard and Virginia Woolf* (London: Hogarth Press, 1972), 32. Bertrand Russell likewise notes the power of Moore's physical presence, "beautiful and slim, with a look almost of inspiration." See Bertrand Russell, *The Autobiography of Bertrand Russell, 1872–1914* (London: Allen & Unwin, 1967), 64.

24. For more on this topic, see chapter 6 below; *Pragmatist Aesthetics*, 127–28, 134–35, 259–61; and Richard Shusterman, "Die Sorge um den Körper in der heutigen Kultur," in A. Kuhlmann (ed.), *Philosophische Ansichten der Kultur der Moderne* (Frankfurt: Fischer, 1994), 241–77.

25. For an excellent account of Alexander Technique and Dewey's relationship to Alexander, see Frank P. Jones, *Body Awareness in Action: A Study of the Alexander Technique* (New York: Schocken, 1976).

26. Letter to Joseph Ratner, July 24, 1946; cited in Rockefeller, 343.

27. Foucault writes: "But if the Kantian question was that of knowing what limits knowledge has to renounce transgressing, it seems to me that the critical question today has to be turned back into a positive one. ... The point, in brief, is to transform the critique conducted in the form of necessary limitation into a practical critique that takes the form of a possible transgression" (FR 45).

28. Michel Foucault, "The West and the Truth of Sex", *Sub-Stance*, 20 (1978), 5,7 (cited in Mi 269).

29. See Michel Foucault, "An Interview: Sex, Power, and the Politics of Identity", *The Advocate*, 400 (August 7, 1984), 27; "Le gai savoir", *Mec*, 5 (June 1988), 36; and "Sade, sergent du sexe," *Cinematographe*, 16 (1975–1976), 5.

30. "Sade, sergent du sexe," 3–5. These descriptions of Foucault's somatic aims are made through his praise of the cinematic work of Werner Schroeter, not of his own S/M encounters.

31. Charles Baudelaire, "The Painter of Modern Life," in *The Painter of Modern Life and other Essays* (London: Phaidon, 1964), 27–28.

32. See Alexander Lowen, *Bioenergetics* (New York: Penguin, 1976). For philosophical analysis of this somatic practice and others (including Alexander Technique and Feldenkrais Method), see my paper "Die Sorge um den Körper in der heutigen Kultur."

33. See Rhees, 172.

34. See Fania Pascal, "Wittgenstein: A Personal Memoir," in Rhees, 18 and Ma 29. Wittgenstein once told Rhees that philosophy demanded a constant readiness for change, which is why he advised Rhees against joining the communist party (Rhees, 208).

35. The cited words (the German reads *Niedrigkeit und Gemeinheit*) come from a letter to Engelmann, 33. See also N 74–75, 81.

36. See, for example, Marcus Aurelius's demand for integrity. "Your every action should contribute to an integrated life," in his *Meditations* (New York: Penguin, 1964), 127. Aquinas makes *integritas* the first of his three conditions for beauty in *Summa Theologiae*, I, 39, 8c. The best (though rather different) interpretations of it are in James Joyce's *Portrait of the Artist as a Young Man* and in Umberto Eco's *The Aesthetics of Thomas Aquinas* (London: Hutchinson, 1988).

37. Change is also an evident goal of Wittgenstein's philosophical pedagogy: "A present-day teacher of philosophy doesn't select food for his pupil with the aim of flattering his taste, but with the aim of changing it" (CV 17).

38. Wittgenstein's remark to Engelmann, cited in Mc 227.

39. Fania Pascal, in Rhees, 37.

40. *The Complete Essays of Montaigne* (Stanford: Stanford University Press, 1958), 614,852,857. Similar themes of the good life as a simple, tranquil life without hardship or spectacular heroism can be found in Epicurean thought.

41. From Rhees, 174. See also CV 49: "a man will never be great if he misjudges himself."

42. Augustine's *Confessions* were an avowed influence on Wittgenstein, and Wittgenstein's frequent complaints (like Foucault's) of the inadequacy of his previous writings express the perpetual provisionality and self-overcoming of philosophical work.

43. The logical problem can be resolved in terms of a set of identifying descriptions that all interlocutors in a given context would provisionally ac-

cept as true of the individual in question. For a more detailed treatment of this and the distinction between referential and substantive identity, see *Pragmatist Aesthetics*, 93–94.

44. See, for example, Epictetus, *The Handbook* (Indianapolis: Hackett, 1983), 17–22; and Marcus Aurelius, *Meditations*, 176.

45. From a diary entry, cited in Rhees, 196.

46. One destabilizing discontinuity in Wittgenstein's life was his status as a foreigner in England, a land to which he was tied professionally but in whose culture and society he felt neither at home nor understood (see Mo 267–68).

47. Macey's *The Lives of Michel Foucault* construes this variety as the leading of "many different and very compartmentalized lives" and notes the connection Foucault made between madness and the absence of an *oeuvre*, a coherent body of work (xiv, 102).

48. See Montaigne, 55, who cites Seneca's view that death "is the day that must judge all my past years." Montaigne, however, ultimately prefers to judge life on the whole rather than on the basis only of its end. For a discussion of the theme of death in ancient philosophy, see Hadot's *Philosophy as a Way of Life*, and (the much lighter) Anne Coquelin, *La mort des philosophes* (Paris: Presses Universitaires de France, 1993).

49. On Wittgenstein's preoccupation with suicide and his great admiration for Otto Weininger who theatrically killed himself in the home where Beethoven died, see Mo 19–25, 185–86. Monk's book highlights the theme of death not only textually but pictorially. Among the photos selected to represent Wittgenstein's life, we find one of his grave at Cambridge as well as an especially grim deathbed shot. Foucaults's interest in death is emphasized in Miller's biography, which describes how his lovingly close and often lurid studies of murderers, suicides, and executions earned him the reputation of a thinker obsessed (in Julia Kristeva's phrase) with "the adoration of death" (Mi 129). With Baudelaire, Foucault notes "the essential, permanent, obsessive relation that our age entertains with death" (FR 40).

50. M. Foucault, "Le recherche scientifique et la psychologie", in J-E. Morère (ed.), *Des Chercheurs français s'interrogent* (Paris: Presses Universitaires de France, 1957), 194.

51. The real difficulties in philosophical understanding, Wittgenstein argues, are not the result of "abstruse" subject-matter but rather the lack of courage to see things other than how we like to see them. "What has to be overcome is a difficulty of the will, rather than of the intellect" (CV 17).

52. McGuinness discusses three of Wittgenstein's citations for outstanding bravery in Mc 240–44, 262–63. The confessions of cowardice come from notebooks cited in Rhees, 183, 189.

53. See Wittgenstein's letters to Russell and Engelmann, cited in Mc 166, and Engelmann, 57.

54. M. Foucault, "Conversation" in Gérard Courant (ed.), *Werner Schroeter* (Paris: Cinemathèque Francais and Goethe Institute, 1982), 45; cited in Mi 460.

55. Foucault also notes that we think of "sex" as something "worth dying for." But given Foucault's insistence on experiential truth (which would include carnal knowledge, long associated with death) and his treatment of sex as a historical construct we seek "to formulate ... in truth", the quest for sex must, for Foucault, be closely related to the quest for truth, even if "sex itself" is a "fictitious point" (HS 156).

56. Montaigne, 269–72.

57. This was reported at a meeting of Wittgenstein scholars in May 1995, organized by the Bergen Wittgenstein Archives and held at the Sogne Fjord where Wittgenstein had his hut. The information was received from Mrs. Bevan by Bo Göranzon, who was researching his play on Wittgenstein, *Beyond All Certainty*, repr. in B. Göranzon (ed.), *Skill, Technology and Enlightenment* (London: Springer, 1994).

58. McGuinness notes how Wittgenstein's "family provided its own severest critics," 30–31.

59. See Xenophon, *Conversations of Socrates* (London: Penguin, 1990), 211–213; Seneca, *Letters from a Stoic* (London: Penguin, 1969), 159; and Montaigne's long essay, "Apology for Raymond Sebond," 318–457.

60. At one point, Wittgenstein invoked Lessing's idea of preferring "the single and untiring striving after truth" over truth itself, thus suggesting that truth is not the ultimate value but a useful target whose pursuit provides an effective discipline or *askesis* that can give one's life beauty and happiness. This notion of ascetic aestheticism explains how Wittgenstein reconciles his aim of happiness with his view "that we are not here to have a good time." Happiness can come through the joyful renunciation of a mere "good time." The quotations are from Rhees, 88, 134.

61. It even disturbs Rockefeller's deeply admirative biography of Dewey, which centers on issues of religious faith and humanism. Concerned with reconciling Dewey's naturalism with "ultimate meaning," Rockefeller notes that this problem becomes evident "only when one faces squarely the problem of death and nothingness, which Dewey's writings avoid doing" (534).

62. See "To Death." In the poem "Life," death is described as "a sleep—end of desire"; in poem # 60, he writes how death can "blend the struggling spirits of severed men" in its embracing unity; and in "Two Births" he welcomes death as a unifying part of nature:

No thief is nature but mother
Whose power shall not lack
To turn me in time to clean brother
Worm and sister flower and laden air
To feed the tender sprouting plants
Till in their mingled life I share
And in new measures tread creation's dance.

See Jo Ann Boydston, ed., *The Poems of John Dewey* (Carbondale: Southern Illinois University Press, 1977).

63. One could further argue that the very preoccupation with death and its mastery represents a failure to accept it as part of life. Full acceptance would involve taking death for granted as an essential fact of life, but not one requiring intense philosophical absorption. Dewey's student Sidney Hook takes a still stronger line, denying that death even provides "the tragic sense of life." Blasting existential philosophers like Heidegger for their concentration on death, he asserts that "death as such is not a tragic phenomenon." Instead, he locates life's tragedy in "the tragic conflicts of goods and rights and duties," much as Dewey complained of these unreconciliable claims in "Three Independent Factors in Morals" (LW: 5, 279–88). See Sidney Hook, *Pragmatism and the Tragic Sense of Life* (New York: Basic Books, 1974), 12–13, 19.

64. Milan Kundera, *Immortality* (New York: Harper Collins, 1992), 48–49.

65. In his Collège de France Lecture of February 29, 1984, Foucault portrays the modern artist's life of self-sacrificing dedication to his art (with its radical difference or "rupture" from conventional living) as a modern variation of the heroism of the ancient philosophical life. The life of the modern political revolutionary is similarly portayed in the lecture of March 7, 1984. The typed French transcripts of this last series of Foucault's lectures were generously shown to me by biographer James Miller.

66. This account of Socrates comes from Foucault's Collège de France Lectures of February 8 and 15, 1984.

67. Wittgenstein inherited his family's sense of duty for artistic and civic patronage. Before giving away his entire inheritance to his brothers and sisters after World War I, he gave (in 1914) a large donation to Austrian artists, and later, while a soldier, made a huge gift of a million crowns to the Austrian state for the purchase of artillery. For details, see Mc 206–208, 257, 278.

68. His problematic social relations led him to consider retreating to monastic life in a religious house. As he complained to Engelmann, "Normal hu-

man beings are a balm to me, and a torment at the same time" (Engelmann, 21).

69. See Ma 28. His friends report that Wittgenstein liked American but not European cinema because the former had no artistic pretensions (see Rhees, 71, 120). Compare Wittgenstein's earlier remark to Russell that "nothing is tolerable except producing great works or enjoying those of others" (cited in Mc 112).

70. Wittgenstein also complained that "books which attempt to popularize science are an abomination." Reported in M.O'C. Drury, "Conversations with Wittgenstein," in Rhees, 117.

71. This is not to deny Dewey's awareness of his work's distinction. His four-line poem "My Road" describes it as "a little lane of light that none but I could mark" (*The Poems of John Dewey*, 24). His recognition of individuality was not, however, one of proud superiority, since Dewey seemed to have had no sense of pride. Sidney Hook speaks for many in asserting that: "Dewey was a man of no pride — no pride of dress, literary style, social origins, or intellectual achievement. He was prepared to learn from anyone.... There were no hidden ambitions, no vain regrets, no sense of being anything more than a citizen, a neighbor, a teacher, a friend — and a philosopher." ("Some Memories of John Dewey," in *Pragmatism and the Tragic Sense of Life*, 111, 113). Biographical accounts of Wittgenstein and Foucault testify, in contrast, to their pride.

72. See Jane Dewey, ed., "Biography of John Dewey," in P. A. Schilpp, ed. *The Philosophy of John Dewey* (La Salle: Open Court, 1989), 7; and Sidney Hook, "Some Memories of John Dewey," in *Pragmatism and the Tragic Sense of Life*, 102. Many have commented on the external signs of Dewey's repression, like his painful shyness and lack of spontaneity. Hook (in "Materials for a Biography," *New Republic* 169, October 27, 1973, 28) remarks for example: "His speech and judgements were so deliberate and qualified that they suggested a mass of inhibitions and repressions. Yet he himself was always impressed — and sometimes too much so — by the spontaneous, colorful, unguarded expression of emotion." In his poetry, Dewey refers to his repressed self as "the choked up fountain" (in "Two Weeks," *The Poems of John Dewey*, 16).

73. From a letter to Scudder Klyce in 1927, quoted in Rockefeller, 318.

74. See, for example, Nietzsche's "On the uses and disadvantages of history for life" in his *Untimely Meditations* (Cambridge: Cambridge University Press, 1983); and Montaigne, 319, 769. Even this supreme self-examiner admits the need to look away: "This common attitude and habit of looking elsewhere than at ourselves has been very useful for our business. We

are an object that fills us with discontent; we see nothing in us but misery and vanity. In order not to dishearten us, Nature has very appropriately thrown the action of our vision outward" (766).

75. Dewey's own thinking reflects such change. Facing the challenge, in the late 1930s, of totalitarian regimes in Europe, he expressed the "wish to emphasize more than I formerly did" the ultimate importance of individuals, even if the nature of their individuality is strongly influenced by their social conditions. For "individuals who are democratic in thought and action are the sole final warrant for the existence and endurance of democratic institutions," while democratic institutions have been shown to be "no guarantee for the existence of democratic individuals." See "What I Believe, Revised," LW 5:422.

76. Interview with Foucault's close friend Daniel Defert (cited in Mi 253).

77. Eribon describes Foucault's activism for Poland's Solidarity movement and other causes in 1981–1983, and notes that in 1984, although the year of his death, he volunteered to organize a relief boat for Vietnam (Er 296–308).

78. See Foucault's Collège de France Lecture of March 14, 1984, where he notes how Cynicism "introduced at once into ethics, the art of conduct, and unhappily also into philosophy values of ugliness which have not yet departed." Nietzsche similarly attests to the Greek demand for beauty. In discussing the ugliness of Socrates, he remarks: "But ugliness, in itself an objection, is among the Greeks almost a refutation." *Twilight of the Idols*, "The Problem of Socrates," para. 3, in W. Kaufmann (ed.), *The Portable Nietzsche*, (New York: Viking, 1954), 474.

79. Another aesthetic problem Foucault fails to consider is whether the stark simplicity universally prescribed by the Cynic's philosophical life does not risk, or even demand, a homogenizing normalization of its own, however transgressively nonconformist it be with regard to society's norms. One way to handle this problem would be by recognizing a variety of ways to live simply, rather than preaching a single, fixed code of simplicity.

80. In this connection, Foucault seems to share Cynicism's critique of Socrates' personal life as being too average and conventional in its care for house, wife, and children "as being content with the petty mediocrity which constitutes his existence" (Lecture of March 14, 1984).

81. Foucault asks rhetorically, "Mustn't the philosophical life, the true life, be obliged to be a radically other life?" (Lecture of March 14, 1984). But earlier that year, he suggested in an interview, that philosophical otherness might be seen as more a difference in degree. For the philosopher and for "any free man," "care for the self is the same in its form", but the philosopher is

distinctive "in intensity, in degree of zeal for self—and hence in zeal for others" (FF 13). Recognizing degrees of philosophical self-care is already a promising step toward making philosophical life more possible for more people, and I develop this gradable logic below.

82. See M. Weber, "On Science as a Vocation" in H.H. Gerth and C. Wright Mills eds., *From Max Weber: Essays in Sociology* (New York: Oxford University Press, 1958), 142–51.

83. For an analysis of range concepts, see Max Black, *Problems of Analysis* (London: Routledge and Kegan Paul, 1954), 24–45. Application of the range approach to art can be found in Richard Shusterman, *The Object of Literary Criticism* (Amsterdam: Rodopi, 1984), 136–48.

Notes to Chapter Two

1. See Richard Rorty, "Postmodernist Bourgeois Liberalism," in *Objectivity, Relativism, and Truth: Philosophical Papers, vol. 1* (Cambridge: Cambridge University Press, 1991), 197–202. I shall be referring to this and other essays in this volume, using the abbreviation ORT. References to the companion volume of Rorty's *Philosophical Papers, Essays on Heidegger and Others* (Cambridge: Cambridge University Press, 1991), will use the abbreviation EHO. The other works of Rorty cited in the paper are as follows: *Contingency, Irony, and Solidarity* (Cambridge: Cambridge University Press, 1989), CIS; "Thugs and Theorists," *Political Theory*, 15 (1987), 564–80, TT; "Intellectuals in Politics," *Dissent* (Fall, 1991), 483–90), IP; "Social Hope and History as Comic Frame," published in French translation as "L'espoir social et la fin du socialisme," in *Les lettres françaises*, January, 16, 1992. I quote from the original English typescript, an abbreviated version of which has been published as "The Intellectuals at the End of Socialism," in the *Yale Review* 80 (1992), 1–6.

2. Richard Bernstein, *The New Constellation* (Cambridge: Polity Press, 1991), 233.

3. John Dewey, *Liberalism and Social Action* (Carbondale: Southern Illinois University Press, 1991), 45; henceforth referred to as LSA. Other books by Dewey will be referred to as follows: *The Public and its Problems* (Carbondale: Southern Illinois University Press, 1984), PP; *Ethics* (1932) (Carbondale: Southern Illinois University Press, 1989), E; *Philosophy and Civilization* (New York: Capricorn, 1963), PC; *Experience and Nature* (Carbondale: Southern Illinois University Press, 1981), EN; *The Quest for Certainty* (Carbondale: Southern Illinois University Press, 1988), QC; *Art as Experience* (Carbondale: Southern Illinois University Press, 1987),

AE; *Individualism Old and New* (Carbondale: Southern Illinois University Press, 1984), I. Further Dewey references will be to his collected works published by Southern Illinois University Press, and according to volume number of *Early Works*, *Middle Works*, and *Later Works* (EW, MW, and LW).

4. If these themes and his democratic ideal of individual flourishing through participation in public life make Dewey sound like Aristotle, we should briefly recall a few salient differences. First, Dewey's embodied pragmatism was inimical to the intellectualist Aristotelian ideal of *theoria*, not only in ethics but in epistemology. Secondly, Dewey was an egalitarian liberal who prized individuality and could not tolerate the idea of slavery, class, or acquiescence to a fixed station or function in life. Third, Dewey's idea of human flourishing has no fixed teleology; new ends and visions of the good are always emerging, and the fundamental "end is growth itself" (E 306).

5. Robert Westbrook makes a good case for viewing Dewey's metaphysics of *Experience and Nature* and *The Quest for Certainty* as "an effort to provide a philosophical anthropology for democracy," in *John Dewey and American Democracy* (Ithaca: Cornell University Press, 1991), 320–66.

6. The former is the realm of strict logical argument based on shared premises and evaluated by formal criteria of logical validity, the latter is the realm of rhetorical persuasion, whose discourse is assessed by its "aesthetic" appeal, i.e. by how attractive it renders the position it advocates and how bad it makes the rivals look (CIS 9, 44). Rorty locates his discourse in this aesthetic realm, where most of Dewey's is. But there is no reason, particularly for a pragmatist, to declass such discourse as unphilosophical simply because it relies on these broadly conceived aesthetic criteria.

7. This point requires two cautionary precisions. I am not claiming that America's professional philosophers (i.e. those academics who dominate our philosophy departments) have no political role or influence whatever. John Rawls' work has had some influence on Supreme Court decisions, and other professional philosophers sometimes get a hearing on public issues as diverse as abortion, ecology, euthanasia, and the logic of deterence. My point is that influential policy initiatives are not coming out of philosophy departments. Secondly, I am not denying that there are other sources for political philosophy, in the university and elsewhere, which may be more empowered and influential. Departments of political science may be one source.

8. I thus resist Bernstein's suggestion that Rorty's "aestheticized pragmatism" is what makes him diverge from Deweyan liberalism (Bernstein, 233). For Dewey's privileging of aesthetic experience, see also AE 90–92, 278; and Richard Shusterman, *Pragmatist Aesthetics: Living Beauty, Rethinking Art* (Oxford: Blackwell, 1992), 10–12, 25–33.

9. The same sort of misleading confusion is often made by philosophers with respect to the alleged arbitrariness of convention, where two different senses of "arbitrary" or "contingent" are conflated: not logically or ontologically necessary versus totally capricious, haphazard, unreasoned, and easily reversible. I elaborate on these confusions and their philosophical consequences in "Convention: Variations on a Theme," *Philosophical Investigations*, 9 (1986), 36–55.

10. See Donald Davidson, "Paradoxes of Irrationality," in R. Wollheim and J. Hopkins (eds.), *Philosophical Essays on Freud* (Cambridge: Cambridge University Press, 1982), and Rorty's use of this paper in his "Freud and Moral Reflection," EHO, 143–63.

11. It speaks also to our postmodern aesthetic of fragmentation, typified by multichannel cable TV, remote-control channel zapping, split-screen viewing, and refined into MTV's style of rapid-fire disjoint images. Of course, this postmodern aesthetic pervades not only TV culture but intellectual culture with its ever increasing numbers of "new" books, theories, and mammoth conferences with their mazes of parallel sessions. Critics of late-capitalist consumerism like to doubt whether such variety is any less superficial than the difference between a Whopper and a Big Mac, and whether we are really enjoying our alleged bounty of choices. On the other hand, it is not clear that depth is the highest value and that we would be happier if our choices were more strictly limited to provide greater convergence.

12. Similarly, the ideal of privatized self-realization through a randomly contingent, centerless, and divided self is especially apt for a society where the individual's different social roles do not lend themselves to a unified self-definition, where the individual feels so baffled by the multiple roles she has to play that she can hardly think of trying to harmonize them into what Dewey recommends as "the fullness of integrated personality" (PP 328). This desired disposition toward harmonized wholeness, one that is open to change and growth but aims at constantly integrating them into a coherent but ever evolving complex unity, is the stable, stabilizing integrity that Dewey offers without resorting to a fixed, essential self that both he and Rorty reject.

13. Charles Taylor formulates (without reference to Dewey) a very similar argument in *The Ethics of Authenticity* (Cambridge: Harvard University Press, 1991), emphasizing the inescapable social horizon and dialogical process of recognition that are presupposed in the very idea of distinctive self-realization. This background presupposition does not, however, entail that a life of public action and concern for others is either necessary or best for self-realization. Alan Ryan notes Taylor's striking but unacknowledged

Deweyanism, though he does so with regard to a different issue — objectivity's link to community. See Alan Ryan, *John Dewey and the High Tide of American Liberalism* (New York: Norton, 1995), 361–62.

14. To make this point one need not maintain the illusion that community life in Dewey's day was a perfectly integrated *polis* led by a philosopher king. Dewey himself was already complaining of the disruptions and divisions caused to community life by the technological, industrial, and economic changes of his day. One need only recognize that in postmodern times these socially decentering, fragmenting, and destabilizing forces have been greatly intensified and increasingly destructive to community coherence. David Harvey's socio-economic narrative of the transition from Fordist modernism to the "flexible-accumulation" economy of postmodernism makes this clear, in *The Condition of Postmodernity* (Oxford: Blackwell, 1990). See also the account of the increasing erosion of community in Robert Bellah et. al., *Habits of the Heart* (New York: Harper and Row, 1985). Even earlier sociological studies that affirm (up to the 1970s) the continued existence of active community life, nonetheless see it as increasingly "fragmented," "disarticulated," or incoherent and poorly integrated with larger public structures, resulting in "the decline of public confidence and trust in the political process." See Morris Janowitz, *The Last Half-Century: Societal Change and Politics in America* (Chicago: University of Chicago Press, 1978), especially pp. 9, 22–23, 271–319.

15. It is therefore ironic though understandable that Rorty so stridently attacks the philosophy of campus, cultural politics. We shall consider his critique below.

16. I should make clear that the problem with Anglo-American linguistic philosophy was not its concentration on language, which, of course, has deep socio-political dimensions, but rather its excessively formalist and socially neutered analysis of language. Even the apparent great exceptions here, like Austin and Wittgenstein, who stress the crucial social dimension of langugage, never engage in detailed empirical study of the actual socio-political factors and struggles governing linguistic meaning, in the manner suggested by Foucault and Bourdieu. I make this case in Richard Shusterman, "Bourdieu et la philosophie anglo-américaine, *Critique* 579/580 (1995), 595–609; while I discuss the formalizing and professionalizing pressures of analytic philosophy in greater detail in "Analysing Analytic Aesthetics", in Richard Shusterman (ed.), *Analytic Aesthetics* (Oxford: Blackwell, 1989), 1–19.

17. Rorty was professionally formed by philosophy's logico-linguistic turn, so it is not surprising that he regards language as the only social dimension

that is crucial to self-realization. But even here he problematically divides the self's language into public and private idioms, privileging the private and idiosyncratic as what is essential to self-realization, while regarding public language as merely a means to provide the secure environment to realize ourselves through our private language. For critique of this divison of linguistic labor and more generally of Rorty's disembodied textualization of the self, see chapters 4 and 6; and also *Pragmatist Aesthetics*, 101–106, 255–58.

18. Besides urging philosophy to propose concrete means, Dewey often recommends its general utility as a guide to social reform through its embodiment of "intelligence" and "experimental method." But these notions remain too vague to be helpful, and Rorty, in ignoring them, could be seen as reading Dewey more charitably by being more faithful to pragmatism's spirit of shunning empty "solving names."

19. See, for example, SH and IP, cited in note 1.

20. Lingering communal religious sentiments, deeply imbued through Dewey's long association with the Congregationalist Church, may provide yet another explanation of his commitment to community and to the fusion of private and public perfection: as if the salvation of the individual soul depended on the strengthening purity of the community of faithful. The religious aspect of Dewey's democratic views receives most detailed attention in Steven C. Rockefeller, *John Dewey: Religious Faith and Democratic Humanism* (New York: Columbia University Press, 1991). See also James Kloppenberg, *Uncertain Victory: Social Democracy and Progressivism in European Thought, 1870–1920* (New York: Oxford University Press, 1986).

21. Dewey anticipates this response of Rortian privatism in his criticism of Epicureanism as a selfish retreat of the privileged from the harder struggle to improve themselves through improving society. "It is a doctrine that will always flourish, though probably under some other name as Epicureanism, when social conditions are troubled and harsh, so that men of cultivation tend to withdraw and devote themselves to intellectual and esthetic refinement" (E 202).

22. Ironically, in Rorty's text, this quote reads "For Dewey," etc.

23. Dewey himself already recognized in 1927 "the eclipse of the public" as a substantive, harmonious community. He attributed this loss to the disruptive effects of industrial, economic, and administrative forces that imposed new impersonal forms of societal organization necessary for the complexity and vastness of our technological "Great Society." But he thought philosophy had a crucial role to play in "the search for the conditions under which the Great Society could become the Great Community," insisting

that one necessary condition was the renewal of "local communal life" (PP 327, 370), an option I discuss below.

24. The feminist community is another, overlapping, public. Indeed, it is one whose progressive theory and politics Rorty commends, and to which he even recommends pragmatist philosophy as "useful". (See Richard Rorty, "Feminism and Pragmatism," *Michigan Quarterly Review*, Spring 1991, 247–50.) Yet he contrastingly denigrates, for reasons I explore below, the project of cultural politics, even though feminism is surely one of its forms. His advocacy of feminist theory and cultural politics (even to the point of recognizing the value of forging separatist feminist culture) leads me to think that Rorty's diatribe on cultural politics is not really directed against this project *per se*, but merely against the negative extremism of what may be its most dominant and radical academic form, a form combining themes of Marxism and poststructuralism.

25. Without real contact, as Rorty suggests in "Love and Money" (*Common Knowledge*, 1 [1992], 12–17), poor people tend to become "unthinkable" abstractions to whom it is easy to be cruel, since (in Levinas's words) "we do not see their face." Self-deceptively narcissitic as Rorty may consider us to be, we cultural, campus politicians may learn how to progress from caring about our sometimes quasi-invisible students to caring about far more unthinkable, invisible masses.

Notes to Chapter Three

1. The texts of Putnam and Cavell that I use here will be cited with the following abbreviations: Hilary Putnam, *The Many Faces of Realism* (La Salle: Open Court, 1987), MFR; *Realism With a Human Face*, (Cambridge: Harvard University Press, 1990), RHF; *Renewing Philosophy* (Cambridge: Harvard University Press, 1992), RP; and *Words and Life*, (Cambridge: Harvard University Press, 1994), WL; Stanley Cavell, *In Quest of the Ordinary: Lines of Skepticism and Romanticism* (Chicago: Chicago University Press, 1988), QO; *Conditions Handsome and Unhandsome: The Constitution of Emersonian Perfectionism* (Chicago: Chicago University Press, 1990), CH; *A Pitch of Philosophy: Autobiographical Exercises* (Cambridge: Harvard University Press, 1994), AP; and *Philosophical Passages: Wittgenstein, Emerson, Austin, Derrida* (Oxford: Blackwell, 1995), PP. The quotations here are from QO 10, 12; RP 200; MFR 50. Putnam's RHF and WL include fine introductory essays by James Conant.

2. Putnam's account of this demand and "the absolute conception of the world" is based on the work of Bernard Williams, which he criticizes in

"Bernard Williams and the Absolute Conception of the World," RP 80–107.

3. I doubt that Dewey would have used the term "epistemological" to characterize the argument for democracy that Putnam finds in his work, since "epistemology" had for Dewey rather narrow and negative connotations, identified as "intellectual lockjaw." He probably would have preferred the term "logical" in the general sense he gave it as ordered, rational inquiry.

4. See John Dewey, *The Public and its Problems* (Carbondale: Southern Illinois University Press, 1988), 319; and *Ethics* (Carbondale: Southern Illinois University Press, 1989): 347, hereafter abbreviated as E. Other works of Dewey will be cited with the following abbreviations *Art as Experience* (Carbondale: Southern Illinois University Press, 1987), AE; *Experience and Nature* (Carbondale: Southern Illinois University Press, 1981), EN; *Liberalism and Social Action* (Carbondale: Southern Illinois University Press, 1987), LSA. Other references to Dewey's writings will simply use the volume numbers in the complete edition of his collected works — early, middle, and later (EW, MW, LW) — published by Southern Illinois University Press.

5. Part of Putnam's aim in invoking the notion of "right" is to criticize Dewey's ethics for reducing the idea of right and duty to questions of good consequences. "Like all consequentialist views," Putnam argues, "Dewey's has trouble doing justice to considerations of right" as opposed to questions of good. But this charge of pure consequentialism should not be taken too seriously. First, it is valid only for Dewey's earlier ethical theory. By 1930 and with the publication of the second edition of his and Tufts' *Ethics* (1932), Dewey insisted that right and obligation (and also virtue) were "independent factors in morals," irreducible to consequentialist considerations of good. Moreover, we should note that Putnam himself ultimately formulates the personal ethical question in terms of good rather than right ("whether it is good that I, Hilary Putnam, do that thing," RP 194).

6. In other writings, Putnam also links James' "will to believe" with existentialism and notes James' own allusion to Kierkegaard, "the Danish thinker," when advocating the individual's right to believe in cases "that cannot ... be decided on intellectual grounds," "the right of the existentialist to believe ahead of the evidence." The difference Putnam draws between pragmatism and existentialism is that only the former can see one's leap of faith as fallible and "subject to revision." "William James' Ideas," RHF 227, 229.

7. See Michel Foucault, "What is Enlightenment?," in *The Foucault Reader* (New York: Vintage, 1984), 35.

8. Rorty's creative misprision of Deweyan democratic theory is discussed in the previous chapter, and earlier in Richard Bernstein, *The New Constellation* (Cambridge: Polity Press, 1991).

9. But we never enjoy the radical freedom existentialists claim, because our behavior, desires, and beliefs have always been partly prestructured by habits that are shaped (though not mechanically determined) by our social conditions, training, and past experience. By turning to existentialism to maintain individual freedom against social determination, Putnam courts an unhappy opposition between individual and society that risks forgetting that individual freedom is largely an emergent product of social structures rather than an autonomous, oppositional force.

10. Cavell would regard such a view as a form of moralism morally inferior to perfectionism, "the form of moralism that fixates on the presence of ideals in one's culture and promotes them to distract one from the presence of otherwise intolerable injustice." The other form of moralism "is the enforcement of morality, or a moral code, by immoral means." "It is," Cavell adds, "to John Dewey's eternal credit to have combated, unrelentingly, both forms of moralism" (CH 13).

11. John Rawls, *A Theory of Justice* (Oxford: Oxford University Press, 1973), 325.

12. In this conversation, perfectionism "is the idea of the cultivation of a new mode of human being, of being human where the idea is not that this comes later than justice but that it is essential in pursuing the justice of sharing one another's fate without reducing that fate, as it were, to mitigation" (CH 25).

13. Ralph Waldo Emerson, *The Journals and Miscellaneous Notebooks of Ralph Waldo Emerson* (Cambridge: Harvard University Press, 1960–82), vol. 15, 462.

14. Such *ad hominem* arguments that appeal to the attraction of a life can cut both ways, involving the judger as well as the judged. In other words, my judgment of whether Cavell's philosophical life of perfectionism has enough democratic (or other) attraction will be a comment not only on his life, but on my own aesthetic taste and the life it reflects.

15. At one point, Cavell speaks of the self's need to exemplify its intelligibility not only "when words are called for" but "when there are no words" (CH xxvii). But this vague idea is never developed.

16. See my case for philosophical intervention in the praxis of cultural and university politics, ch. 2.

17. See Pierre Hadot, "Spiritual Exercises" in his *Philosophy as a Way of Life* (Oxford: Blackwell, 1995), 81–125. The book's editor Arnold Davidson

himself suggests the connection between this idea and Cavell's view of philosophical writing, 40 n. 91.

18. Alexander Nehamas, *Nietzsche: Life as Literature* (Cambridge: Harvard University Press, 1985), 233–34.

19. Friedrich Nietzsche, "Schopenhauer as Educator," in *Untimely Meditations* (Cambridge: Cambridge University Press, 1983), 187.

20. Henry David Thoreau, *Walden*, in *The Portable Thoreau* (New York: Viking, 1969), 270; henceforth abbreviated W.

21. Putnam and Cavell, of course, recognize our embodied condition. As Putman critiques mind-body dualism (e.g. WL 3–61), so Cavell praises Austin's account of excuses for turning attention to "something philosophy would love to ignore—to the fact that human life is constrained to the life of the human body, to what Emerson calls the giant I always take with me. The law of the body is the law." But in treating embodiment as governed by unmodifiable law beyond our control and thus constituting the realm for excuses, Cavell effectively excludes the body from his perfectionist project. In contrast to bodily efforts, "the saying of words is not excusable" and marks the realm of responsibility. Hence it is here that Cavell urges perfectionist striving, assuming "the unending responsibility of responsiveness, of answerability, to make [oneself] intelligible." Similar demands (even if likewise not fully achievable) might be directed toward somatic improvement; and it is hard to see how Cavell would wish to separate words and voice from the body from which they issue and in which they resonate. Quotations here are from PP 53, 63, 65; AP 87, 126.

22. I take this issue up in chapters 1 and 6, but give it a far more detailed treatment in my comparative analysis of today's more popular and promising somatic techniques of emancipatory self-realization (e.g. Alexander Technique, Feldenkrais Method, and Bioenergetics), in Richard Shusterman, "Die Sorge um den Körper in der heutigen Kultur," in A. Kuhlmann (ed.), *Philosophische Ansichten der Kultur der Moderne* (Frankfurt: Fischer, 1994), 241–77.

Notes to Chapter Four

1. Jürgen Habermas, *The Philosophical Discourses of Modernity* (Cambridge: MIT Press, 1987), 185–210; henceforth referred to as PDM.

2. Richard Rorty, *Contingency, Irony, and Solidarity* (Cambridge: Cambridge University Press, 1989), 44–45, 48, 53; henceforth CIS. He glosses the notion of poeticized culture as "substitut[ing] the hope that chances for equal fulfillment of idiosyncratic fantasies will be equalized for the hope that everyone will replace 'passion' or fantasy with 'reason'" (53). See also

his critique of Habermas's use of communicative reason to answer modern culture's " 'need for unification' in order to 'regenerate the unifying power of religion in the medium of reason' "; in Richard Rorty, "Habermas and Lyotard on Postmodernity," in his *Essays on Heidegger and Others: Philosophical Papers, vol. 2* (Cambridge: Cambridge University Press, 1991), 169 (citing PDM 19, 20), henceforth EHO. In that volume's introduction, Rorty retrospectively regrets his usage of the contested term "postmodernism" in defining his position as "postmodern bourgeois liberalism" and in characterizing other contemporary philosophy. Instead he offers "post-Nietzschean" as a more precise, uncontroversial label for philosophers (e.g. Heidegger, Derrida, Lyotard) earlier defended under the notion of postmodern (EHO 1–2). Since Habermas identifies the postmodern with Nietzsche, Rorty's terminological substitution does not effect the sense of their debate. Rorty's "Postmodern Bourgeois Liberalism" is reprinted in his *Objectivity, Relativism, and Truth: Philosophical Papers, vol. 1* (Cambridge: Cambridge University Press, 1991), henceforth ORT.

3. This chapter was originally written for a conference "Modernity in Question: Habermas and Rorty" that was held in 1993 at Cerisy-la-Salle with the participation of both philosophers. Its location near the beaches of Normandy only intensified the sense of philosophical conflict that the program's oppositional facing off of German and American philosophers (respectively representing modernity and postmodernity) was meant to evoke. Despite the preconference "hype" of world-historical philosophical conflict, substantive agreement clearly prevailed over difference. So did the philosophical habit of endless paper reading, which provoked this paper's closing call for alternative expression.

4. The compartmentalization of Habermas's aesthetic of modernity is confirmed in a later, less polemical work. "The aesthetic experiences are not admitted into forms of praxis; they are not referred to cognitive-instrumental skills and moral respresentations, which are developed from innerworld learning processes; they are tied up [*verwoben*] with the world-constituting, world-disclosing function of language." From "Handlungen, Sprechakte, sprachlich vermittelte Interaktionen und Lebenswelt," in Jürgen Habermas, *Postmetaphysisches Denken: Philosophisches Aufsätze* (Frankfurt: Suhrkamp, 1988), 63–104 (quotation from p. 94, my translation). This essay was not included in the book's English version, *Postmetaphysical Thinking: Philosophical Essays* (Cambridge: MIT Press, 1992), henceforth PT.

5. Jürgen Habermas, "Modernity—An Incomplete Project," repr. in Hal Foster (ed.), *The Anti-Aesthetic* (Port Townsend, Washington: Bay Press, 1983), 11.

6. For more detailed argument, see Richard Shusterman, *Pragmatist Aesthetics: Living Beauty, Rethinking Art* (Oxford: Blackwell, 1992), 46–49.

7. Habermas's theory of communicative reason does not simplistically limit the connection of validity and meaning to the standard notion of truth as the representation of facts, but concerns also the speech-act's dimension of "rightness" (in the sense of moral normativity) and "truthfulness" (in the sense of authenticity of expression). This tripartite analysis of validity is explicitly meant to parallel "the three fundamental functions of language" (representative, appelative-regulative, and expressive), but also clearly suggests modernity's division of spheres into representative science, regulative ethics and politics, and expressive art (PDM 313–315). Earlier, in *The Theory of Communicative Action*, vol. 1 (Boston: Beacon Press, 1984), 335, he cites "works of art" as "exemplary" of the "rationality" of "expressive knowledge" which "can be criticized as untruthful." In short, modernity's tripartite differentiation of cultural spheres appears as the rational development of the essential tripartite logic of language itself. Rorty is right to object that our cultural institutions and language are more contingent in origin. But given his own problematically vague and radical sense of contingency (already criticized in chapter two), Rorty's contrasting account of all language and culture as "sheer contingency" should likewise be resisted (CIS 22). Habermas returns to his tripartite analysis of the validity-dimension of all speech acts in PT 74–79. But the conclusion of that book's essay "Philosophy and Science as Literature?" presents a seemingly different suggestion for artworks: that validity claims, though still present in fictional texts or utterances, are only binding for the people in the fiction, "not for the author and the reader" (223–24). This greatly limits the role of expressive truthfulness for the validity of aesthetic discourse.

8. Through a critical reading of Calvino's experimental novel *If on a winter's night a traveler*, Habermas tries to show how the leveling of the aesthetic-fiction/everyday-real world distinction will not succeed even in aesthetic practice. His central point is that "Everyday life [with its discourse to solve problems] continues to place limits around literary texts" that are essential for the differentially determined identity and proper functioning of these artworks. See "Philosophy and Science as Literature?", in PT 205–227, especially 218, 223.

9. For a critique of this metaphysics, see *Pragmatist Aesthetics*, 79–82.

10. Rorty's plea that philosophy become privatized and avoid all claims to general authority over others can be read as a confession of his own choice not to presume the role of a dominating major philosopher whose views claim to be definitive, preferring instead what he calls a style of "weak

thought" (EHO 6). Such a position dovetails neatly not only with an-
tifoundationalism but with his liberalist pluralism. Rorty also commends
Derrida's later writing as moving in this more personal direction (CIS
135–37).

11. For detailed critique of this conflation, see *Pragmatist Aesthetics*, 253–55.

12. For elaboration of this point, see *Pragmatist Aesthetics*, 255–57.

13. Though Rorty always insists on the primacy of the sentential, he is forced
by his privileging of the private and the idiosyncratically creative to admit
the presence and value of associations and images of words below the level
of propositional attitudes. These nevertheless depend for their possibility
on sentential meaning (CIS 153).

14. See *Pragmatist Aesthetics*, ch. 7, 8, 9; and my "Die Sorge um den Körper in
der heutigen Kultur", in A. Kuhlmann (ed.), *Philosophische Ansichten der
Kultur der Moderne* (Frankfurt: Fischer, 1994), 241–77.

15. See Jürgen Habermas, "Philosophy as Stand-In and Interpreter", in *Moral
Consciousness and Communicative Action* (Cambridge: MIT Press, 1990), 3,
4. His linking of philosophy with science as opposed to the aesthetic is
underlined in "Philosophy and Science as Literature?", where both the
former (as opposed to the latter) cannot "give up the orientation toward
questions of truth" (PT 225).

16. Though Rorty has recently tried to address a wider public by occasionally
writing for the general press, these articles remain largely centered on issues of the academy in contrast to Habermas's broader scope.

17. Two substantial and convincing (though very different) cases for the continuity of modernity and postmodernity are found in Albrecht Wellmer's
The Persistence of Modernity (Cambridge: MIT Press, 1991) and David Harvey, *The Condition of Postmodernity* (Oxford: Blackwell, 1989).

18. See Xenophon's *Symposium*, in his *Conversations on Socrates* (London: Penguin, 1990), 233–34.

Notes to Chapter Five

1. My most extensive case is made in *Pragmatist Aesthetics: Living Beauty, Rethinking Art* (Oxford: Blackwell, 1992). But see also "Art in a Box," in
Mark Rollins (ed.), *Danto and his Critics* (Oxford: Blackwell, 1993) and my
interview ("Breaking Out of the White Cube") in Suzi Gablik's *Conversations Before the End of Time* (London: Thames and Hudson, 1995).

2. The editions of Goodman's works to which I shall be referring (in abbreviation) are as follows: *Languages of Art* (Oxford: Oxford University Press,
1969), *LA*; *Fact, Fiction, and Forecast* (Indianapolis: Hackett, 1977), *FFF*;

Ways of Worldmaking (Indianapolis: Hackett, 1978), *WWM*; *Of Mind and Other Matters* (Cambridge: Harvard University Press, 1984), *OMM*.

3. See John Dewey, *Art as Experience* (Carbondale: Southern Illinois University Press, 1987), 52, 202, 323. For a more detailed account of Dewey's critique of dualisms in aesthetics and elsewhere, see *Pragmatist Aesthetics*, ch.1.

4. Goodman and Dewey also agree that what distinguishes art from science is their different form of symbolization, aesthetic symbols being characteristically richer or, in Goodman's terms, more replete, dense, and ambiguous. Dewey further distinguishes the aesthetic from the scientific in terms of greater immediacy of experience and full-bodied satisfaction; but immediacy is a very suspect notion for Goodman.

5. *OMM*, 44. Goodman here self-conciously refers to his style by exemplifying it in the stylized passage in which he makes its point, a passage full of Goodman's characteristic alliterative parallelisms. "Readers often find in my work—to their delight or disgust—many quips and cracks, puns and paradoxes, alliterations and allegories, metaphors and metonymies, synechdochies and other sins. If there are as many routes to reference as I think, perhaps some of these devices are not mere decoration or unsuccessful attempts to keep the reader awake but part and parcel of the philosophy presented and the worlds made."

6. Goodman's views on the nature and problems of art's appreciation and his critique of the museum's difficulties in advancing this aim are admirably based on his own exploratory work on art education, conducted as founder of the Harvard Graduate School of Education's Project Zero which he directed from 1967 to 1971. His conclusions are presented in the chapter "Art in Action" of OMM, 146–87.

7. How Goodman can handle the apparent clash between his dynamic function-centered aesthetic and his strict definitions of work-identity is discussed at the end of this chapter, along with rap's own deep tensions. I criticize Goodman's logicistic approach to work-identity in *Pragmatist Aesthetics*, 30, and in *The Object of Literary Criticism* (Amsterdam: Rodopi, 1984), 130–39.

8. See *Pragmatist Aesthetics*, ch. 7, 8; "Légitimer la légitimation de l'art populaire," *Politix*, 24 (1993), 153–67; "Don't Believe the Hype: Animadversions on the Critique of Popular Art," *Poetics Today*, 14 (1993), 101–122, and "Popular Art and Education," *Studies in Philosophy and Education*, 13 (1994), 203–212. This last paper critiques the limits of Dewey's approach to popular art.

9. Though also known offstage as Kris Parker, his original first name was

Lawrence, and he is musically identified with the group BDP (Boogie Down Productions), which he founded with Scott Larock in 1986. For an illuminating sketch and interview of KRS-One, see Michael Lipscomb, "Can the Teacher Be Taught?", in *Transition*, 57 (1993), 168–89.

10. Goodman particularly insists on the importance of entrenchment of categories as a way of explaining the logic of induction in FFF; and he likewise makes antecedent practice of individuation a condition for notational definitions of works of art in LA.

11. See William James, *Pragmatism and Other Essays* (New York: Simon and Schuster, 1963), 26–27, 88–103. For an example of rap's lyrical privileging of the future and present over the past, take KRS-One's "I manifest the future, the present, followed by the past./Everything in nature rules by kickin' ass" ("Health, Wealth, Self").

12. LA, xii. One of Goodman's violations of common sense is the view that a copy of a novel with one misprinted letter or punctuation mark is not an instance of the novel in question, but another work.

13. First published in skeletal form in Richard Shusterman, "The Fine Art of Rap," *New Literary History*, 22 (1991), 613–632, but later with much more detail as chapter 8 of *Pragmatist Aesthetics*. The rap–pragmatism connection is further clarified in my "Rap Remix: Pragmatism, Postmodernism, and Other Issues in the House," *Critical Inquiry*, 22 (1995), 150–58. For more on rap's aesthetic import, see Tim Brennan, "Off the Gangsta Tip: A Rap Appreciation, or Forgetting About Los Angeles," *Critical Inquiry*, 20 (1994), 663–93, who also provides an instructive critical review of rap criticism. Among the most notable works are Tricia Rose's multidimensional study, *Black Noise: Rap Music and Black Culture in Contemporary America* (Hanover: Wesleyan University Press, 1994) and Houston Baker's *Black Studies, Rap, and the Academy* (Chicago: University of Chicago Press, 1993). See also the collection of essays edited by Andrew Ross and Tricia Rose, *Microphone Fiends* (New York: Routledge, 1994); W. E. Perkins (ed.), *Droppin' Science: Critical Essays on Rap Music and Hip-Hop Culture* (Philadelphia: Temple University Press, 1995), and David Toop's classic *Rap Attack 2: African Rap to Global Hip-Hop* (London: Serpent's Tail, 1991).

14. One should not forget that even Ice-T (saddled with gangsta notoriety not only for his *Original Gangster* album but especially for the later scandal concerning his "Cop Killer") first claims: "My lethal weapon is my mind" ("Lethal Weapon," 1989).

15. Guru, "Lifesaver" from his superb 1995 album *Jazzmatazz II, the New Reality*, whose title I sample in tribute. On these black diasporic traditions, see, for example, Roger Abrahams, *Deep Down in the Jungle* (Chicago: Aldine

Press, 1970), whose study of a Philadelphia ghetto reveals that speaking skills "confer high social status" and that even among young males "ability with words is as highly valued as physical strength" (39,59). Studies of Washington and Chicago ghettos have confirmed this. See Ulf Hannerz, *Soulside* (New York: Columbia University Press, 1969), 84–85, which notes that verbal skill is "widely appreciated among ghetto men," not only for competitive practical purposes but for "entertainment value"; and Thomas Kochman (ed.), *Rappin' and Stylin' Out* (Urbana: University of Illinois Press, 1972). Along with its narrower use to designate the traditional and stylized practice of verbal insult, black "signifying" has a more general sense of encoded or indirect communication which relies heavily on the special background knowledge and particular context of the communicants. For an analysis of "signifying" as a generic trope and its use "in black texts as explicit theme, as implicit rhetorical strategy, and as a principle of literary history," see Henry Louis Gates Jr., *The Signifying Monkey: A Theory of Afro-American Literary Criticism* (Oxford: Oxford University Press, 1988); citation from 89. The rich complexities of Afro-diasporic culture have been powerfully demonstrated by Paul Gilroy, *There Ain't No Black in the Union Jack* (Chicago: University of Chicago Press, 1987) and *The Black Atlantis* (Cambridge: Harvard University Press, 1993).

16. Goodman's later theorizing indeed notes that "not every art can be classed as autographic or as allographic" (OMM, 139).

17. See, respectively, "My Philosophy," "Ghetto Music," and "Out for Fame." Public Enemy's "Don't Believe the Hype" has a 1988 time-tag, and similar dates can be found in the lyrics of Ice-T, Kool Moe Dee, NWA, Guru, MC Solaar, and many others.

18. MC's references to their creative rap locales (especially Compton and South Central Los Angeles or Brooklyn and the South Bronx) abound in rap's lyrics. Public Enemy's Chuck D explains the local musical variations: "Rap has different feels and different vibes in different parts of the country.... So rap music in New York City [where one mainly walks] is [now, after the end of the boom-box phase, discontinued because of violence over them] a headphone type of thing, whereas in Long Island or Philadelphia, where ... people have cars ... , rap is ... more of a bass type of thing." See Mark Dery, "Public Enemy: Confrontation," *Keyboard* (September, 1990), 90. As Tricia Rose (9–12) notes, rappers also manifest their neighborhood loyalty by typically insisting that their videos be filmed in their ghetto. It is therefore striking that a group like Brand Nubian, who seek to dispel the friction between East and West coast rap, have made a point of coming from their East coast home to film a video in

L.A.'s Watts ghetto. See The Bishop of Hip-Hop, "Gods in the City of Angels," *The Source* (January 1995), 64–65. Regional differences and rivalries can also be found in French rap, e.g. the North Parisian suburb sound of Suprême NTM as contrasted to Marseille's IAM.

19. The recognition that rap can simultaneously celebrate its works' temporality and its art's (and artists') survival is underlined by KRS-One in his late-1995 album (simply titled by his name). Insisting that his musical longevity is the product of "lyrical persistence" in "changin' with the times" and "still growin,'" that it depends on his image of being true to continuing hip-hop creativity rather than to any permanent "platinum" hit or Grammy, KRS raps: "I start from 1986 and bring you into '96/No gimmicks, tricks, or lip-sync lyrics." While this "image is respected,/Records come and go and get collected./ Even records of platinum artists that used to rip shot/Can be bought for a quarter at the thrift shop" (from "De Automatic" and "Health, Wealth, Self"). I should also note that rap's intertextual allusions include the visual, e.g. appropriatively restaging in album and publicity photos famous images from black history, for example KRS-One's Malcolm X-armed-at-the-window pose in his album *By All Means Necessary*.

20. These include Presidents Bush and Clinton (who respectively condemned Ice-T and Sister Souljah in the 1992 election campaign) as well as 1996 Presidential candidate Robert Dole who vehemently attacked rap's gangsta values.

21. For an example of how rap has been effectively used in high school teaching, see Dimitri Leger, "Hip-Hop High," *The Source*, October 1994, 22. See also Jeffrey Decker, "The State of Rap: Time and Place in Hip-Hop Nationalism," in *Microphone Fiends*, 99–121. In 1996, the Hip-Hop Coalition for Political Power has been active in getting inner city youth to register to vote, see R. Harrington, "Hey Man, Get Out There and Register to Vote," *International Herald Tribune*, April 13, 1996, 20. Condemnations of rap for having no political efficacy or agenda (even by sympathetic experts like Greg Tate in "The Sound and the Fury," *Vibe* 1 [Fall 1993, 15] are the products of ignoring the political importance of these everyday (educational and socio-economic) uses of rap by falsely assuming that rap's politics should deliver a dramatically rapid revolution. They forget rap's crucial message that political revolution requires the slow, often invisible revolution of individual self-mastery. As rapped by Disposable Heroes of Hiphoprisy in their "Music and Politics," "the personal revolution is far more difficult and is the first step in any revolution." I develop this theme below; it shares the perfectionist ideal expressed in Wittgenstein's "That man will be

revolutionary who can revolutionize himself." See Ludwig Wittgenstein, *Culture and Value* (Oxford: Blackwell, 1980), 45.

22. For a critical survey of this trend, see Brennan, 667–73.

23. T.W. Adorno, *Minima Moralia* (London: Verso, 1978), 85. Adorno borrows the line from F. H. Bradley.

24. See also his "Who Protects Us From You?", "Gimme Dat, Woy," and "Squash All Beef." Jeru the Damaja likewise stresses the scientific role of his rap in "Mental Stamina" and "Mind Spray" (where he claims "I am a scientist and an activist").

25. From "I'm still #1." For KRS-One's attack on establishment history, media, and stereotypes, see especially "My Philosophy," "You Must Learn," "Why is That?", "The Blackman's In Effect," and "Squash All Beef." The critique of institutional religion expressed in "The Holy Place" is continued in "The Truth."

26. This phrase and notion, for example, provides the central theme of Kool Moe Dee's "Do You Know What Time It Is?" and appears in many other raps (e.g. Public Enemy's "Don't Believe the Hype," X-Clan's "Grand Verbalizer: What Time Is It?"). Hip-hop's heightened sense of temporality is expressed in other striking ways. For example, Flavor Flav of Public Enemy always wears a large clock around his neck, explaining "I wear a clock around my neck because time is the most important thing in life; it brought us into the world and it will take us out." Quoted from Robert Marriott, "Resurrection of the Jester King," *The Source*, August 1994, 76. For rappers connected to the Nation of Islam, the notion of "knowing the time" further alludes to that movement's familiar cry "Do you know what time it is? It's nation time."

27. The citations are from "Living in this World" and "New Reality Style."

28. Goodman's pragmatist aesthetic seems imperfect in another way: by ignoring the human intentionality and phenomenal subjectivity of aesthetic experience, defining such experience merely in terms of formal symbolic properties. I offer a more detailed critique of Goodman's view of aesthetic experience in "The End of Aesthetic Experience," *Journal of Aesthetics and Art Criticism,* 55 (1997).

29. I should note that MC Solaar has recorded with Guru in "Le bien/Le mal" in the first *Jazzmatazz* album, while *Jazzmatazz II*'s "Lifesaver" also includes French lyrics (from another MC). If rap can be bilingual, so can its citations for philosophical discussion here. A rough translation of the lines would go: Science without conscience equals the science of unconscious thoughtlessness. It doesn't give a damn about progress, but wants the progression of all the processes that lead to elimination.

30. See, for example, Ice-T's "High Rollers" and "Drama" or Kool Moe Dee's "Monster Crack."

31. From Guru's "Looking Through the Darkness," "Living in This World," "Lost Souls," "Nobody Knows." The idea of rap as a thoughtful tool for the sublimation of anger and aggression into lyrically intelligent symbolic combat is reinforced by KRS-One: "Rappers display artistic cannibalism/ Through lyricism./We fight each other over rhythm./Through basic animal instincts/We think./So the fight for mental territory/Is glory./End of Story." This comes from the song "R.E.A.L.I.T.Y.", whose refrain unpacks the title: "Reality ain't always the truth/Rhymes Equal Actual Life Into Youth." That reality is not always the truth, because not always linguistic, is a Deweyan point I develop in chapter 6.

32. From Guru's "Choice of Weapons" and KRS-One's "My Philosophy."

33. In this context, I should note Crispin Sartwell's *The Art of Living: Aesthetics of the Ordinary in World Spiritual Traditions* (Albany: SUNY Press, 1995) which suggests some connections between pragmatism, American popular culture, and the philosophies of Zen, Tao, and Confucianism.

34. His more recent "Squash All Beef" exploits the double meaning of beef in order to link the self-mastery of vegetarianism with the self-control needed to stop street violence. Even those addicted to meat are urged to at least "be mental vegetarians" by refraining from internecine hate. Here is a good place to note that the highbrow postmodern poet John Ashbery also is drawn to the idea of a total, diet-encompassing, philosophical life, though he treats it with characteristic, devastating irony in his "My Philosophy of Life" from his *Can You Hear, Bird* (New York: Farrer, Strauss, & Giroux, 1995), 73–75:

> Just when I thought there wasn't room enough
> for another thought in my head. I had this great idea—
> call it a philosophy of life, if you will. Briefly,
> it involved living the way philosophers live,
> according to a set of principles. OK, but which ones?
>
> That was the hardest part, I admit, but I had a
> kind of dark foreknowledge of what it would be like.
> Everything from eating watermelon or going to the bathroom
> or just standing on a subway platform, lost in thought

35. Respectively from "Et Dieu Créa L'homme" and "C.R.E.A.M."

36. This final track is entitled "Health, Wealth, Self."

37. Sister Souljah, "Survival Handbook vs. Global Extinction"; MC Solaar "Et Dieu Créa L'homme" and "Temps Mort"; and Guru, "Living in This World."

38. Quoted from an interview in Kierna Mayo Dawsey, "It's all in the Mind: Philosophies of Jeru the Damaja," *The Source*, September 1994, 58. Making the point musically (in "Ain't the Devil Happy") Jeru urges, "You must discover the power of self./Know thyself,/Find thyself./Hate in thyself/Kill in thyself." KRS-One offers a related argument in advocating that "violence in society would be minimal [if] education here would be...metaphysical, not livin' by laws, but livin' by principle" ("Squash All Beef").

39. This view of hip-hop as a life-philosophy is widely shared. The rap group Brand Nubian, for example, claims its music is for "the hip-hop nation," meaning those who "who live it every day! Not just the motherfuckers who 'like the music,'" but those who "breathe it and taste it ... love it; willin' to die for it." Quoted from "Gods in the City of Angels" (see note 18), 64. Guru's already cited account of hip-hop life surprisingly does not include graffiti. This is because he seeks to give hip-hop a purely positive image. But KRS-One continues to celebrate graffiti as an essential, positive, "visual" part of hip-hop culture, affirming its Egyptian roots and explaining its criminal status through its inability to generate corporate wealth as rap music has done. See his "Out For Fame," whose refrain goes "I'm writin' my name in graffiti on the wall."

40. I should note here (what I argued in *Pragmatist Aesthetics*) that modernity's ideal of pure aesthetic autonomy was not, for its time, a bad idea; it was a valuable ideology to help art free itself from strict servitude to the undemocratic domination of Court and Church. The doctrine, however, has outlived its usefulness.

41. See Queen Latifah, "Dance For Me" and Ice-T's "Hit the Deck." For a similar emphasis on the mesmerizing possession and physically and spiritually moving power of rap in performer and audience, see Kool Moe Dee's "Rock Steady," "The Best," and "Get the Picture." This aesthetic of divine yet bodily possession is strikingly similar to Plato's account of poetry and its appreciation as a chain of divine madness extending from the Muse through the artists and performers to the audience, a seizure which for all its divinity was disparaged as irrational and inferior to true knowledge. The spiritual ecstasy of divine bodily possession should also remind us of Vodun and the metaphysics of African religion to which the aesthetics of African-American music has often been traced. Rap here represents a clear infraction not only of modernism's distanced, disembodied, and formalized aesthetic, but of modernity's whole project of secular, disenchanting rationalization.

42. Jerry Levinson raises this worry in his sympathetic review of *Pragmatist Aesthetics* in *Mind*, 102 (1993) 682–86. In that book I showed the complexities

of rap's textual meanings through a detailed analysis of Stetsasonic's "Talkin' All That Jazz."

43. For Goodman's insistence on the actively embodied nature of cognition, the cognitive role of feeling, and the importance of nonverbal forms of cognition, see the chapter "Art in Action" of OMM and LA 241–51. That rap recognizes its twin roles as knowledge and dance is lyrically underlined in Guru's "The Traveler," who goes to "Holland and England with knowledge to bring in" and "to France with a chance to enhance the dance."

44. These contradictions are discussed further in *Pragmatist Aesthetics*, 208–214. Good examples of some of these tensions can be found in Ice-T's "High Rollers," "Drama," "6'n the Mornin'," "Somebody Gotta Do It (Pimpin' Ain't Easy!)," "Radio Suckers"; in Big Daddy Kane's "Another Victory" and KRS-One's "The Blueprint," "R.E.A.L.I.T.Y.," and "Health, Wealth, Self." For a good discussion of the contradictory pressures facing female rappers who want to combat rap's misogynous expression without aiding those trying to condemn rap for oppressive exploitation and violent abuse of women, see Tricia Rose, 146–82.

45. See, in particular, the work of Pierre Bourdieu, *Distinction* (Cambridge: Harvard University Press, 1984) and *The Rules of Art* (Stanford: Stanford University Press, 1995); and Lawrence Levine, *Highbrow/Lowbrow* (Cambridge: Harvard University Press, 1988).

46. See Houston Baker Jr., *Blues, Ideology, and Afro-American Literature: A Vernacular Theory* (Chicago: University of Chicago Press, 1984), 57. Rap artists not only recognize this relation of economic power and expression, thematizing it in their music, but are developing new ways to secure greater artistic control of (and financial benefits from) their music by securing more power in the corporate structures of its production. One notable example is the Wu-Tang Clan, whose artistic-business creativity is described in Selwyn Seyfu Hinds, "The Wu-Gambinos," *The Source*, October 1995, 84–88.

47. KRS-One makes this point in "Why is That?" from his *Ghetto Music* album: "The stereotype must be lost/That love and peace and knowledge are soft/For love, peace must attack and attack real strong/Stronger than war." He is also exemplary in realizing that the double vision of judicious vacillation is an answer to hip-hop's basic dilemma of positive message versus effective depiction of the real ghetto negativities emphasized in rap's criminal style. Opposing the one-sidedness of censors and "rap-positivity" purists, KRS-One demands that just as rap should show both "the good and bad of society," so listeners should have the chance to hear rap's negative as well as positive forms. Critique, not censorship, is the an-

swer. "If you show just one aspect of rap, it's damaging because [listeners] are not getting the truth but rather a made-up version." Quoted in Anita M. Samuels, "Rap Family Values," *New York Times*, September 14, 1995, C10.

48. Alive to the troubling contradictions between hip-hop's high ideals and its negative realities, KRS-One notes how ghetto life itself demands a juggling of multiple lives: "Hip-hop as a culture is really what we're givin'./ But sometimes the culture contradicts how we're livin'./ 'Cause every black kid lives two or three lives./ The city's a jungle only the strong will survive" ("R.E.A.L.I.T.Y.").

49. The undermining of dichotomies was already begun in *Languages of Art* by linking art with science. This shows that although analytic and pragmatist aesthetics are usefully contrasted, they are not always inconsistent and can be usefully combined. For their more salient contrasts, see *Pragmatist Aesthetics*, ch. 1. I discuss their combination in my *Analytic Aesthetics* (Oxford: Blackwell, 1989), 13–15; and "On Analysing Analytic Aesthetics," *British Journal of Aesthetics*, 34 (1994), 390–94.

Notes to Chapter Six

1. See Richard Rorty, "Dewey Between Hegel and Darwin," in Dorothy Ross, ed., *Modernism and the Human Sciences* (Baltimore: Johns Hopkins University Press, 1994), 60, henceforth referred to as DHD; and also "Dewey's Metaphysics" in *Consequences of Pragmatism* (Minneapolis: University of Minnesota Press, 1982), henceforth DM. Dewey's second thoughts about the efficacy of the term "experience" are forcefully expressed in a letter to Bentley, when he toyed with the idea of changing the title and content of a new edition of *Experience and Nature* by substituting the term "culture" for "experience." In the end, however, Dewey refused to renounce the notion of experience—as the unfinished revisions for the new edition make clear: "We need a cautionary and directive word, like experience, to remind us that the world which is lived, suffered and enjoyed, as well as logically thought of, has the last word in all human inquiries and surmises." See John Dewey and Arthur Bentley, *A Philosophical Correspondence 1932–1951* (New Brunswick: Rutgers University Press, 1964), 643; and "Appendix 2" in John Dewey, *Experience and Nature 1925*, rev. 1929 (Carbondale: Southern Illinois University Press, 1981), 372, henceforth EN.

2. Rorty underlines this point in his *Objectivity, Relativism, and Truth* (Cambridge: Cambridge University Press, 1991), 16–17.

3. Dewey writes of such immediate experiences that we "*have* them, but ... do not know [we] have them" (EN 198). Moreover, in the following paragraph Dewey goes on to deny the empiricist idea of immediate nondiscursive knowledge: "The notion that sensory affections discriminate and identify themselves, apart from discourse, as being colors and sounds, etc., and thus *ipso facto* constitute certain elementary modes of knowledge, even though it be only knowledge of their own existence, is inherently so absurd that it would never have occurred to any one to entertain it, were it not for certain preconceptions about mind and knowledge" (199).

4. Ludwig Wittgenstein, *Philosophical Investigations* (Oxford: Blackwell, 1968), para. 190, 197, 217, 485, 654; II: 208, 226.

5. John Dewey, "Qualitative Thought," repr. in *Philosophy and Civilization* (New York: Capricorn, 1963), henceforth abbreviated as Q; and *Logic: The Theory of Inquiry* (Carbondale: Southern Illinois University Press, 1986), henceforth L.

6. "Confusion and incoherence are always marks of lack of control by a single pervasive quality.... The underlying unity of qualitativeness regulates pertinence or relevancy and force of every distinction and relation; it guides selection and rejection and the manner of utilization of all explicit terms.... For the latter things are *its* distinctions and relations" (Q 98–99).

7. Dewey later adds: "Were not the sequence [of inquiry] determined by an inclusive situation, whose qualitative nature pervades and holds together each successive step, activity would be a meaningless hop-skip-jump affair" (L 126).

8. Such unity is largely prospective, an impulse or aim of coordinated action. See John Dewey, *Human Nature and Conduct*, 1922 (Carbondale: Southern Illinois University Press, 1983), henceforth HN, ch. 2, 4.

9. For Dewey, "habits are abilities" that provide the initial, prereflective structure for "all the perceiving, recognizing, imagining, recalling, judging" we perform, while the "selective-restriction" that determines more specific situational subjects or elements is "made for a definite purpose" (HN 47, 121, 124; L 131).

10. John Dewey, *Ethics* (Carbondale: Southern Illinois University Press, 1985), 185.

11. This point, of course, has been emphasized by Merleau-Ponty. His account of the lived body as the experiential unifying ground of perception has many similarities to Dewey's use of the unifying ground of felt quality; and it could be vulnerable to similar criticisms. There is no space to pursue this here, nor to pursue what I think is a more important criticism: Merleau-Ponty's lack of attention to the project of how to *improve* somatic

experience rather than simply describe it as it is and show its philosophical importance. This suggests a basic difference between phenomenology and pragmatism as I conceive it.

12. Rejecting dualism to embrace an emergent naturalism, I share Dewey's view that all experience, even abstract thinking, is body-dependent, just as our bodily functioning is often influenced by thought. Body and mind are functional distinctions of an organic whole that Dewey called "body-mind" (EN 191). My ensuing emphasis on the soma should not therefore be taken as implying a new inverted dualism. Nor should the notion of nondiscursive immediacy be seen as limited to the somatic disciplines I later cite. Nondiscursive immediacy plays a wide-ranging role in everyone's everyday understanding and praxis. Though insisting that everyday experience is not an intrinsically inferior realm, pragmatism still advocates that it can be bettered through intelligent means. Somatic disciplines claim to provide such means and therefore warrant pragmatist consideration.

13. Robert Westbrook's fine biography mentions Alexander only once in a footnote; and even there he is mentioned not in terms of his own work or relationship to Dewey but only as an "occasion" for polemical exchange between Dewey and Randolph Bourne. See Robert Westbrook, *John Dewey and American Democracy* (Ithaca: Cornell University Press, 1991), 221 n26. Alan Ryan gives Alexander a rather dismissive short paragraph in his *John Dewey and the High Tide of American Liberalism* (New York: Norton, 1995), 187–88. This neglect is sadly the norm in Dewey studies. But there is a longer discussion of Alexander's influence on Dewey in Steven Rockefeller, *John Dewey: Religious Faith and Democratic Humanism* (New York: Columbia University Press, 1991), 333–44. For a deeper account of Dewey's relations with Alexander and of the scientific evidence for Alexander's theories, see F. P. Jones, *Body Awareness in Action: A Study of the Alexander Technique* (New York: Schocken, 1979). For a philosophical analysis of Alexander work and other popular somatic therapies, see Richard Shusterman, "Die Sorge um den Körper in der heutigen Kultur," in A. Kuhlmann (ed.), *Philosophische Ansichten der Kultur der Moderne* (Frankfurt: Fischer, 1994), 241–77.

14. John Dewey, "Introduction" to F. Matthias Alexander, *Constructive Conscious Control of the Individual* (New York: Dutton, 1923), reprinted in John Dewey, *The Middle Works*, vol. 15 (Carbondale: Southern Illinois University Press, 1983), 313.

15. John Dewey, "Reply to Reviewer" (R. Bourne) of F. Matthias Alexander, *Man's Supreme Inheritance* (New York: Dutton, 1918), henceforth MSI; in *New Republic* 15 (1918), repr. in John Dewey, *The Middle Works*, vol. 11

(Carbondale: Southern Illinois University Press, 1982) 354, henceforth abbreviated RR. The same volume also contains Dewey's "Introductory Word" to the book, henceforth abbreviated ISI. Dewey also wrote an "Introduction" to a third book by Alexander, *The Use of the Self* (New York: Dutton, 1932), reprinted in John Dewey, *The Later Works*, vol. 6 (Carbondale: Southern Illinois University Press, 1985), 315–320, in which Dewey describes his long experience as a pupil of Alexander.

16. This is reflected in the title of Alexander's book, *Constructive Conscious Control of the Individual*. Dewey also advocates Alexander's idea of "conscious control" in EN 225.

17. The question of what exactly qualifies as "conscious" is a complex problem that I should raise but cannot answer here. In describing certain habits or experiences as unconscious, I mean simply that they are not thematized objects of consciousness or objects of reflection. I am not implying that we are unconscious when they occur, nor that they are not in some way mentally processed or noticed. John Searle, for example, argues that such unthematized events or objects in sentient experience are conscious, though they are not objects of attention. He thinks that "we need to distinguish the conscious/unconscious distinction from the center of attention/periphery distinction." See John Searle, *The Rediscovery of the Mind* (Cambridge: MIT Press, 1992), 138. Certainly, we need to distinguish different levels of attention, if we do not distinguish different levels or degrees of consciousness. But the point I am making about the unappreciated somatic background can be made just as easily in terms of the "unattended" as the "unconscious."

18. Rorty's argument against using the concept of experience for ontological and epistemological puzzles of continuity is as follows:

> The problem with this way of obtaining continuity between us and the brutes is that it shoves the philosophically embarassing discontinuity back down to the gap between, say, viruses and amoebae.... Only by giving something like experience to protein molecules, and perhaps eventually to quarks — only a full-fledged pan-psychism — will eliminate such embarassment. But when we invoke panpsychism to bridge the gap between experience and nature, we begin to feel that something has gone wrong. For notions like "experience," "consciousness," and "thought" were originally invoked to *contrast* something which varied independently of nature with nature itself. The philosophically interesting sense — the only sense relevant to epistemology — of *experience* ... [applies] to a realm that might well be "out of touch" with nature because it could vary while nature remained the same, and remain the same when nature varied. (DHD 58–59)

I doubt that our notions of experience, consciousness, and thought were first invoked for philosophical purposes of epistemological contrast with nature rather than for more practical functions of interacting with it. I also question Rorty's narrow identification of "the philosophically interesting sense" of "experience" with its traditional epistemological use of contrast to reality. There are other interesting senses to which Dewey's philosophy of experience is, in fact, directed (e.g. aesthetic and ethical). For an account of Dewey's aesthetic use of the concept of experience, see Richard Shusterman, *Pragmatist Aesthetics* (Oxford: Blackwell, 1992), 25–33, 46–59.

19. The quote is taken from *Collected Papers of Charles Sanders Peirce* (Cambridge: Harvard University Press, 1960) vol. 5, para. 314.

20. In *Dialectic of Enlightenment* (New York: Continuum, 1986), 234, Horkheimer and Adorno savage the idea of "remaking the body into a noble object," and Susan Bordo's *Unbearable Weight: Feminism, Western Culture, and the Body* (Berkeley: University of California Press, 1993) provides usefully updated critiques of today's ideals and ideologies of somatic plasticity. It is Foucault, rather than the Frankfurt school, that informs her work; but he is an ambiguous ally here. Though critical of society's use of "biopower" to normalize and subjugate the subject, Foucault also urged the emancipatory potential of powerful somatic experiences (see ch. 1 above). He therefore advocated an experiential somatic plasticity, even though he recognized that the initial forms of such experience are conditioned by society's discursive forms. Another Foucauldian feminist, Judith Butler, emphasizes the body's plasticity but concentrates on gender and the body's discursive nature. See *Gender Trouble: Feminism and the Subversion of Identity* (New York: Routledge, 1990) and *Bodies That Matter: On the Discursive Limits of "Sex"* (New York: Routledge, 1993). There is thus room for a philosophy that takes nondiscursive somatic transformation more seriously, yet discusses it more clearly than do Deleuze and Guattari. I develop this project in "Die Sorge um den Körper in der heutigen Kultur" and in "Soma und Medien," *Kunstforum International*, 132 (1996), 210–215.

21. Richard Rorty, *Philosophy and the Mirror of Nature* (Princeton: Princeton University Press, 1980), 183; henceforth PMN.

22. See Richard Rorty, *Contingency, Irony, and Solidarity* (Cambridge: Cambridge University Press, 1989), henceforth CIS, where Rorty argues that the privileged use of language is not to represent or justify something already there, but to cause something different, "to make something that never had been dreamed of before" (CIS 13).

23. Wilfred Sellars, *Science, Perception, and Reality* (London: Routledge & Kegan Paul, 1963) 60; Hans-Georg Gadamer, *Philosophical Hermeneutics*

(Berkeley: University of California Press, 1976), 19; Rorty, CIS 88; Jacques Derrida, *Of Grammatology* (Baltimore: Johns Hopkins University Press, 1976), 158. I provide a more detailed critique of these textualists in the chapter "Beneath Interpretation," of *Pragmatist Aesthetics*.

24. See Richard Rorty, "Introduction: Pragmatism and Philosophy," in *Consequences of Pragmatism*, xix. The other citation in this paragraph is from another essay in that volume "Nineteenth-Century Idealism and Twentieth-Century Textualism," 140.

25. Despite its dominant trend to deprecate the body, Christianity included several thinkers and sects who saw the body—despite its material inferiority and even because of it—as a central tool to achieve greater spirituality, notably through somatic asceticism. Jesus, after all, needed incarnation to go through the passion of crucifixion. Origen, in the third century, urges this ascetic route to making the body into a "temple to the Lord," using the following metaphorical injunction: "You have coals of fire, you will sit upon them, and they will be of help to you." For more on this topic, see Peter Brown, *The Body and Society: Men, Women, and Sexual Renunciation in Early Christianity* (New York: Columbia University Press, 1988); citations from 165, 175.

26. This tradition can be traced from Democritus, Epicurus, and Lucretius to Hobbes, La Mettrie, Marx, and into our own century. For all the merit and influence of these thinkers, they obviously do not constitute the core of the academic discipline of philosophy. Hobbes and Marx are, of course, more central, but this is mainly because of their influential political philosophy.

27. Daniel Stern, *The Interpersonal World of the Infant* (New York: Basic Books, 1985).

28. I take up this project by examining the techniques and ideologies of three popular body practices (Alexander Technique, Feldenkrais Method, and Bioenergetics) and trying to explain our culture's growing concern with somatic techniques of self-transformation. See Richard Shusterman, "Die Sorge um den Körper in der heutigen Kultur."

29. See Henry David Thoreau, *Walden*, ch.1 ("Economy") in *The Portable Thoreau* (New York: Viking, 1964), 270; and Ralph Waldo Emerson, "Experience," in *Essays* (London: Everyman, 1942), 236. Thoreau likewise insists that philosophy's life is embodied, urging that man's "mind descend into his body and redeem it" (469).

30. From the conclusion of Michel Foucault's Collège de France Lecture of March 14, 1984.

Notes to Chapter Seven

1. Jean-Paul Sartre, *Réflexions sur la question juive* (Paris: Gallimard, 1954), 166. My English translation is: "Jewish authenticity consists in choosing oneself *as a Jew*, that is to say, in realizing one's Jewish condition. The authentic Jew abandons the myth of universal Man; he knows and wants himself in history as an historical and damned creature; he has ceased to flee from himself and to be ashamed of his own people."

2. For an insightful and balanced discussion of such issues, see Seyla Benhabib, *The Situated Self: Gender, Community, and Postmodernism in Contemporary Ethics* (New York: Routledge, 1992).

3. This difficulty of secular Jewish self-expression in America is recognized by many. Bernard Berofsky, for example, explains "the disappointing condition of American Jewish life" as resulting from the fact that the dominant secular Jewish community "no longer discerns the eternal verities of the Jewish faith and is not prepared to uproot itself from its native land in order to redefine this faith in national terms." Hence, "there is no positive goal or meaning in continued Jewish existence." Not surprisingly, Berofsky recommends *aliyah* to Israel as the best solution for expressing Jewish identity. See Bernard Berofsky, "Jewish Spirituality in the Diaspora," in Etan Levine (ed.), *Diaspora: Exile and the Jewish Condition* (New York: Scribner, 1983), 123–33; quotations from 128.

4. Michel Foucault, "What is an Author?", in *Language, Counter-Memory, Practice* (Ithaca: Cornell University Press, 1977), 138.

5. The concepts of person and self may be usefully distinguished for a variety of contexts and issues. We can use them, for example, to allow for the existence of a single person having many selves, or for a radical transformation of self that would still not entail the assignment of a different personal identity. My discussion of Jewish identity does not require elaboration of the self/person distinction, but those interested in it may consult Rom Harré, *Personal Being* (Cambridge: Harvard University Press, 1984).

6. See, for example, Moshe Feldenkrais, *The Potent Self* (New York: Harper, 1985), 68, 71–72.

7. See Richard Rorty, *Contingency, Irony and Solidarity* (Cambridge: Cambridge University Press, 1989); Michel Foucault, "On the Genealogy of Ethics: An Overview of Work in Progress," in Paul Rabinow, ed., *The Foucault Reader* (New York: Pantheon, 1984), 340–72; Charles Taylor, "What is Human Agency?" and "Self-interpreting Animals," in *Human Agency and Language: Philosophical Papers, vol. 1* (Cambridge: Cambridge University Press, 1985), 15–76; *Sources of the Self* (Cambridge: Harvard University

Press, 1989); and *The Ethics of Authenticity* (Cambridge: Harvard University Press, 1991); and Alasdair MacIntyre, *After Virtue* (London: Duckworth, 1982).

8. Recent continental theory often uses "the Jew" as a symbol for the oppressed other, for example as when Jacques Derrida (in *Writing and Difference* [Chicago: Chicago University Press, 1976], 75) describes "the Jew [as] but the suffering allegory." For more detailed and empirically based accounts of Jewish "Otherness," see Jonathan Boyarin, *Storm from Paradise: The Politics of Jewish Memory* (Minneapolis: University of Minnesota Press, 1992) and Sander Gilman, *Jewish Self-Hatred: Anti-Semitism and the Hidden Language of the Jews* (Baltimore: Johns Hopkins University Press, 1986). Though the Jew's role as victimized Other is hardly questionable, I neither want to see it as an ideal nor exploit it as a strategy for claiming superior discursive authority through the contemporary tendency of privileging the victims' perspectives.

9. The term's primary sense of forced expulsion and prolonged separation from one's native land is arguably no longer applicable, since with respect to most Jews (at least since the demise of the Soviet Union) there is no political power or even force of circumstances that compels their separation from Israel.

10. MacIntyre, 191.

11. The distinction between logical or referential identity and substantive identity is elaborated in *Pragmatist Aesthetics* (Oxford: Blackwell, 1992), 93–95.

12. This does not mean that national and religious interests cannot be powerfully combined, as they sometimes are with fanatical vehemence in religious-nationalist extremism. But one should not forget how the national/religious tension is confirmed by the ultra-orthodox rejection of the very legitimacy of the Israeli state. The primacy of religion as self-definition explains why devout American Jews who make *aliyah* for religious reasons seem to move more easily between their Israeli and American Jewish identities, because religion is the foremost determinant of both. The same goes for devout Israeli Jews, who feel much more at home in Orthodox communities in America than secular Israelis do in progressive and essentially secular American Jewish communities.

13. A. B. Yehoshua, "Exile as a Neurotic Condition," in Levine (ed.), *Diaspora*, 15, 16; henceforth abbreviated as E. The second main reason Yehoshua gives for the attraction of *golah* is that it provides an easy solution for the felt Jewish injunction "to be different" as a special chosen people." As a distinct minority living in a foreign land rather than their own homeland, it was easy to be different.

14. Nor do I see much hope in the inverse strategy of those (like the Boyarin brothers) who "propose a privileging of Diaspora ... as the only social structure that even begins to make possible a maintenance of cultural identity." See Daniel and Jonathan Boyarin, "Diaspora: Generation and the Ground of Jewish Identity," *Critical Inquiry*, 19 (1993), 723.

15. Though now primarily associated with varieties of poststructuralism, this logic can be traced back to Hegel's principle of organic unity. For a genealogical account of its development from Hegel through Nietzsche to deconstruction, see "Organic Unity: Analysis and Deconstruction", in *Pragmatist Aesthetics*.

16. Yehoshua recognizes that the religious element cannot be completely expunged from Jewish identity, but he means to give it a very subordinate role in Jewish experience, by having it radically reformed by secular thought and experience. He wants orthodox religious authority (but not Israeli national authority) to be decentered "through the creation of additional centers of authority" in religion. To this purpose, "secular Jews ... must become involved in religious affairs ... as daring reformers" (E. 30, 31).

17. Theorists argue that such multinational cultural mixing is characteristic of postmodern life. In Lyotard's account, "one listens to reggae, watches a western, eats McDonald's food for lunch and local cuisine for dinner, wears Paris perfume in Tokyo and 'retro' clothes in Hong Kong." Jameson explains the multinational postmodern style as a function of our current phase of multinational capitalism (the successor of capitalism's classical and national imperialist phases). See Jean-François Lyotard, *The Postmodern Condition: A Report on Knowledge* (Minneapolis: University of Minnesota Press, 1984), 76; and Fredric Jameson, *Postmodernism: or, The Cultural Logic of Late Capitalism,* (Durham: Duke University Press, 1991), ch. 1.

18. Young Israelis who are especially keen for adventure in the radically alien *do* sometimes choose a long voyage to more exotic destinations like the South American jungles or the Far East, though this is typically a one-shot affair, after completing one's army service and before starting the university.

19. Isaac Deutscher, *The Non-Jewish Jew and Other Essays* (New York: Oxford University Press, 1968).

20. Deploying this pragmatico-aesthetic logic, C. S. Peirce suggests that the perceived value of beautiful living is even enough to justify such life as implying an "ought": "what one ought to desire ... is ... what he will desire if he sufficiently considers it, and that will be to make his life beautiful, admirable." See Peirce's letter to Lady Welby, cited in Joseph Brent, *Charles Sanders Peirce: A Life* (Bloomington: Indiana University Press, 1993), 49.

INDEX